D0276681

THE
BIRDS
OF BRITAIN AND EUROPE
with North Africa and the Middle East

Hermann Heinzel · Richard Fitter

John Parslow

Collins St James's Place, London

William Collins Sons & Co Ltd

London · Glasgow · Sydney · Auckland

Toronto · Johannesburg

First published 1972
Second edition 1973
Third edition 1974
Reprinted 1976
Reprinted 1977
Fourth edition 1979
© 1972 R. S. R. Fitter, H. Heinzel, J. L. F. Parslow
Paperback edition 0-00-219210-1
Hardback edition 0-00-219234-9
Filmset by Jolly & Barber Ltd, Rugby
Made and printed in Great Britain
by Wm. Collins Sons & Co. Ltd., London and Glasgow

Contents

3

4

Introduction

The Text

All the birds of Europe, North Africa and the Middle East are described in the text, species by species, arranged in their families.

The text stresses the characters which are most important for identifying birds in the field, and especially those which are less obvious or which cannot be shown in the illustrations, such as song, call notes, mode of flight and other habits, and habitat.

The **size** of each bird, indicated by its length from the tip of the bill to the tip of the tail, is given at the end of the description of each bird in both inches and centimetres. When a bird is perched or resting, it may be hunched up and not revealing its full length.

Voice is often one of the most important clues to a bird's identity, and in a few cases, for instance Chiffchaff and Willow Warbler (p. 237), Reed and Marsh Warblers (p. 225), is almost essential to identification. Birds utter two

Measuring a Robin

main kinds of sound, song and call notes. Song is a specialised utterance, usually in order to establish and maintain a male bird's rights to a territory, which it will defend against other males of the same species in the breeding season. Song is therefore usually loud and fairly continuous, and is normally only heard in the breeding season. Some species, however, also sing again in the autumn, after their moult. On the other hand, in the great majority of species call notes, the normal conversation of a bird, which express alarm, anger, warning or the need to maintain contact, can be heard all the year round. Only a very few birds are silent outside the breeding season.

Habitat, the type of country where the bird is usually found, where it feeds or roosts or makes its nest, is another vital clue to the identity of some birds, for instance the Meadow and Rock Pipits (p. 209). Most birds are rather conservative in their choice of breeding-habitat, but less so after the breeding season, when they may wander a good deal and be found in quite different types of country. See also p. 18.

Not all birds are resident or present in Britain or even in Europe throughout the year. Some migrate here in spring to breed, returning southwards to spend the winter, perhaps in Africa. Others come here each autumn from places further north to spend the winter in what is to them a warmer climate or a better feeding ground. A few species, passage migrants, visit us in both spring and autumn on their way to and from breeding grounds further north. Less frequent visitors can be divided into those which appear annually in small numbers, and those which appear in Britain only irregularly, perhaps at intervals of several years.

Swallows on migration

The status and relative abundance of each bird within the British Isles are indicated in this book by the following symbols and letters, which follow the text description of each bird:

● Occurs regularly: widespread and common. Likely to be seen annually by most bird-watchers.

☉ Occurs regularly: local or uncommon. Can be seen annually if species' favoured localities are visited.

○ Occurs regularly: very local or rare. Usually occurs in very small numbers, or restricted to a very few localities.

— Occurs only as vagrant, 'A' — annually,

	Main status	Lesser status
Resident	R	r
Summer resident (breeds)	S	s
Migrant	M	m
Winter visitor	W	w
Annual vagrant	A	
Irregular vagrant	V	
Has bred in British Isles (not regularly now)		(b)

Thus **Kestrel** is Rsmw = Widespread and common **Resident**, some also occurring as **summer residents** (i.e. wintering outside the British Isles), as **migrants** (i.e. breeding and wintering outside the British Isles, though passing through them on migration) or as **winter visitors** (i.e. breeding outside the British Isles but spending the winter here).

As other examples, the resident House Sparrow is just R, but the Blackbird, which occurs also as a common migrant and winter visitor, is RMW.

The Maps

The maps in the text show the status and distribution of all breeding birds and regular visitors in the region. For explanation see pages 11—13.

On pp. 321—336 are a further set of maps giving similar information for the British Isles only. A reference to each follows the abundance and status symbols of the birds in question. Thus **Kestrel**

● Rsmw— Map 62.

The Illustrations

The illustrations are carefully designed to show all significantly distinct plumages of each bird that breeds in the region or occurs there regularly. In many cases typical flight and other attitudes are also shown. The main picture of each bird is always in breeding plumage. This is in fact the plumage that is seen in spring and summer, except in the ducks, which assume their breeding plumage in late autumn and go into "eclipse", as their moult plumage is called, about midsummer. Plumages get worn as time goes on, and birds seen in late summer just before the moult may look a good deal dowdier than they appear in the plates.

For the great majority of birds, every distinct plumage is given, breeding and winter, male and female, juvenile and immature, where these are sufficiently distinct, but in a few groups, notably the waders and gulls, where there are many plumages, often only slightly different, this has not been possible. Juvenile plumage is the first feathered as distinct from downy plumage, and immature plumages are any others that intervene between the juvenile and adult stages, as for instance with the birds of prey and gulls, many of which take several years to attain adult plumage. Some winter plumages may start to appear immediately at the end of the breeding season, in summer.

Also shown where relevant are important colour variations or phases, both spread throughout the whole population as with the Cuckoo, Ruff and Eleonora's Falcon, or on a geographical basis, as with subspecies. Most of the numerous instances of partial albinism, melanism, or other colour forms that occur as freaks or sports are, however, omitted.

partial albino   albino   flavistic   melanistic

Bullfinches (p. 287): all males

Family or group to which the birds on the plate
belong

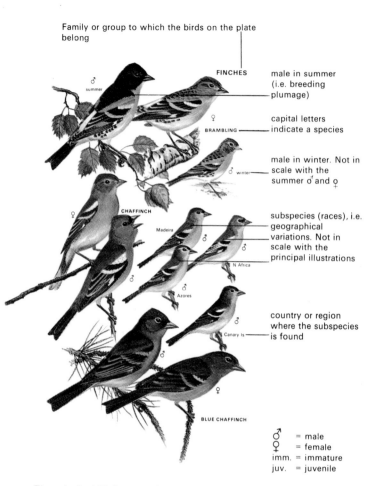

FINCHES — male in summer
(i.e. breeding
plumage)

capital letters
BRAMBLING — indicate a species

male in winter. Not in
scale with the
summer ♂ and ♀

subspecies (races), i.e.
geographical
variations. Not in
scale with the
principal illustrations

country or region
where the subspecies
is found

♂ = male
♀ = female
imm. = immature
juv. = juvenile

The principal birds on each page are painted to scale, but colour and
other variants, flight and other behaviour sketches, birds put in for the sake
of comparison and rare visitors are distinguished by being shown on a
smaller scale.

A change of background colour on a plate indicates the start of a new
family or group.

The Birds in the Book

This book includes all birds which either breed in, or visit regularly in the winter or on passage, any part of Europe, North Africa south to a line drawn eastwards from southern Morocco, and the Middle East, east to a line drawn from the head of the Red Sea to the head of the Gulf and thence more or less due north to the Arctic Ocean. It thus includes the whole of the Western Palaearctic Region (except for parts of the Sahara and Arabia, central and eastern Iran, Afghanistan and Baluchistan), and so covers the Azores, the Canaries, Madeira, all Morocco, northern Egypt, all Iraq, the whole European part of the USSR, and Iceland. The breeding birds of Greenland are all included, since they are all also European birds.

Birds which do not occur regularly present a problem, partly because now that bird watching is so intensive, birds new to the European list of vagrants are being added every year. Already most of the North American migratory birds have been recorded as vagrants in Europe, and by the end of the century all North American migrants that use either the east coast or the Mississippi flyway will probably have been seen in Europe at least once. A book overloaded with North American vagrants would not be useful to the European birdwatcher. The majority of accidentals, especially of those from across the Atlantic, are therefore only listed, on p. 312. Those vagrants most likely to be seen, based on recent frequency of occurrence rather

American visitor among European birds: Pectoral Sandpiper and Dunlins

than by total numbers ever seen, are, however, scattered through the text, and also clumped on pages 136–7 (waders), 260–1 (thrushes) and 282–3 North American passerines.

Scientists classify all animals in a series of groupings, starting with 22 phyla and proceeding downwards through classes, orders, families (ending in -idae), subfamilies (ending in -inae) and genera to the actual species, below which there are sometimes subspecies or races based on geographical variation. Birds belong to the Phylum Chordata, along with the mammals, reptiles and fishes, and are themselves distinguished as the Class Aves. Within the Class Aves, there are 27 orders of living birds, much the largest of which is the Passeriformes, loosely known as song birds, perching birds or passerines. The passerines comprise more than half the known bird species of the world, and more than a third of the 154 bird families. They are all terrestrial and very diverse in shape and form, but

Osprey *(Pandion haliaetus)*

generally adapted to perching in trees and often have a very well developed song. The Passeriformes in this book start with the larks (p. 199) and end with the crows (p. 305).

The basic unit of classification used in this book is the family, of which 74 are represented. The beginning of all but the smallest families is indicated by a solid blue circle beside the heading.

For the actual arrangement of birds in the text, we have adopted, subject to the exigencies of fitting birds on to the plates, the order of families originally devised by Alexander Wetmore and used in such standard works as *A New Dictionary of Birds* (1964), edited by Sir Landsborough Thomson, as amended in recent volumes of Peters's *Birds of the World*.

The scientific name of an animal is part of the international language of science, enabling naturalists in one country to know what those in another are talking about. For instance "Osprey" might not mean anything to a Chinese ornithologist, but *Pandion haliaetus* would. The scientific name of an animal consists of two Latinised words, a generic name, which has a capital initial, followed by a specific name, which always has a small initial. Where subspecies or geographical races are referred to, a third word is added to the name. For instance the European White Wagtail is *Motacilla alba alba*, and its British race, the Pied Wagtail, *Motacilla alba yarrellii*. Without necessarily always agreeing with him, for the sake of standardisation we have in almost all cases followed the scientific names used in *The Birds of the Palaearctic Fauna* (1959–65), by Charles Vaurie. The few exceptions are mostly where we have treated as species birds he has treated as subspecies, and *vice versa*.

Maps

The various colours, shadings and symbols used on the distribution maps in this book are explained in the sample map overleaf. The main features to remember are that **yellow** represents breeding distribution, and **blue** winter distribution, while the combination of these two colours **(green)** indicates that the bird both winters and breeds — i.e. it is present throughout the year. Areas of **blue hatching** show that the bird occurs on spring and/or autumn migration, but does not usually breed or overwinter. A **blue arrow** indicates the general direction of migration for a bird flying over an area; some may alight, but generally too few do so, or they do so

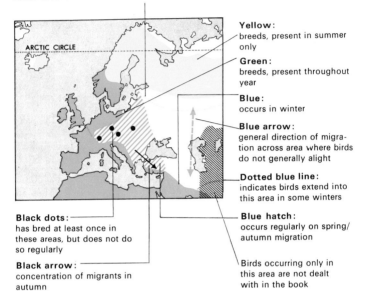

Dotted yellow line indicates that birds breed as far south as this in some summers

Yellow:
breeds, present in summer only

Green:
breeds, present throughout year

Blue:
occurs in winter

Blue arrow:
general direction of migration across area where birds do not generally alight

Dotted blue line:
indicates birds extend into this area in some winters

Black dots:
has bred at least once in these areas, but does not do so regularly

Black arrow:
concentration of migrants in autumn

Blue hatch:
occurs regularly on spring/ autumn migration

Birds occurring only in this area are not dealt with in the book

ARCTIC CIRCLE

so locally that it would give too misleading an impression of their abundance to blue-hatch the areas concerned.

The question of how to indicate abundance, or rather relative abundance, is one which faces all compilers of range maps such as these; on such small-scale maps it is not possible to show how common a bird is within the range in which it occurs. For example, the Kestrel and the Blackbird both occur throughout the British Isles and so their ranges for this area are similar; yet there are many more Blackbirds than Kestrels. Small-scale range maps also tend to exaggerate the distributions of species – all birds have certain habitat preferences and limitations. A breeding bird may perhaps be associated only with large bodies of fresh water (e.g. Great Crested Grebe) or have altitudinal preferences linked with local climate or habitat (e.g. Dartford Warbler). Some birds tend to be rather nomadic, breeding in one region one year, but not the next; the Black-necked Grebe, which requires areas of fresh water at a critical, shallow depth for breeding, is one such example; when the waters dry out during droughts the birds move elsewhere. In the case of some birds which breed very locally, often colonially, their distributions have been deliberately exaggerated on these maps; had this not been done, the areas in which they nest would have been too small to have shown up at all.

The mapping of wintering ranges is also difficult since these partly depend on the severity of the winter, or in the case of berry- and seed-eating birds on the abundance of their food supply which may fluctuate from one year to the next. For example, in a normal winter many thousands of Lapwings, of north European as well as local origin, are found throughout most of Britain, but in a severe one, as for example in 1962–3, practically all depart for southern Europe, leaving none in Britain. Birds such as Fieldfares may linger through most of a mild winter in parts of Scandinavia, including even the far north of Norway; but in a cold one, or when food is short, none remains there.

The information on which these maps are based has been derived from many sources. All compilers of such maps are indebted to Dementiev and Gladkov, *The Birds of the Soviet Union* (1954), who produced the first extensive series of range maps for Palaearctic species: despite many inaccuracies, their maps have formed the basis of all future work. Outstanding among the latter, so far as maps of European bird distribution are concerned, have been the maps produced by P. A. D. Hollom for the *Field Guide to the Birds of Britain and Europe* (1954; revised 1966) and by K. H. Voous *Atlas of European Birds* (1960). The maps in the present book owe much to the pioneering work of these earlier authors. Up-to-date information has been obtained from the great many national bird checklists and other ornithological publications produced in the last few years. The information from western Europe tends to be more complete, accurate and up-to-date than information from elsewhere, simply because there are more ornithologists and more regular ornithological publications in these countries.

The main aim of these maps is to provide an indication to the general reader of the distribution of every species which is found in Europe, N. Africa and the Middle East. Errors will have been made in these maps, and information from ornithologists which correct any errors will be welcomed by the publishers.

Identifying Birds

The rules of bird identification are few and simple. The first is to be patient. You cannot expect, especially when you are still a beginner, to identify every bird you see the first time you see it. You must have a good enough view, and birds go about their own affairs oblivious, or sometimes all too conscious, of a bird watcher eagerly trying to find out whether it is a Whitethroat or a Lesser Whitethroat. The second rule is to be quiet. You will certainly not see or hear many birds if you plunge noisily through the undergrowth, or chatter unheedingly to a friend. An invaluable asset, however, is a knowledgeable friend, to set your footsteps on the right path. Alternatively join a local society, most of which have field excursions for beginners; or visit a bird observatory. The addresses of local societies and observatories in Britain can be had from the Council for Nature (see p. 19). The full recipe for successful bird identification is patience, quietness, a reasonably sharp eye and ear and a good bird book.

Although the common garden birds can readily be identified by attracting them within close range at a well sited bird table, for general bird watching a pair of binoculars is essential. The best magnifications for binoculars are 7× and 8×. Their most important quality is light-gathering power, measured by the figure that represents the diameter of the object-lens and is usually engraved after the magnification, e.g. 7 × 40 or

8 × 50. The key figure is obtained by dividing the magnification into the diameter, e.g. 7 into 40 goes 6 (or near enough) and any result between 4 and 7 is satisfactory.

Before starting out, it is helpful to memorise the names for the various parts of a bird on the pictures below. You can then make notes on what you have seen, for checking afterwards, if you are in doubt. It also helps to have in your mind the following eleven points (pp. 15–16) to look for in identifying a new or doubtful bird.

Topography of a Bird

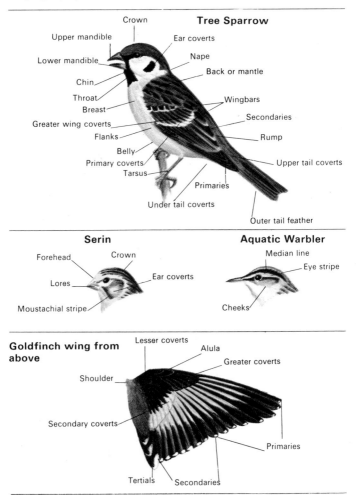

Tree Sparrow

Crown
Upper mandible
Ear coverts
Lower mandible
Nape
Back or mantle
Chin
Throat
Wingbars
Breast
Secondaries
Greater wing coverts
Flanks
Rump
Belly
Primary coverts
Upper tail coverts
Tarsus
Primaries
Under tail coverts
Outer tail feather

Serin

Forehead
Crown
Lores
Ear coverts
Moustachial stripe

Aquatic Warbler

Median line
Eye stripe
Cheeks

Goldfinch wing from above

Lesser coverts
Alula
Greater coverts
Shoulder
Secondary coverts
Primaries
Tertials
Secondaries

1. Size, compared with some fairly common bird, and general shape. Among land birds, for instance, the Blue Tit, House Sparrow, Starling, Lapwing, Rook and Pheasant represent six well-known birds that you can usefully compare sizes with. On the water you might have Moorhen, Mallard and Mute Swan.

2. General colour, above and below. A bird the size of a Rook that is grey with black head and wings, for instance, can only be a Hooded Crow (p. 311).

3. Any conspicuous marks or patches, their colour and approximate position on the bird. An all black bird, smaller than a Rook, with a grey patch on the nape must infallibly be a Jackdaw (p. 311).

4. Size and shape of bill, legs, wings, tail and neck. A black and white bird, nearly rook-sized, with a long tail, is clearly a Magpie (p. 307). A long-legged brown bird with a markedly down-curved bill, on the other hand, may be either a Curlew or a Whimbrel, or in some parts of the region also a Slender-billed Curlew (p. 139)

5. Colour of bill, legs feet and eyes. Bill colour separates the Chough and Alpine Chough (p. 307), and eye colour distinguishes the Tawny and Short-eared Owls (pp. 179, 183).

6. Actions and character of flight or gait, e.g. whether flight bounding, like a finch, woodpecker or Little Owl, or direct like a crow or wader, and whether the bird runs like a Starling or hops like a Blackbird. Some birds also have helpful mannerisms of behaviour, such as the tail-wagging of wag-tails, hovering of Kestrel and some other birds of prey, and plummet-diving of gannets and terns.

Kestrel hovering

7. Any call notes or song. Voice is one of the most helpful aids to identification. Some birds with very similar plumage, such as Chiffchaff and Willow Warbler (p. 237) or Marsh and Willow Tits (p. 269), can much more readily be distinguished by their calls than by sight. An experienced bird watcher in woodland or scrub will detect twice as many birds by ear as by eye.

8. Comparisons with any other birds that come to mind. For instance, a small falcon that "flies like a swift" may well prove to be a Hobby (p. 95), and a small brown bird that creeps about tree trunks will be either a

Marsh Tit   Willow Tit   Willow Tit, northern form

Treecreeper or a Short-toed Treecreeper (p. 273), unless indeed it is large enough to be a Wryneck (p. 197), in which case you will see that it has a straight not a curved bill.

9. Date, time, place and weather are important clues to identity. A wagtail with yellow underparts in southern England in November is much more likely to be a Grey Wagtail than a Yellow Wagtail (p. 214), which as a summer visitor to Britain should at this time be in Africa. A brown owl seen beating over the heather at 12 noon is more likely to be a Short-eared Owl (p. 179), which does fly by day, than a Tawny Owl (p. 183), which very rarely does so, and then usually near sunrise or dusk. A singing Reed Warbler need only be checked to see if it is in fact a Marsh Warbler (p. 225) if it is somewhere near the zone of overlap between these two very similar species in southern England. A small white-rumped black bird seen over Lake Windermere is much more likely to be a House Martin (p. 207) than a small petrel (p. 29).

10. Habitat and general surroundings. A red-tailed bird seen in an oak forest in Gloucestershire is likely to be a Redstart, but a similar bird seen on an industrial site in East London is almost certain to be a Black Redstart (p. 251). However, birds can and do turn up in the most unlikely surroundings. One can see a Peregrine Falcon in the centre of a large city, a Green Woodpecker on a treeless cliff slope, or a lost migratory bird almost anywhere.

11. Angle of vision, conditions of light, distance of bird from observer, and whether bird was at rest, swimming or in flight should all be noted. A Magpie flying towards you so that you cannot see its tail looks very odd indeed, and birds flying directly towards and away from the observer are often almost impossible to identify. When gulls are directly overhead it is often very hard for the observer to see the colour of their upperparts which would reveal whether they are Herring Gulls or Lesser Blackbacks (p. 151). In poor light or misty conditions all kinds of strange illusions may occur.

Attracting Birds

There are two main ways of attracting birds nearer to the observer: by feeding them and by encouraging them to nest in nest-boxes. In winter many birds can be induced to come quite near the windows of a house by a suitably sited bird table, kept supplied with household scraps, bits of fat, nuts and so forth. A coconut or an old bone hung up will bring the tits. By careful varying of the food supply, such apparently unlikely species as Great Spotted Woodpecker and Nuthatch can be tempted in. In really hard weather the mass feeding of birds by housewives in northern and western Europe is probably responsible for saving the lives of hundreds of thousands of birds.

Nestboxes are of two main types, those with a small hole, for tits, Pied Flycatchers, Redstarts and Nuthatches (which will plaster up the hole), and those with an open front for ledge-builders like the Robin, Wren and Spotted Flycatcher. Special boxes or ledges can also be constructed for Treecreepers, Tawny Owls, Swallows and House Martins, while Mallards can be induced to nest in wicker baskets.

Nestboxes, bird tables and other bird feeding equipment can be obtained from the Royal Society for the Protection of Birds (see p. 19).

Tits at nuts

Pied flycatcher

Robin

Types of nest box

Where to Look for Birds

The key to successful bird watching is to know where to look for birds, which vary in kind greatly from one habitat to another. In the agricultural countryside, with its mixture of farmland, houses with gardens and scattered broad-leaved woodlands, you can see a fair variety of birds in the course of a morning's or afternoon's walk. If the patchwork of habitats also includes some wetlands, marshes, lakes or rivers, a total of 50–60 species in a few hours is by no means impossible, especially in spring and summer, and keen motorised bird-spotters intent on their sport can knock up 100 or more in a day.

Habitats are best classified as land, waterside and water. Land habitats proceed by natural processes from bare ground with increasing vegetation cover to dense woodland. In deserts, lack of rainfall prevents all but the sparsest vegetation, and leads to a characteristic assemblage of larks, wheatears, sandgrouse and other birds. The Arctic and sub-Arctic tundra is the northern counterpart of the desert, but during the spring and summer it is mostly waterlogged and so holds waders and other birds of the waterside. Desert merges imperceptibly into semi-desert and grassy steppe, represented in settled Britain and western Europe by the artificially maintained chalk downs, grass moors, and agricultural grasslands. Here there are still birds of open country, such as larks, pipits, partridges and Stone Curlew. In northern Europe the hill grasslands, maintained as such largely by sheep grazing, merge into the heather moors, with their special group of birds, including Red or Willow Grouse, Meadow Pipit, Ring Ouzel and Skylark.

Heather moor is botanically a scrub formation, heather being a woody undershrub. Scrub, the intermediate stage between grassland and woodland, is one of the most important bird habitats of the region, and is favoured by many thrushes, warblers, finches and other song birds. A mixture of patches or glades of open grassland, scrub and scattered trees affords a wide range of ecological niches to birds, and while this is found often enough on wood edges and in open woodlands of much of western Europe this type of habitat includes houses and gardens, in' villages, suburbs and towns. The characteristic garden birds are also those of scrub and woodland, Blackbird, Song Thrush, Robin, Hedgesparrow, Wren, Great and Blue Tits, Chaffinch, Greenfinch. On acid soils scrub takes the form of heath.

Scrub develops naturally into woodland, which is of two main kinds: coniferous, in a broad belt across northern Europe, called the taiga, and in a corresponding zone in the Alps and other mountains further south; and broad-leaved, mainly oak and beech, occupying the central and southern lowlands of Europe. Millennia of human destruction have made extensive woodland a rare habitat in North Africa and the Middle East. Besides the familiar garden birds, woodlands hold many birds, such as woodpeckers, Pied Flycatcher and Woodcock, which are seen only in large country gardens, if at all, and some, such as Black Stork or Lesser Spotted Eagle, which are never seen in gardens at all. Coniferous woodland has a special assemblage of birds, including Goldcrest, Coal and Crested Tits and crossbills.

Waterside habitats consist of both waterlogged swamps and bogs, and the more open margins of lakes and rivers. The long-legged wading birds, herons, rails, snipe and sandpipers, are the typical birds of these habitats, which also contain a few song-birds, such as the acrocephaline (reed) warblers. Many plovers, on the other hand, are open country birds. By the sea the waterside habitat consists mainly of cliff and saltmarsh, where many birds of the open sea nest, but numerous waders feed on the mud flats along the shore.

The birds of open water, both sea and fresh water, must of course come to land to breed, but grebes, diving ducks, swans, auks, gannets, cormorants, petrels and many others spend most or all of the rest of their lives on the water.

Ornithological Societies

British Ornithologists' Union, c/o Zoological Gardens, Regent's Park, London N.W.1.

British Trust for Ornithology, Beech Grove, Tring, Herts.

Council for Nature, c/o Zoological Gardens, Regent's Park, London N.W.1. will supply addresses of local bird clubs, bird observatories and natural history societies in the British Isles.

International Council for Bird Preservation, c/o British Museum (Natural History), Cromwell Road, London S.W.7, has national sections in Britain and most European countries.

Irish Wildbird Conservancy, c/o Royal Irish Academy, 19 Dawson St., Dublin 2, Ireland.

Ornithological Society of Turkey, c/o The Lodge, Sandy, Beds.

Pheasant Trust, Great Witchingham, Norwich, Norfolk.

Royal Society for the Protection of Birds, The Lodge, Sandy, Beds.; 17 Regent Terrace, Edinburgh EH7 5BN, Scotland; 58 High St., Newtownards, Co. Down, N. Ireland.

Scottish Ornithologists' Club, 21 Regent Terrace, Edinburgh EH7 5BN. Scotland.

Seabird Group, c/o British Ornithologists' Union.

Wildfowl Trust, Slimbridge, Glos.

DIVERS: *Gaviidae*. The most primitive bird family in Europe, and one of the five main groups that dive from the surface of the water. The others are the grebes (p. 23), cormorants (p. 33), diving ducks (p. 59) and auks (p. 165). Divers are larger than grebes and are highly adapted to their aquatic way of life, both by their short-tailed cigar-shape and by the position of their legs set far back on the body. This gives them a powerful thrust when swimming but makes them clumsy on land, which they rarely visit except to breed. At rest divers hold their heads more horizontally than cormorants, but less so than the saw-bills. In flight head and neck are held straight out, slightly below the plane of the body, giving the bird a rather humped look. Vocal mainly in breeding season, with various loud wailing and laughing notes. Sexes alike. Winter plumage dark above, white below. They breed close to fresh water inland in moorland or forested districts; winter at sea inshore, rarely inland, sometimes in small loose parties.

GREAT NORTHERN DIVER *Gavia immer*. Unmistakable in spring and summer with black head, alternating dark and light horizontal bands around neck, and conspicuously spotted upper parts. In winter stout bill and more peaked forehead are best distinctions from smaller Black-throated Diver; crown and hind neck usually darker than back. Has a loud eerie wailing cry; flight-note 'kwuk-kwuk-kwuk'. Breeds by larger lakes, often on islands. 27–32 in. (68–81 cm.).
⊙ **W(b)**   **Map 1**

WHITE-BILLED DIVER *Gavia adamsii*. Differs from the much commoner Great Northern Diver mainly in its bill, which is pale yellowish-white and angled below, and so appears distinctly tip-tilted. But beware some Great Northerns which have paler bills than the normal greyish-black. Voice and behaviour also similar to Great Northern. 33–34 in. (84–87 cm.).   **—V**

BLACK-THROATED DIVER *Gavia arctica*. Easily told from the larger and commoner Great Northern Diver in breeding plumage, when head is grey and neck a combination of grey and black with vertical black and white stripes. Bill less stout and forehead more receding are all-the-year distinctions. In winter crown and hind neck usually appear paler than blackish back and white patch at rear of flanks is distinctive. Voice and behaviour similar to Great Northern.
23–27 in. (58–68 cm.).   **RW   Map 2**

RED-THROATED DIVER *Gavia stellata*. The smallest and commonest diver, readily told by neck pattern in breeding plumage, combining red and grey with vertical black and white stripes. In winter back is finely spotted with white and face appears whiter than other divers. At all times angled lower mandible gives bill a distinctive tip-tilted appearance. Lack of wing-bar in flight distinguishes from Great Crested and Red-necked, the largest grebes (p. 23). Flightnote more quacking than other divers. Breeds on quite small lakes and tarns on open moorland and tundra. 21–23 in. (53–58 cm.).
⊙ **RmW   Map 3**

DIVERS

Shag

Diver

Shag

Diver

'rolling preen'

winter

summer

GREAT NORTHERN DIVER

WHITE-BILLED DIVER

winter

summer

winter

summer

BLACK-THROATED DIVER

winter

summer

on nest

RED-THROATED DIVER

21

GREBES: *Podicipitidae*. Smaller, longer-necked and generally dumpier than the divers (p. 21), and with lobed toes, but otherwise very similarly adapted to aquatic life. Sexes similar. Winter plumage dark above, white below. Juveniles striped vertically on head and neck. In flight hold head and neck at angle below body. Breed always on fresh water, sometimes in colonies, the nest a mass of floating vegetation; in winter also in estuaries and coastal waters.

GREAT CRESTED GREBE *Podiceps cristatus*. Breeding adult unmistakable with dark double-horned crest and rufous tippets, used in mutual head-wagging and other striking courtship displays. In winter white cheeks conspicuous. At rest often holds neck erect. In flight shows pale wing-bar. Song a crooning note; call a harsh bark or honk; juvenile has shrill piping hunger call. 19 in. (48 cm.). ●Rw Map 4

RED-NECKED GREBE *Podiceps grisegena*. Easily told from larger Great Crested Grebe in breeding plumage by chestnut neck, pale grey cheeks and lack of head ornaments; in winter by stockier build, black and yellow bill, lack of stripe over eye, and dark of crown coming down below eye and shading off gradually into much less white cheeks. Song, wailing or whinnying; call, a high-pitched 'keck, keck'. Winters mainly in coastal waters. 17 in. (43 cm.). ⊙W Map 5

SLAVONIAN GREBE *Podiceps auritus*. The largest and longest-necked of the three smaller, dumpier and shorter-billed grebes, most easily recognised in its striking breeding plumage. In winter differs from Black-necked Grebe by black crown contrasting sharply with white of cheeks at eye-level, and by straight bill. Calls include a low rippling trill. Winters mainly in coastal waters. 13 in. (33 cm.). ⊙rW Map 6

BLACK-NECKED GREBE *Podiceps nigricollis*. Slightly smaller than Slavonian Grebe, from which it differs in breeding plumage in its black neck and golden-chestnut ear-tufts pointing downwards, in winter in black of crown merging gradually into white of cheeks below eye-level, and at all times an angled lower mandible giving bill a tip-tilted appearance. Calls include a soft 'preeip'. 12 in. (30 cm.). ⊙ sMW Map 7

LITTLE GREBE or **DABCHICK** *Tachybaptus ruficollis*. The smallest European grebe, distinctive for its brown plumage, with chestnut cheeks and throat and white patch at base of bill in breeding plumage. Autumn juveniles have some white on cheeks. Song a whinnying trill; alarm note, 'whit, whit'. More frequent on rivers and less so in coastal waters than other grebes. 10½ in. (27 cm.). ●Rw Map 8

winter

Pied-billed Grebe

PIED-BILLED GREBE *Podilymbus podiceps*. A transatlantic vagrant, now seen almost annually in England. A stocky, short-necked, large-headed grebe best told by short thick, almost rounded bill, white at the base, and white under tail coverts. Call a gruff bark followed by a short wail, 'bn-aah'. 12–15 in. (30-38 cm.). —V

GREBES

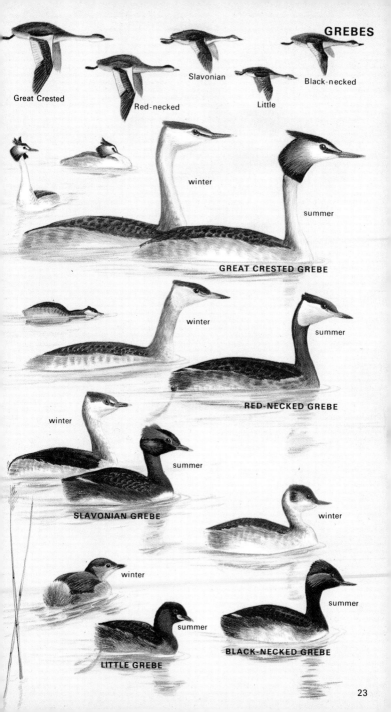

Great Crested

Red-necked

Slavonian

Little

Black-necked

winter

summer

GREAT CRESTED GREBE

winter

summer

RED-NECKED GREBE

winter

summer

SLAVONIAN GREBE

winter

winter

summer

LITTLE GREBE

summer

BLACK-NECKED GREBE

23

● ALBATROSSES, SHEARWATERS AND PETRELS:

Diomedeidae and Procellariidae. pp. 25–27. Long-winged seabirds, characterised by their tube-noses, their nostrils lying in two short tubes on the bill, and by their strong musky smell. Exclusively pelagic, they come to land voluntarily only to breed and are highly adapted to gliding; they also swim. The albatrosses (Diomedeidae), the largest seabirds, noted for their great wing-span and sustained gliding flight are only vagrants in the region. The shearwaters and petrels (Procellariidae) are medium-sized, and distinctive for their stiff-winged mode of flight, 'shearing' the waves as they skim the surface, tilting alternately from one wing-tip to the other.

BLACK-BROWED ALBATROSS *Diomedea melanophris.* Resembles a giant Great Black-backed Gull (p. 151), with its dark mantle and wings and white head and underparts, but has 6–8 ft wing-span, dark tail, blackish line through eye and white stripe along dark underwing. Immatures are generally greyer, especially on the head, the white stripe only developing gradually. Bill starts blackish-grey, becoming horn-coloured and finally yellow, with black tip when fully adult. Call 'gah' or 'gah-gah-gah', sometimes with bill clattering. Rare visitor from S Atlantic. 32–34 in. (81–86 cm.).   —V

YELLOW-NOSED ALBATROSS *Diomedea chlororhynchos.* The only other albatross at all likely to be seen in the North Atlantic is rather smaller, with pale grey head, much more white on underwing, and black bill with yellow stripe and pink tip; immatures have head pure white and bill all black. 30–34 in. (76–86 cm.).

SOFT-PLUMAGED PETREL *Pterodroma mollis.* A medium-sized petrel, the size of a Manx Shearwater, but with upperparts grey, dark patch on ear coverts, partial grey chestband, dark underwings, shorter bill and quite different, more darting or undulating flight. Breeds on desolate marine islands, rarely wandering to continental inshore waters. 14 in. (35 cm.).

CAPE PIGEON or PINTADO PETREL *Daption capensis.* A rare vagrant from the Antarctic and South Atlantic Ocean with notably dappled black and white plumage, which has reminded successive generations of seamen of a pigeon. Only doubtfully recorded in the region and probably released from ships. 14 in. (35 cm.).

FULMAR *Fulmarus glacialis.* A rather large gull-like petrel, typically with silver-grey upperparts and white head and underparts, but in Arctic may be partly or wholly dark grey-blue, and also has a rare almost all-white form. Readily told from herring-type gulls (p. 151) by shearwater-like flight with rigid wings, by lack of black wing-tips and at close range also by tubular nostrils. Guttural growls, chuckles and grunts heard mainly at breeding sites. Has defensive habit of spitting foul-smelling oil at intruders. Nests colonially on cliffs, occasionally on ruined buildings or a few miles inland; mainly pelagic outside long breeding season. 18½ in. (47 cm.).

●Sr   Map 9

YELLOW-NOSED ALBATROSS

BLACK-BROWED
ALBATROSS

SOFT-PLUMAGED
PETREL

CAPE
PIGEON

light phase

FULMAR

dark phase

storm petrels, p. 28

terns, p. 158

fulmars, p. 24

gulls, p. 146

shearwaters, p. 26

MANX SHEARWATER *Puffinus puffinus.* The commonest shearwater of the region, the Atlantic and E Mediterranean breeding forms being recognised by sharp contrast of dark upperparts and white underparts, revealed by characteristic shearwater flight; also has pink legs and black bill. W Mediterranean race *mauretanicus* (Balearic Shearwater), which reaches Western Approaches in autumn, has underparts much darker, and is best told from Cory's and Sooty Shearwaters by much smaller size and 'scuttling' flight. E Mediterranean race *yelkouan* is browner above. Very noisy at breeding places at night, with loud cooing and caterwauling cries. Breeds on marine islands, sometimes high up and well inland. 14 in. (35 cm.). ⊙ **Sm Map 10**

LITTLE SHEARWATER *Puffinus assimilis.* A smaller version of the Manx Shearwater, with more flapping, less gliding flight; also has bright blue feet and black of crown not extending below eye. Calls on breeding grounds like Manx but less noisy. Rocky shores of Atlantic islands, wandering to N W Africa, Iberia and W Ireland. 10½ in. (27 cm.). —**V**

GREAT SHEARWATER *Puffinus gravis.* Differs from Cory's Shearwater especially in the marked capped effect of its dark crown, sharply defined by white sides of neck, also by dark bill, larger and more constant white patch at base of tail, and dark patch on belly (not easily seen in field). Has typical low skimming shearwater flight, but sometimes soars. Late summer and autumn visitor from S Atlantic, sometimes inshore near promontories. 18 in. (46 cm.). ○**M Map 11**

SOOTY SHEARWATER *Puffinus griseus.* Can be told from both Great and Cory's Shearwaters by all dark plumage, except for pale stripe on underwing, but flight resembles Great rather than Cory's with strong scything action of wing-beats. Larger and darker than Balearic Shearwater. Another southern visitor to N W European waters in autumn, occasional inshore. 16 in. (41 cm.). ○**M Map 12**

CORY'S SHEARWATER *Calonectris diomedea.* The largest tube-nose breeding in Europe, best told from the two other large shearwaters by its combination of uniformly ash-brown upperparts, lack of any capped effect, white underparts and (at close range) yellow bill; may have a small white patch at base of tail. Flight often more gliding, soaring and albatross-like or gannet-like than the other two, wings being characteristically bowed when gliding. Raucous wailing cries at breeding colonies, on rocky islands and cliffs. 18 in. (46 cm.). ○**M**

26

SHEARWATERS

W. Mediterranean race

Atlantic race

adult

MANX SHEARWATER

GREAT SHEARWATER

LITTLE SHEARWATER

SOOTY SHEARWATER

CORY'S SHEARWATER

27

STORM PETRELS: *Hydrobatidae.* Small white-rumped black tube-noses (p. 24) of the open sea, flying or fluttering low over the surface, and coming to land, except when storm-wrecked, only to breed in holes on rocky coasts, where exclusively nocturnal. Sexes alike; bill short, black.

STORM PETREL *Hydrobates pelagicus.* The smallest European seabird, looking not unlike a large square-tailed House Martin (p. 207), white rump contrasting strongly with otherwise almost all black plumage; pale patch on underwing; feet black. Habitually follows ships, with weak but direct flight; also has fluttering feeding flight. Nightjar-like purring note, ending in a hiccuping 'chikka' only heard at nest, usually at night. 6 in. (15 cm.). ⊙ **Sm   Map 13**

LEACH'S PETREL *Oceanodroma leucorrhoa.* Larger than Storm Petrel, and differs in its forked tail (hard to see in flight), greyish centre to white rump (not visible in field), paler basal part of wing, dark underwing, and especially in characteristic buoyant darting zigzag flight. Does not follow ships. Churrs gutturally at nest. More widespread in winter. 8 in. (20 cm.). ◯**Sm   Map 14**

MADEIRAN PETREL *Oceanodroma castro.* Rather browner than other small petrels, and chiefly notable for variable flight, which can resemble Storm, Leach's and Wilson's, but extremely hard to distinguish in field. Is larger and longer-winged than Storm Petrel, and differs from Leach's in its pure white rump, and from Wilson's in its shorter all-black legs. Slightly forked tail is almost useless field character; in the hand black tips to white tail coverts are also distinctive. Call at nest, 'kair chuck-a-chuk chuck chuck'. May sometimes follow ships. Does not disperse far from breeding islands in winter. 7½ in. (19 cm.).   —**V**

WILSON'S PETREL *Oceanites oceanicus.* Differs from Storm Petrel chiefly in characteristic gliding flight, with yellow-webbed feet extending well beyond tail; also has pale patch on wing. Sometimes appears to patter along surface of water with outspread wings. Visitor from Antarctic, common in Bay of Biscay but rare inshore. 7 in. (18 cm.).   —**V**

FRIGATE PETREL *Pelagodroma marina.* The only small North Atlantic petrel with white on face and white underparts; feet with orange webs. Flight wavering and erratic, with long legs extending beyond tail. 8 in. (20 cm.).   —**V**

BULWER'S PETREL *Bulweria bulwerii* (Procellariidae) The only small all black petrel at all likely to be seen in the North Atlantic, with longish wedge-shaped tail, black bill and black and pink feet. Call on breeding grounds a croaking bark. Nests in rocky places on marine islands, likely to be seen inshore only off N W Africa. 10½ in. (27 cm.).   —**V**

House Martin

petrels feeding

STORM PETREL

LEACH'S
PETREL

MADEIRAN
PETREL

WILSON'S PETREL

FRIGATE PETREL

BULWER'S PETREL

GANNET *Sula bassana* (Sulidae). A large white seabird with black wing-tips, easily recognised even at great distances by habit of diving steeply into sea from a height, with wings folded. At close range, yellow-buff head and neck, stout bluish-white bill, blackish-brown legs and grey eye surrounded by bare blue-grey skin. Sexes alike. Juvenile dark brown speckled white, immatures gradually becoming whiter with each moult. Harsh voice heard only at nest. Flight direct, also glides, soars and swims. Breeds on rocky coasts and marine islands; at other times on open sea. Masked or Blue-faced Booby *S. dactylatra*, with wing-tips, whole trailing edge of wing and tail chocolate-brown, might occur off Moroccan coast. 36 in. (90 cm.). ●**Smr   Map 15**

BROWN BOOBY *Sula leucogaster*. Much smaller than Gannet, and with all plumage except white breast and belly dark brown. Immature similar but paler, differing from immature Gannet in sharp two-tone appearance. (64 cm.).

RED-BILLED TROPICBIRD *Phaethon aethereus* (Phaethontidae). An almost all-white seabird, more than half of whose length is an immensely long pointed tail; black bar on wing, black mark through each eye, dark barring on upperparts; red bill. Shrill rasping call often heard at sea. Flies with strong, rather pigeon-like beats, diving from a height. 42 in. (107 cm.).

FRIGATEBIRDS : *Fregatidae*. Ungainly looking dark birds of tropical seas, piratical on other seabirds. Most likely to be seen as a wanderer on Moroccan coast is the Magnificent Frigatebird or Man o' War Bird *Fregata magnificens*, with long forked tail, marked crook in long wings, red pouch in male, white breast in female, and white head and underparts in immature.   **—V**

WHITE PELICAN *Pelecanus onocrotalus* (Pelecanidae). A very large heavy white bird, tinged pink and crested in breeding plumage; wing-tips black, yellow patch on breast, bill bluish and pink, pouch pale pink or yellow, legs pink or orange. Sexes alike. Immature pale brown, becoming whiter with each moult. Guttural voice heard mainly at nest. Flight majestic, with neck retracted; Soars, glides and flies in formation. Fresh and brackish lakes and marshes, shallow coastal water. Smaller, more crested, pale grey Pink-backed Pelican *P. rufescens* has wandered to Palestine. 55–70 in. (140–180 cm.).

DALMATIAN PELICAN *Pelecanus crispus*. Rather larger than white pelican, from which it differs in its greyer white (never pink) plumage, lack of crest, yellow eyes and especially grey legs. Easier to distinguish when in flight overhead, no black showing in underwings. 63–70 in. (160–180 cm.).

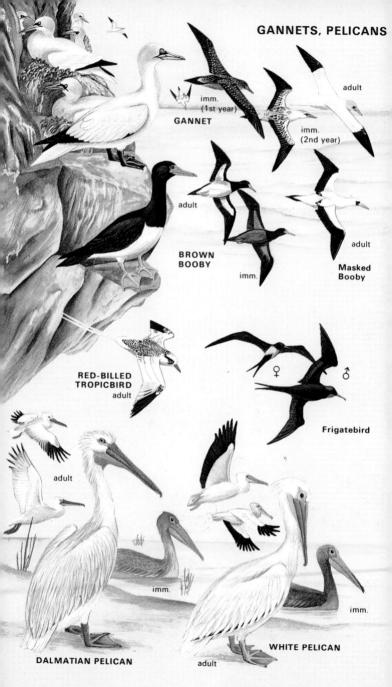

GANNETS, PELICANS

GANNET

imm. (1st year)

adult

imm. (2nd year)

BROWN BOOBY

adult

imm.

Masked Booby

adult

adult

RED-BILLED TROPICBIRD

adult

Frigatebird

♀

♂

adult

DALMATIAN PELICAN

imm.

WHITE PELICAN

imm.

adult

31

● **CORMORANTS** : *Phalacrocoracidae*. Large dark-plumaged aquatic diving birds, with long neck, long stout hooked bill, rather short wings, fairly long tail and webbed feet. Sexes alike. Juveniles mostly brown with paler underparts. On land often hold wings out to dry; on water hold head at marked upward angle; in air fly, often in V-formation, with neck held level. These traits, together with longer tail, distinguish them from the divers. Breed colonially on cliffs or rocks, or inland in trees.

SHAG *Phalacrocorax aristotelis*. Smaller than Cormorant and all dark except for yellow patches at base of bill and around eye; distinctive recurved crest in breeding season. Juvenile brown with whitish chin and throat. Harsh croak, at nest only. Has faster wing-beats than Cormorant. Exclusively marine, nesting on rocky coasts and rarely wandering to muddy or sandy shores or inland. 30 in. (76 cm.).   ●R   Map 16

CORMORANT *Phalacrocorax carbo*. The largest all-dark European sea-bird, with yellow patch at base of bill, white patch on face, and in breeding season white patch also on each thigh. Many older birds, especially of Continental and N African races *sinensis* and *maroccanus*, have head and neck predominantly white in breeding season. Juvenile brown with whitish throat and underparts. Various guttural notes at nest. Inshore waters on all types of coast, also on lakes inland. 36 in. (90 cm.).   ●Rmw   Map 17

PYGMY CORMORANT *Phalacrocorax pygmeus*. The smallest European cormorant, easily told by its short head, and in breeding season also by its red-brown head and neck and speckled appearance, though sometimes with head and neck black just before breeding. Fresh and brackish water with extensive reed-beds; often at quite small ponds. A south-eastern species. 19 in. (48 cm.).

LONG-TAILED CORMORANT or REED CORMORANT *Phalacrocorax africanus*. A small cormorant, the black breeding plumage relieved only by grey speckling on wing coverts, a small crest and briefly by white plumes behind eye. In winter browner with white throat and paler underparts. Hisses at nest. Fresh and coastal waters. 23 in. (58 cm.).

SOCOTRA CORMORANT *Phalacrocorax nigrogularis*. All dark, with some white on cheeks, neck and rump in breeding plumage. Breeds on islands off S. Iraq. 32 in. (80 cm.).

DARTER or SNAKE-BIRD *Anhinga rufa* (Anhingidae). Like a slender, long-tailed, long-necked cormorant, with a pointed bill and apparently a curious kink in its neck; black, with vertical chestnut and white stripes on neck. Immature paler, with whitish underparts. Grunts at nest. Often swims with only head and neck above surface; typically makes snake-like movements with neck. Holds out wings like cormorants. Lakes, rivers and estuaries; nests colonially, in trees and bushes near water; Middle East (perhaps now extinct at most localities), Egypt. 38 in. (100 cm.).

CORMORANTS

adult

imm.

Shag

Cormorant

SHAG

adult
Moroccan
breeding

adult
Continental
breeding

adult
Atlantic breeding

imm.

CORMORANT

breeding

winter

imm.

PYGMY CORMORANT

breeding

imm.

imm.

DARTER

**LONG-TAILED
CORMORANT**

33

● HERONS, EGRETS AND BITTERNS: *Ardeidae.* pp. 35–39.

Large to very large wading birds, with long legs, bill and neck — all of which are adaptations to feeding in shallow water. Head often adorned with elongated plumes. Wings broad and rounded in flight, tail rather short. Neck held retracted in flight and often also at rest; legs outstretched in flight. Storks, spoonbills, ibises and cranes fly with both legs and neck outstretched. Sexes usually alike. Colonial nesting, usually in trees or reed-beds.

GREY HERON *Ardea cinerea.* Generally the commonest of the large herons, mainly grey, with white head and neck and black crest; immature has crest grey. Commonest call a harsh 'kraaaank'; varied raucous vocabulary at nest, including castanet-like bill-snapping. Flight slow and majestic, with outer half of wings black. Often stands still in water, with neck either outstretched or hunched up. (In N Africa vagrant Black-headed Herons *A. melanocephala* from tropical Africa could occur; they are easily recognised by their black head, back of neck and mantle.) Nests in trees, or rarely on cliffs and in reed-beds. Feeds in shallow fresh or coastal water or in marshes. 36 in. (90 cm.). **●Rw   Map 18**

Grey Herons in a field

PURPLE HERON *Ardea purpurea.* Smaller, more rakish looking and much darker than Grey Heron, with black crown and belly, striped rufous neck and chestnut breast; immature brown, lacking most of black on crown and stripes on neck. In flight whole wing uniformly dark, legs project further beyond tail, and neck bulge deeper and much more marked. Calls similar to Grey Heron, but less deep; generally a more silent bird. More of a skulking marsh or reed-bed bird, not normally nesting in trees. 31 in. (79 cm.).   **—A**

GOLIATH HERON *Ardea goliath.* Much the largest heron of the region, but only likely to be seen at heads of Red Sea and Gulf. Most resembles much smaller Purple Heron, which, however, has black crown. Substantially larger also than Grey Heron, from which it differs most conspicuously in its rufous head, neck and belly. Has a loud, harsh deep call, likened to the baying of a hound. Marshes and shallow water. 47 in. (120 cm.).

HERONS

juv.

adult

GREY HERON

adult

juv.

PURPLE HERON

GOLIATH HERON

35

| Cattle Egret | Squacco Heron | Little Egret | Great White Egret |

GREAT WHITE EGRET *Egretta alba*. Much the largest of the white herons or egrets of the region. No visible crest, but long wing plumes in breeding season, legs black; bill black, black and yellow, or yellow. Confusable only with rare albino of Grey Heron (p. 35) or with possible vagrant Yellow-billed Egret *E. intermedia* from S of Sahara, which is smaller (26 in.), with shorter yellow bill, a not very obvious yellow patch above knee-joint, and shorter legs, not protruding so far beyond tail in flight. Silent, even at nest, though young are noisy. Marshes, shallow fresh and brackish water, usually nesting in reed-beds. 35 in. (89 cm.).   —V

LITTLE EGRET *Egretta garzetta*. A small pure white heron with black bill and legs, best told by its yellow feet, which show clearly in flight. In breeding season has long drooping crest and long fuzzy wing plumes. Dark form rare. A harsh bark at nest. Marshes, shallow fresh and coastal waters, usually breeding in trees and near water. 22 in. (56 cm.).   —A

REEF HERON *Egretta gularis*. A pitfall for the unwary, having two distinct races, each with two plumage phases; both races have crest, plumes and yellow soles to feet, like Little Egret. Eastern race *schistacea* has dark phase (all blackish except for white chin and throat) rather more numerous than white phase, which differs from Little Egret mainly by yellow bill. Western race *gularis* has dark phase greatly predominant, but the few white ones are very hard to tell from Little Egrets because of brownish bill. However, Reef Heron only likely to be seen on coast, wading deep into water to feed. In Morocco confusable with possible vagrant Black Heron *Hydranassa ardesiaca*, which is all dark and also frequents fresh water. 22 in. (56 cm.).

CATTLE EGRET *Bubulcus ibis*. Slightly smaller and compacter than Little Egret, and in non-breeding and immature plumages and in flight appears similarly all white. In breeding plumage has distinctive dark buff plumes on crown, breast and mantle, also legs and feet reddish (dark greenish at other times). Bill yellow. Various guttural notes at nest. Often feeds in grassland in characteristic association with domestic livestock. Expanding its range. 20 in. (51 cm.).   —V

SQUACCO HERON *Ardeola ralloides*. The smallest white heron of the region, but appearing white only in flight. At rest is mainly tawny buff with white wings, tail and belly; in breeding season has crown and long crest streaked black and bill bluish (otherwise greenish); legs yellow-green. Immature streaked on buff parts. Call a high-pitched 'kerr'. Marshes, swampy riversides, nesting in trees. 18 in. (46 cm.).   —V

POND HERON or PADDYBIRD: *Ardeola grayii* is like Squacco Heron, but with back deep chestnut. Mangroves in Kuwait. 18 in. (46 cm.).

EGRETS

non-breeding

display

GREAT WHITE EGRET

breeding

black phase

display

LITTLE EGRET

white phase

non-breeding

CATTLE EGRET

breeding

black phase

REEF HERON

breeding

non-breeding

display

SQUACCO HERON

37

NIGHT HERON *Nycticorax nycticorax.* A small black, grey and white heron, whose habitual hunched attitude makes it look compacter than its length suggests. Distinctive black back and crown with narrow, greatly elongated white crest, bill greenish, legs yellow or pink, eye red. Immature mainly brown, spotted white like a Nutcracker (p. 305), resembling a small, boldly marked Bittern. Call, a hoarse croak. Very broad-winged in flight, and showing marked dark/light contrast; wing-beats faster than the larger herons, often flies in lines. A skulking, mainly nocturnal bird, most often seen flying at dusk or crouched on secluded bough in densely vegetated swamp or marsh, fresh or salt, or even well away from water; nest usually in tree or bush. A feral colony exists at Edinburgh Zoo, Scotland. 24 in. (61 cm.). **—A**

LITTLE BITTERN *Ixobrychus minutus.* Much the smallest heron-like bird of the region, and the only one with a prominent whitish wing-patch, which is especially conspicuous in flight, when wings have strong dark/light contrast. Female brown, with black crown and nape and less conspicuous wing-patch; juvenile similar but appearing more streaked. 'Song' a toad-like croak; various more or less croaking other notes, and flight-note 'quar'. Flight fast with intermittent glides. A very skulking bird, but sometimes climbs about reeds, like a giant Reed Warbler; will also freeze upright, like Bittern. Densely vegetated swamps and freshwater margins. 14 in. (35 cm.). **—A(b)**

BITTERN *Botaurus stellaris.* A rather large brown heron, very skulking and so more often heard than seen; heavily mottled black, crown black. Looks very different when hunched up like a large domestic fowl from when its neck is elongated in alert or frozen upright alarm positions, or from its striking crouched threat posture. Looks owl-like with rounded, somewhat down-bent wings in flight, but has long bill and trailing legs. 'Song' a penetrating low booming or mooing, like distant foghorn or cow; flight call a harsh 'kwow' or 'kwah'. Extensive reed-beds, fens and swamps. 30 in. (76 cm.). ⊙**Rw Map 19**

AMERICAN BITTERN *Botaurus lentiginosus.* A vagrant from N America, slightly smaller than Bittern and recognisable by lack of black crown and possession of black stripe down each side of neck, showing as patch when neck retracted; also less distinct black mottling on upperparts and wing-tips black. Flight notes, a hoarse 'kok-kok-kok' and a nasal 'haink'. Trisyllabic boom note, likened to old-fashioned water pump, unlikely to be heard in Europe. Flies more frequently than Bittern. Most often reported British Isles, Faeroe, Iceland; wet places. 26 in. (66 cm.). **—V**

BITTERNS

adult

imm.

NIGHT HERON

imm.

alarm posture

LITTLE BITTERN

♂

BITTERN

Bittern alarm posture

AMERICAN BITTERN

Bittern
threat posture

39

IBISES AND SPOONBILL: *Threskiornithidae*. Fairly large, long-necked, long-legged wading birds, habitually flying with neck outstretched; a useful distinction from herons. Bill long and curved in ibises, straight and spoon-shaped at the tip in spoonbills.

SPOONBILL *Platalea leucorodia*. The only large white heron-like bird with a long broad black bill, spoon-shaped at the tip. Adult has yellowish breast-band and in breeding season a long yellowish crest. Immature has wing-tips blackish and no crest. Normally silent, but may grunt in breeding season. Shallow fresh and coastal waters, nesting colonially in trees, bushes and reed-beds in marshy areas. 34 in. (86 cm.).   ○M   **Map 20**

juv.   adult

Curlew   Godwit   Glossy Ibis.

GLOSSY IBIS *Plegadis falcinellus*. Like a large dark round-winged Curlew (p. 139); the only blackish long-legged bird of the region with a curved bill. Plumage purplish-brown, wings and tail glossed green; legs greenish-brown. Call a harsh grating croak. Often flies in lines. Habitat as Spoonbill, with which and various egrets and herons it often breeds. 22 in. (56 cm.).   **—V**

BALD IBIS or WALDRAPP *Geronticus eremita*. Larger than Glossy Ibis, from which it differs especially in its bald red head, red bill and legs, and neck ruff of long pointed feathers, which wave in the wind and give the bird a somewhat shaggy appearance at rest. Call a rather high-pitched 'kay-kay'. Not a waterside bird, frequenting dry country and nesting on rocky cliffs and stream banks, sometimes on ruined buildings. A local and decreasing species. 30 in. (75 cm.).

SACRED IBIS *Threskiornis aethiopicus*. Unmistakable with its black and white plumage, black on the bare head and neck and plumed wings. Immature has head and neck feathered black and white and no plumes. Rather silent, but sometimes croaks. Margins of fresh and coastal water, marshes and cultivated land. No longer breeds Egypt, and now confined in our region to S Iraq. The emblem of the British Ornithologists' Union. 25 in. (64 cm.).

SPOONBILL, IBISES

adult

juv.

SPOONBILL

juv.

adult

juv.

GLOSSY IBIS

BALD IBIS

juv.

adult

SACRED IBIS

41

STORKS AND WOOD IBISES: *Ciconiidae.* Large to very
large long-legged long-necked birds, with long stout bills and black and/or white
plumage, flying with neck and legs both outstretched (unlike herons), legs trailing
slightly downwards; stately gait.

WHITE STORK *Ciconia ciconia.* One of the largest land
birds of the region, differing from all its other large white
birds by combination of long red bill and legs, long neck,
short tail and black wings with white patch. Normally silent,
but will hiss when annoyed and clatters mandibles together
during courtship, at same time holding neck backwards in a
U-bend. Farmland and open marshes, nesting in trees or in
W Europe on buildings, usually on specially erected platforms.
Decreasing in W Europe. (The huge Marabou Stork
Leptoptilos crumeniferus, 5 ft. long, with large air-filled
pouch hanging from neck, has occurred in Palestine.) The
national bird of Germany. 40 in. (102 cm.).   —V

BLACK STORK *Ciconia nigra.* Differs from White Stork most
notably in being all black except for white underparts. Immature browner, especially on head and neck. Less gregarious
but more vocal, chief call being 'he lee, he lee'. A retiring
forest bird, feeding at freshwater margins and in open marshy
areas in well wooded country; on migration in more open
country. Nests in trees. 38 in. (97 cm.).   —V

WOOD IBIS *Mycteria ibis.* Most confusingly named as it is a
stork not an ibis. Differs from White Stork in its yellow bill,
black tail and bare red face; pink on back and wings. Juvenile
has no red, and is brownish on head, neck and upperparts;
immature is grey where juvenile brown, but has reddish under
wing coverts. Generally silent, but may croak or grunt rather
weakly. A rare vagrant to N W Africa from further S, on both
fresh and coastal waters. 39 in. (100 cm.).

GREATER FLAMINGO *Phoenicopterus ruber* (Phoeni-
copteridae). The only flamingo of the region, easily recognised by its pink plumage and striking red and black contrast
of wings in flight; also by 'Roman nose' effect of uniquely
curved flamingo-type bill, specially adapted to sieving animal
and vegetable food from shallow water. Other species not
infrequently escape from bird collections and zoos in Europe,
including Chilean race of Greater Flamingo, which has red
'knees' and feet, and smaller and much brighter pink Lesser
Flamingo *Phoeniconaias minor* of East Africa, which has
dark red bill. A noisy and highly gregarious bird, uttering
loud goose-like honking cries in flight. Extensive shallow
lakes or lagoons of salt or soda water, where it builds conical
heaps of mud on which to lay its eggs. In our region breeds
only in S Morocco, S Tunisia, S Spain, Rhone delta, S E
Russia and N W Iran. 50 in. (127 cm.)

STORKS, FLAMINGO

adult

juv.

adult

WHITE STORK

juv.

WOOD IBIS   juv.

adult

adult

BLACK STORK

chick

imm.

GREATER FLAMINGO

43

SWANS, GEESE AND DUCKS: *Anatidae*. pp. 45–69. Aquatic birds characterised by long neck, comparatively narrow and usually pointed wings, webbed feet, and (except in the sawbills) bill flattened and blunt. Young, thickly covered in down, leave nest soon after hatching. Two main groupings: swans and geese, subfamily Anserinae (pp. 45–9) and ducks, subfamily Anatinae (pp. 51–69). Many species not native to region are liable to escape from waterfowl collections. SWANS: *Cygnus*. The largest waterfowl, northern swans are all white, the young (cygnets) being ash-brown, becoming whiter as they grow older; sexes alike. Ungainly and waddling on land, swans swim gracefully, taking off from the water with ponderous flapping to sail majestically through the air. No black on wings and no long trailing legs distinguish them from all other large white birds in flight. Still and slow-moving fresh water, estuaries, sheltered coastal water, sometimes breeding in swamps.

MUTE SWAN *Cygnus olor*. Adult readily distinguished by orange bill with black basal knob, also by holding neck curved at rest, by habit of slightly erecting tail when swimming, and by loud throbbing of wings in flight. In a rare variety, the Polish Swan, immatures also white. Usually silent, but has twangy trumpeting note and will hiss or snort when annoyed. Mostly semi-domesticated; common in town parks. 60 in. (152 cm.). ●R **Map 21**

WHOOPER SWAN *Cygnus cygnus*. Differs from Mute Swan in yellow base instead of orange tip to knobless bill, also in upright carriage of neck at rest, in whistling rather than throbbing of wings in flight, and in more vocal habits. Has more yellow on bill than smaller Bewick's Swan, reaching below nostril at an acute angle. A loud clanging, somewhat goose-like 'ahng-ha'. 60 in. (152 cm.). ☉W(b) **Map 22**

BEWICK'S SWAN *Cygnus bewickii*. Smaller and shorter-necked than Whooper Swan, yellow on bill ending bluntly above nostrils. Calls 'hoo, hoo' and a higher-pitched and more musical honk than Whooper. Breeds in marshy and swampy tundra. 48 in. (122 cm.). ☉W **Map 23**

BAR-HEADED GOOSE *Anser indicus*. A native of India, now breeding ferally in Sweden; paler grey than other grey geese (p. 46) and easily told by two black bars on white crown. Juvenile has unbarred dark brown crown and nape. Bill yellow, legs orange. Call a musical 'aang, aang'. 30 in. (75 cm.).

SNOW GOOSE and BLUE GOOSE *Anser caerulescens*. A 'grey goose' (p. 46), a rare visitor from Arctic North America, in two colour forms: Snow Goose, all white with black wing-tips; and Blue Goose, with bluish grey-brown back and wings, white head, neck and tail coverts, and underparts of either colour or a mixture. Bill red or pink, legs dull purplish-pink. Black wing-tips always distinguish Snow Goose both from swans and from albino geese of other species; white head distinguishes Blue Goose from other grey geese. Voice mellower and more bell-like than other grey geese, with which it usually consorts in Europe. 25–30 in. (63–76 cm.). —V

SWANS, GEESE

MUTE SWAN

imm.

WHOOPER
SWAN

imm.

imm.

BEWICK'S
SWAN

BAR-HEADED GOOSE

white
phase

blue phase
(Blue Goose)

imm.
white phase

blue phase

SNOW GOOSE

45

GEESE: *Anserinae.* pp. 45–9. Large thickset birds, with necks relatively longer than most ducks, and legs comparatively short. Highly gregarious, and collectively noisy, they fly fast and direct, but often with rather laboured wing-beats and in V-formation. Odd individuals often in flocks of other goose species. Sexes alike. GREY GEESE: *Anser.* pp. 45–7. Plumage grey-brown, darker on underparts, with white under tail coverts. A difficult group: concentrate on bill and leg colour, bill shape and calls. In winter on estuaries, coastal marshes and farmland.

GREYLAG GOOSE *Anser anser.* One of the larger grey geese, with heavy flight and gait, best distinguished by its pale grey forewing, orange bill and pink legs. Flight-note, a clangorous 'aahng-ung-ung', and hissing note when annoyed both similar to farmyard goose, its domestic derivative. Breeds in lowland moors and marshes. Eastern race *rubrirostris* breeding in E Europe and Iraq, has pink bill. 30–35 in. (76–89 cm.).   ⊙**rW   Map 24**

BEAN GOOSE *Anser fabalis.* The other large grey goose, much darker, especially on head, neck and forewing than Greylag; bill rather longer, either all orange-yellow, or orange-yellow at the tip and blackish at the base; legs orange. Less noisy than Pinkfoot, having a tenor version of its notes. Breeds in marshy places and by fresh water on tundra and in taiga. 28–35 in. (71–89 cm.).   ⊙**W   Map 25**

PINK-FOOTED GOOSE *Anser brachyrhynchus.* Markedly smaller than Bean Goose, having similar dark head and neck, but forewing pale, and readily told by pink legs and short black-based pink bill. Very vocal, with a rather shrill medley of 'wink, wink' and 'ung, ung' notes. Breeds on tundra, sometimes on cliff ledges. 24–30 in. (61–76 cm.).
⊙**W   Map 26**

LESSER WHITE-FRONTED GOOSE *Anser erythropus.* The smallest grey goose, adult confusable only with White-fronted Goose, but white on forehead extends much further towards crown, bill much smaller, and has narrow yellow eye-ring, and shriller call. Immature lacks white forehead and eye-ring. Bill pink, legs orange. Can be detected among White-fronts by quicker rate of feeding. Breeds in drier parts of tundra, towards taiga. 21–26 in. (53–66 cm.).   —**A**

WHITE-FRONTED GOOSE *Anser albifrons.* Adult is easiest to identify of northern grey geese, with conspicuous broad white forehead (others occasionally have narrow white band above base of bill) and heavily barred underparts. Bill pink (yellow or orange in Greenland race *flavirostris*) legs orange. Juvenile uniform grey-brown, differing from same-sized Pink-foot in its paler head and neck, darker forewing, lack of black on bill, and orange legs. Calls a babble of 'kow-yow' and 'kow-lyow' sounds, like distant cries of beagle pack; higher-pitched than Greylag but less so than Pink-foot. Breeds on marshy tundra. 26–30 in. (66–76 cm.).   ⊙**W   Map 27**

GREY GEESE

eastern form

western form

GREYLAG GOOSE

PINK-FOOTED GOOSE

BEAN GOOSE

LESSER WHITE-FRONTED GOOSE

Greenland race

imm.

Eurasian race

WHITE-FRONTED GOOSE

47

Black Geese or Brants: *Branta.* A group of mostly rather small (except Canada) geese with crown and whole neck black (except Red-breasted); sexes alike. The three native species are all winter visitors in the central and southern parts of the region.

BRENT GOOSE *Branta bernicla.* The only goose with an all-black head, and smallest and darkest of the three wholly black-necked geese, no bigger than a drake Mallard (p. 53). Also has neck and upper breast black, with a white patch on each side of the neck; back, rump and wings dark grey-brown, tail coverts white. Underparts slate grey in dark-breasted race *bernicla*, breeding in Arctic Europe, but pale grey-brown to white in pale-breasted race *hrota*, breeding in Greenland and Spitzbergen. Immatures distinguished by white speckles on forewing and lack of white neck patch. Call a croaking 'ruk, gruk, grunk'. Breeds on Arctic sea shores and islands and on marshy tundra, wintering in estuaries and coastal mudflats, where highly gregarious. 22–24 in. (56–61 cm.).

⊙W   **Map 28**

BARNACLE GOOSE *Branta leucopsis.* Distinguished from all other true geese by having its whole face white, with crown, nape and neck black; rest of plumage mainly grey more or less barred black and white. *Cf.* however, Canada Goose, much more likely to be seen inland. Call, 'ark', resembles gruff yapping of a small terrier. Arctic coasts and rocky terrain, often nesting on cliff ledges; in winter on coastal flats, marshes, and grassland. Liable to escape from collections of ornamental waterfowl. 23–27 in. (58–69 cm.).

⊙W   **Map 29**

CANADA GOOSE *Branta canadensis.* A well established introduced species from North America, and an occasional genuine transatlantic vagrant. Much larger than the other black-necked geese, and distinguished from Barnacle especially by longer neck, generally brownish plumage and much smaller extent of white on face. Any large black-necked goose inland on lakes almost certainly this species. Call a loud double trumpeting note, 'ker-honk'; noisy during mating period. Ponds, lakes and adjacent marshes and grassland inland; in winter also on coastal flats and marshes. 36–40 in. (92–102 cm.).

●R   **Map 30**

RED-BREASTED GOOSE *Branta ruficollis.* The smallest and most strikingly coloured of the true geese, with a very small bill, chestnut throat, breast and face patch, and rest of plumage black with white lines, including broad one on flanks conspicuous at a distance. Immatures duller. Calls high-pitched and rather musical, 'kee-kwa', 'kik-wit', 'ti-che' and similar disyllables. Winters in steppes and prairies around Caspian Sea, and on W side of Black Sea; more rarely along rivers in Iraq and with flocks of other geese on the Hungarian plains. A popular ornamental waterfowl, which may escape. 21–22 in. (53–56 cm.).

—V

BLACK GEESE

dark-breasted race

pale-breasted race

BRENT GOOSE

BARNACLE GOOSE

CANADA GOOSE

RED-BREASTED GOOSE

49

DUCKS: *Anatinae*. pp. 51–69. A subfamily with seven groups in our region: shelducks (below), perching ducks (below), dabbling ducks (pp. 53–7), and four groups of diving ducks which feed by diving, pochards (pp. 57–9), eiders (p. 61), sawbills and allies (pp. 63–7), and stifftails (p. 67). Ducks are generally smaller and have shorter necks and legs than geese or swans. Most have very distinct male and female plumages, juveniles resembling females. In the eclipse (moult) plumage in late summer males (drakes) temporarily become very like females (ducks), often scarcely separable except by bill colour. Both sexes have a coloured wing-patch (speculum).

SHELDUCK *Tadorna tadorna*. A large, somewhat goose-like duck, with very dark green head, some black markings and chestnut breastband. Legs flesh, bill red, drake usually having a knob in summer; sexes otherwise alike. In eclipse all colours browner and whiter, and in juvenile even more so, with forehead, cheeks and whole underparts white and bill and legs greyish. Drake has whistling flight note, 'sostmieu', not unlike sound of some ducks' wing-beats; duck has a laughing quack, 'ak-ak-ak. . . .'. In the W coastal dunes and heaths, estuaries, sandy, muddy and less often rocky sea-shores, rarely far inland; in the E by brackish or more rarely freshwater lakes and inland seas. A burrow nester. Huge flocks, including most of British breeding population, moult in late summer on coastal flats at mouth of R Elbe. 24 in. (61 cm.). ●**Rw Map 31**

RUDDY SHELDUCK *Tadorna ferruginea*. A large deep buff-brown rather goose-like duck, with head paler and wing-tips black, and white wing-patch conspicuous in flight. Drake has narrow black collar, duck's head whiter; bill and legs black. A loud nasal clanging 'aang, aang', recalling Greylag. Shores of inland lakes, lagoons, rivers and streams, in steppes, deserts and mountains. Decreasing in the region. 25 in. (64 cm.). **—V**

EGYPTIAN GOOSE *Alopochen aegyptiacus*. Another goose-like duck, varyingly grey and buff-brown, slightly larger, longer-necked and longer-legged than Ruddy Shelduck, and so looking more upstanding; also has white shoulders instead of wing-patches and dark chocolate patches round eye and on lower breast, as well as pink bill and feet. Sexes alike; juvenile lacks face patch. A guttural quack, 'kek, kek' and a softer, more whistling call. Marshes and freshwater margins; often perches in trees. Introduced in W Europe. 27 in. (70 cm.). ○**R**

MANDARIN DUCK *Aix galericulata*. Crested drake has strikingly variegated plumage, with conspicuous orange-chestnut wing-fans and side-whiskers. Duck mainly grey-brown, with slight crest, blue hindwing and wing-tips, narrow white ring round eye, black bill and dull yellow legs. Eclipse and immature drakes can be told from duck by bill. Flight notes of drake a sharp little whistle 'wrrick', of duck a plaintive little 'ack'. By fresh water in woods and forests. Native of China, introduced in British Isles. 17 in. (43 cm.). ○**R**

SHELDUCKS

imm.

SHELDUCK

♀ ♂

RUDDY SHELDUCK

♀ ♂

imm.

grey form

brown form

EGYPTIAN GOOSE

♂

♀

MANDARIN DUCK

Dabbling Ducks: *Anas*. pp. 53–7. Dabbling ducks characteristically feed on the surface of the water or by upending, and rarely dive except when young or unable to fly. Females brown; speculum an important field mark. Flight swift, direct.

MALLARD *Anas platyrhynchos*. The largest dabbling duck, the commonest and most widespread duck of the region, and the origin of the farmyard duck. Drake's combination of green head (shot with purple towards the moult), narrow white collar, grey back and underparts and dark purple-brown breast is matched by no other waterfowl. Brown duck has distinctive large blue speculum. Eclipse drake distinguished by yellow bill; duck's is greenish, juvenile's reddish. Familiar loud harsh quack, resembling farmyard duck, uttered by duck only; drake has a softer 'queek'. Breeds not far from all kinds of still and slow-moving water and marshes; in winter also estuaries and seashores. 23 in. (58 cm.). ●Rw **Map 32**

GADWALL *Anas strepera*. Drake is the least brightly plumaged dabbling duck, mainly grey, with contrasting black tail coverts, especially noticeable at rest. In flight shows white belly and black, white and chestnut patches on wing. Duck resembles small duck Mallard, with more peaked forehead, but showing white belly and black and white speculum on wing in flight. Bill of drake grey, of duck dark horn with orange sides, of juvenile yellow. Drake has deep nasal croak 'nhek'; duck's quack is softer than duck Mallard's. Lowland fresh and inland brackish waters, and marshes. 20 in. (51 cm.). ⊙RsW **Map 33**

WIGEON *Anas penelope*. Drake at rest distinctive with shortish bill, chestnut head, buff crown, grey underparts and white line on wing; in flight can be picked out at some distance by conspicuous white forewing. Duck smaller and slenderer than duck Mallard, with shorter bill, more peaked forehead, pointed tail, white belly, and green speculum; cf. duck Pintail (p. 57). Characteristic 'whee-oo' call reveals presence of drake even in fog or at a distance; duck has purring note. Often flies fast in small flocks. Breeds by fresh water on moors and tundra, rarely in coastal marshes; in winter on lakes, reservoirs, estuaries and shallow coastal waters, flocks often grazing on fields. 18 in. (46 cm.). ●rmW **Map 34**

AMERICAN WIGEON *Anas americana*. A rare transatlantic visitor; mainly pinkish-brown drake has quite different green, white and buff head pattern from Wigeon, but shares white forewing, black under tail coverts and distinctive whistling call. Duck almost indistinguishable from duck Wigeon unless greyer head and neck and white axillaries can be seen. Chiloe Wigeon *Anas sibilatrix*, sometimes escaping from waterfowl collections, has white face, green back of head and warm brown flanks. 18–22 in. (46–56 cm.) —A

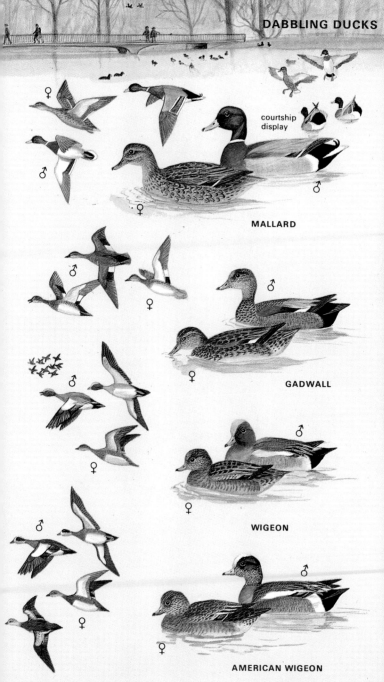

courtship
display

MALLARD

GADWALL

WIGEON

AMERICAN WIGEON

TEAL *Anas crecca*. The smallest duck of the region, very gregarious and often flies, fast and wader-like, in compact flock. Drake has chestnut head with distinctive broad-bordered green stripe, and at rest can be picked out at a distance by horizontal white line above wing and buffish yellow patch behind tail coverts. Bill and legs grey; juvenile's bill pinkish. Drake of rare transatlantic vagrant subspecies, Green-winged Teal *carolinensis*, has vertical white line at side of breast and cream border to green stripe much less conspicuous. Duck of both races like diminutive duck Mallard, with black and green speculum and whitish belly. Bill and legs grey; juvenile's bill pinkish. Call-note of drake a whistling 'crrick, crrick', of duck a short, high-pitched quack; courting parties in spring utter a chorus of bell-like notes. Breeds on still and slow-moving fresh water with dense fringe of vegetation, also marshes, fens, bogs. In winter on lakes, reservoirs, estuaries and coastal water. 14 in. (35 cm.).   ●RmW   Map 35

FALCATED TEAL *Anas falcata*. Rare vagrant from E Asia or escape. Drake easily recognised by long crest and elongated wing feathers. Bill black to dark grey; speculum black and green. 20 in. (51 cm.).

GARGANEY *Anas querquedula*. The second smallest duck of the region, slenderer than Teal and rarely occurring in such large flocks. Drake can be told from all other waterfowl by conspicuous white stripe over eye and from all except Shoveler and Blue-winged Teal by blue-grey forewing. Duck paler and more blotched than duck Teal and has white throat, more distinctive eyestripe, no black in speculum, and pale spot at base of longer and wider bill; in flight blue-grey forewing is distinctive. Bill of drake blackish, of duck greyish. In spring drake has a curious crackling note, like a single match being rattled in a match box; duck has a low quack. Habitat as Teal, but not in mountains. 15 in. (38 cm.).   ⊙Sm   Map 36

BLUE-WINGED TEAL *Anas discors*. A rare transatlantic vagrant, with forewing bluer grey than wing, easily told by conspicuous white crescentic mark in front of eye. Duck very like duck Garganey, but has bluer forewing, blackish bill and yellow legs. Drake has a whistling 'peep' and a soft lisping 'tseef, tseef, tseef'; duck a soft teal-like quack. 15 in. (38 cm.).   —V

BAIKAL TEAL *Anas formosa*. A rare visitor from Siberia, or escape; drake with unique green, cream and black head pattern, slightly recalling Harlequin Duck (p. 63), together with elongated fan of wing-feathers and vertical white mark. Duck resembles large duck Teal, with conspicuous pale spot at base of bill, dark line back through eye, surmounted by a broken pale spot. Drake often repeats a curious clucking 'proop' or 'wot-wot', duck has harsh quack. 16 in. (41 cm.).

DABBLING DUCKS

♀

♂

Mallard

♂

TEAL

♀

♂

♂ Green-winged Teal
N America

♀

♂

FALCATED TEAL

♀

♂

♀

♀

♂

GARGANEY

♀

♂

♀

BLUE-WINGED TEAL

♀

♂

♂

♀

♂

BAIKAL TEAL

PINTAIL *Anas acuta*. The second commonest northern duck of the region. Drake easily told by greatly elongated central tail feathers, 4 in. of total length, combined with striking pattern of dark head and throat and white breast and stripe up side of neck. Duck resembles duck Wigeon (p. 53), but has more pointed tail, slenderer neck, narrower wings, indistinct bronzy speculum and brown belly. Only other white-breasted duck is short-necked heavy-billed Shoveler drake, and only the white-headed maritime drake Long-tailed Duck also has a long tail. Drake has a low moorhen-like weak nasal 'gseee' and in courtship a rather musical croak, and duck a rather hoarse quack. A fast flyer. Freshwater and brackish pools and marshes, on moors and tundra and in taiga; in winter also estuaries and coastal marshes and waters. Drake 26 in. (66 cm.), duck 22 in. (56 cm.). ●rmW **Map 37**

SHOVELER *Anas clypeata*. Both sexes recognisable by heavy shovel-shaped bill producing characteristic head-down attitude when at rest or swimming on water. Drake has striking plumage of dark green (often looking black) head, white breast, chestnut flanks and pale blue forewing and is only dabbling duck with a yellow eye. Duck is like heavy-billed duck Mallard (p. 53), but has green speculum and in flight at once separated by blue forewing. Drake's call a gruff 'took, took', duck's a double quack. Inland and coastal fresh and brackish waters and marshes in lowlands, especially with plenty of vegetation and shallow muddy water. In winter on deeper waters, sometimes also on coastal waters. 20 in. (51 cm.). ●rsmW **Map 38**

MARBLED TEAL *Anas angustirostris*. The only dabbling duck of the region with sexes alike and no obvious speculum; like a rather large longer-necked greyish duck Teal (p. 55), with a dark mark through the eye and contrasting pale lower face; head shaggy rather than crested; tail white. Drake has a weak nasal squeak, duck a double whistle. Breeds on well vegetated fresh or brackish water or marshes; in winter on more open waters, even temporary pools in desert. 16 in. (41 cm.).

RED-CRESTED POCHARD *Netta rufina*. Drake is only red-billed or red-legged diving duck (see p. 58) of the region, further distinguished from smaller drake Pochard by crest and long broad white wing-bar showing in flight. Duck is only uniformly brownish duck with a pale (as distinct from white) cheek, except for maritime Common Scoter (p. 63), which has no white wing-bar Feeds by up-ending as well as diving. Drake has a hard wheezing note, duck a harsh 'kurrr'. Fresh or brackish lakes and lagoons, usually reed-fringed, also marshes. Often escapes from waterfowl collections. 22 in. (56 cm.). **—A**

DABBLING DUCKS

♂

♀

PINTAIL

♀

♂

SHOVELER

♂

♀

MARBLED TEAL

♀

♂

RED-CRESTED POCHARD

57

Pochards *Aythya*. Pochards are the diving ducks *par excellence*, diving frequently and swimming submerged. Usually shorter-necked and compacter than dabblers, drakes with soberer plumage. Drakes have a low often wheezy whistle, and ducks a harsh growling 'kurrr, kurrr'

TUFTED DUCK *Aythya fuligula*. Drake is only waterfowl with a drooping black crest, and is readily recognised, even at some distance, by strongly contrasted black upperparts and white flanks. Short-crested duck mainly brown, with yellow eye, and sometimes white band at base of bill (*cf.* Scaup) or whitish under-tail coverts (*cf.* Ferruginous Duck). Both sexes show a white wing-bar in flight; bill blue-grey. Still and slow-moving fresh water with vegetated margins; in winter also on reservoirs and other bare-banked waters; rarely on salt water. 17 in. (43 cm.). ●RW **Map 39**

RING-NECKED DUCK *Aythya collaris*. A rare vagrant from N America, distinguished from Tufted Duck by more peaked head, due to short crest, and two white rings on bill. Drake also has conspicuous white mark at side of breast; duck has white eye-ring, and obscure whitish patch on face at base of bill. 17 in. (43 cm.). —A

SCAUP *Aythya marila*. In many ways a larger version of Tufted Duck, but drake at once distinguished by grey back, and duck by large white patch at base of bill, much more extensive than occasional white band of duck Tufted. Black head and neck separate drake from similarly patterned drake Pochard. Occasional hybrids of Tufted Duck and Pochard can be distinguished from Scaups by black tip to bill, darker eye and less contrasting wing-bar. Freshwater lakes in tundra and taiga; in winter mainly on estuaries and coastal waters. 19 in. (48 cm.). ⊙mW(b) **Map 40**

POCHARD *Aythya ferina*. Drake is the only waterfowl of region with whole head and neck chestnut and upperparts grey, lacking drake Wigeon's buff crown and white forewing; (shows no white wing-bar in flight). Duck brown in front, grey-brown behind. Both lack a white wing-bar; bill blue-grey with black at tip and base. Habitat similar to Tufted Duck, but also breeds on brackish lakes. 18 in. (46 cm.). ●rmW **Map 41**

FERRUGINOUS DUCK *Aythya nyroca*. Like a warm chestnut brown female Tufted Duck or Pochard but at any distance best distinguished from both by sharp contrast of white under tail coverts. (Tufted Duck may show this but much less contrasted.) Drake also has white eye. Female duller, never with white at base of bill. In flight conspicuous curved white wing-bar separates both from Pochard. Bill blackish. Fresh or brackish still or slow-moving water, well fringed with vegetation, also extensive reedswamps. 16 in. (41 cm.). —A

DIVING DUCKS

diving duck taking off

Mallard

♂

♂

♂

♀

♀

♂

TUFTED DUCK

♀

♂

RING-NECKED DUCK

♂

♀

♂

♀

♂

SCAUP

♀

♂

♂

POCHARD

♀

♂

FERRUGINOUS DUCK

Eiders: *Somateria.* Large heavily built marine ducks, expert divers, rarely seen inland. Drakes strikingly patterned, ducks mottled brown and the only waterfowl with barred breast; both lacking a speculum. Bill continuing in almost straight line from forehead (except drake King Eider). and feathering of forehead descending to a point well down the upper mandible. Ducks show faint line on wing in flight and have harsh pochard-like 'kurrr'

EIDER *Somateria mollissima.* Adult drake unmistakable, being only waterfowl white above and black below; also has crown and tail black, back of head pale green and breast pale pink. In flight forewing almost all white with black tip and trailing edge. Immature and eclipse drakes can be very confusing, with widely varying mixtures of black and white, but head usually dark and underparts black. Duck distinguished from, e.g. duck Mallard (p. 53), by heavy build, distinctive bill outline, and barred breast. Large black and white waterfowl paired with brown one at sea almost certainly eiders. Drake has low crooning or cooing courtship note, 'ah-oo', or 'coo-roo-uh', with accent on second syllable. Rocky and sandy sea coasts, rarely on freshwater lakes a few miles inland. 23 in. (58 cm.). ●Rw   Map 42

KING EIDER *Somateria spectabilis.* Drake very distinctive, being the only waterfowl to appear white in front and black behind when seen at a distance. Quite different from drake Eider, having differently shaped head, markedly peaked orange forehead, red bill, pale grey head and black back. In flight shows large white patch at base of dark wing. Immature and eclipse drakes have confusing mixtures of dark and white plumage, but generally have black head. Duck rather more rufous than duck eider, but otherwise very hard to distinguish except by larger proportion of bill covered with feathers, especially at sides; bare part not extending right back past eye, as with Eider. Drake's coo trisyllabic with accent on last syllable. Arctic coastlines, and fresh water in tundra. 22 in. (56 cm.)   —V

SPECTACLED EIDER *Somateria fischeri.* Rare winter visitor to coasts of N Russia and Arctic Norway. Both sexes distinguished from Eider by large white (drake) or pale (duck) spectacle round eye, and feathers coming much lower down bill; drake also by otherwise green head and black lower breast. Flight pattern more like Eider than King Eider. 21–22 in. (53–56 cm.).

STELLER'S EIDER *Polysticta stelleri.* Drake is only waterfowl with white head, black and white upperparts and rufous underparts; also has green patches on forehead and nape. Dark brown duck best distinguished by white wing-bar and at close range by purple speculum. Both have quite differently shaped head from other eiders. Drake has low croon, duck a harsh wigeon-like quack; both make whistling sound in flight like Goldeneye. Regular visitor off N coast Norway, frequenting only clear water and often coming close inshore. 18 in. (46 cm.).   —V

EIDERS

eclipse plumage

first spring

northern race

♂

imm.

♂

EIDER

♀

♂

KING EIDER

♀

♂

SPECTACLED EIDER

eclipse plumage

♂

♀

♀

♂

STELLER'S EIDER

61

HARLEQUIN DUCK *Histrionicus histrionicus.* An Iceland speciality, very rare elsewhere in Europe. Drake has unique pattern of blue, white, chestnut and black, though looks just dark at any distance, when short bill and white on head may be best clues. Duck plain brown with three pale spots on face, one behind and two in front of eye, readily distinguished from scoters by small size and short bill, and from immature Long-tailed Duck (p. 65) by much less white on belly. No wing-bar a useful pointer in flight. Buoyant on water, often with tail cocked up; fond of surf and rough water. Mainly silent, but drake has low descending whistle, ending in a trill; and duck a harsh croak. Breeds on fast streams, often near waterfalls, wintering at sea off rocky coasts. 17 in. (43 cm.).　　　　—V

Scoters: *Melanitta.* Large diving sea ducks, often breeding on fresh water but normally resorting to salt water at other times. Plumage of drakes predominantly black, of ducks mainly brown; tail short, pointed. Drakes have black bill, marked orange or yellow, with knob at base. Drakes silent, except for low cooing or whistling notes in courtship; ducks have a harsh growling cackle.

COMMON SCOTER *Melanitta nigra.* Drake is the only all-black waterfowl apart from orange mark on upper mandible. Pale lower half of face distinguishes duck from all except ducks of Red-crested Pochard (p. 57), which has white wing-bar, and Long-tailed Duck (p. 65), which has shorter bill, sometimes with a narrow orange stripe, and much whiter underparts. Feet black. Drake often sits on water with tail cocked up. Breeds by still or slow-moving fresh water in tundra, moorland and taiga; winters often in large flocks mainly in coastal waters, many non-breeding birds staying well S of breeding range all summer. 19 in. (48 cm.).

●rMW　Map 43

VELVET SCOTER *Melanitta fusca.* Both sexes distinguished from smaller Common Scoter by white wing-bar, especially noticeable in flight, and red feet. Drake also has small white patch behind eye and orange-yellow sides to instead of patch on bill. Duck and juvenile have a pale patch on either side of eye on otherwise dark face. Freshwater lakes in the taiga, less often on tundra than Common Scoter; in winter mainly in coastal waters, in small parties or with Common Scoters or Eiders. 22 in. (56 cm.).　☉ mW　Map 44

SURF SCOTER *Melanitta perspicillata.* A vagrant from North America to coastal waters of N W Europe, differing from both other scoters in large eider-like bill, strikingly patterned in drake, greenish in duck. Drake also has distinctive white patches on forehead and nape, and duck and immature have pale patch on nape as well as before and behind eye, like Velvet Scoter. Duck sometimes has these patches obscure, when uniform face is best distinction from other two scoters. No wing-bar; legs dull orange. 22 in (56 cm.).　　　　—V

SEA DUCKS

HARLEQUIN DUCK

♀
♂

COMMON SCOTER

♀
♂
♂ American race

VELVET SCOTER

♀
♂

SURF SCOTER

♀
♂

GOLDENEYE *Bucephala clangula.* A diving duck most easily recognised by strikingly peaked, almost triangular shape of head; also has distinctive white neck, broad white wing-bars and yellow eye. Drake has black head, glossed green, with prominent white spot between bill and eye; duck and immature have less peaked head, chocolate-brown with no spot. Usually silent, except in spring, when drake has insistent 'speer, speer' and harsh 'quee-reek', and duck a typical guttural diving-duck 'kurr'. Rises more steeply from water than most diving ducks, wings making a loud singing note in flight. Breeds by fresh water in forests, usually coniferous, nesting in old woodpecker and other tree-holes; in winter on both fresh and coastal waters. 18 in. (46 cm.).
●mW(b) **Map 45**

BARROW'S GOLDENEYE *Bucephala islandica.* Very rarely seen away from Iceland. Differs from slightly smaller Goldeneye in its more rounded, almost bulbous head, and crescentic, instead of round, white mark on drake's purple (not green) glossed head. Drake also has large white spots on closed wing instead of barred appearance of drake Goldeneye, and so appears blacker. Calls and flight-noise similar to Goldeneye. Breeds on freshwater lakes, nesting on cavities in cliffs, rocks, walls and ruined buildings; in winter also on inshore waters. 21 in. (53 cm.).

BUFFLEHEAD *Bucephala albeola.* Rare transatlantic vagrant, drake most easily told by conspicuous white patch at back of head; darker duck has much smaller white patch behind eye. Both sexes show white wing patches in flight, looking rather like small Goldeneye. Short bill distinguishes from equally rare Hooded Merganser (p. 67). Drake has a rolling guttural note and a weak squeak; duck a hoarse 'quack' and a repeated 'guk, guk'. 14 in. (35 cm.). —V

LONG-TAILED DUCK *Clangula hyemalis.* A diving sea duck, rather neat and small, apart from drake's striking 5-in. tail, distinctive for its unusually short bill and lack of any pale wing-bar. Summer drake has front half dark, except for large white face-patch, flanks and rest of underparts white, bill pink at tip; in winter most of head and neck turn white, leaving only a black patch on cheek. Pintail drake (p. 57) the only other long-tailed waterfowl, has quite different head pattern and habits at all times. Duck has dark patch on cheek, bill all grey. Noisy drake has loud musical call, 'ardelow-ar-ardelow' or 'ow, ow, owal-ow', duck has a soft quack. Has a characteristic swinging flight, not raising down-curved wings much above level of body. Breeds by either fresh or salt water on tundra and Arctic coasts, also inland in Scandinavia on mountains; in winter on coastal waters, scarce inland. Drake 21 in. (53 cm.), duck 16 in. (41 cm.).
☉ W(b) **Map 46**

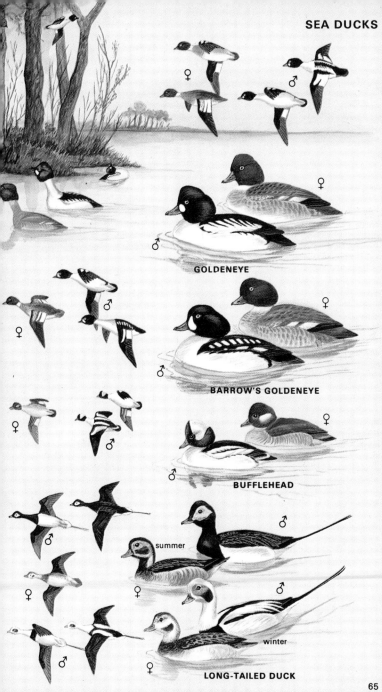

SEA DUCKS

♀

♂

♀

♂

GOLDENEYE

♂

♀

♂

♀

BARROW'S GOLDENEYE

♂

♀

♀

♂

BUFFLEHEAD

♂

♂

summer

♀

♀

♂

♂

winter

♀

LONG-TAILED DUCK

65

Sawbills: *Mergus*. Diving ducks, with distinctive narrow saw-edged bills, well adapted to chasing fish under water. Head crested. Take-off heavy, like Pochard (p. 59), but flight fast and direct, with whistling sound from wings (except Smew). In flight have characteristic cigar-shape, due to holding head and neck straight out level with body; white wing patch distinguishes from divers, and level neck from grebes. Ducks and immatures, known as 'red-heads', have chestnut head and nape, with white chin. Generally silent, except in display. Call of duck a harsh 'karr'.

GOOSANDER *Mergus merganser*. Drakes of two larger sawbills both have dark green head and upper neck and long red bill. Drake Goosander has obscure crest, and white breast and flanks, sometimes tinged pink; smaller Merganser has conspicuous crest, pale chestnut breast and grey flanks. Ducks and immatures harder to tell apart, but duck Merganser is smaller, has crest higher up on nape, upper parts browner and white of chin less sharply defined. Lakes and fast streams or rivers; nesting in tree-holes; rarely on estuaries or rocky coasts; in winter mainly on fresh water inland. 23–26 in. (58–66 cm.).   ●rW Map 47

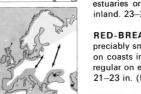

RED-BREASTED MERGANSER *Mergus serrator*. Appreciably smaller than Goosander; see above. More frequent on coasts in breeding season, nesting on ground; in winter regular on estuaries and sea and uncommon on fresh water. 21–23 in. (53–58 cm.).   ●RW Map 48

SMEW *Mergus albellus*. Drake the whitest waterfowl of the region, relieved at rest by only a few black markings, but in flight looks more pied. Red-heads dive constantly like grebes, but have conspicuously whiter cheeks, and are also much whiter than other small diving ducks. Smaller lakes and ponds and slow-moving streams and rivers in coniferous forest; in winter on fresh water and estuaries. 16 in. (41 cm.).   ⊙ W   Map 49

HOODED MERGANSER *Mergus cucullatus*. A rare transatlantic vagrant, drake differing especially from drake Bufflehead (p. 65) in its thin bill. Duck like duck Smew but with whole head rufous. 18 in. (46 cm.).   —V

Stiff-tails: *Oxyura*. Dumpy little short-necked diving ducks, with grebe-like habits including sometimes sinking below water except for head, often swimming with tail cocked up. Generally silent, but drakes cluck and squeak during courtship.

WHITE-HEADED DUCK *Oxyura leucocephala*. Drake has white face and forehead, and in summer blue bill; duck's pale face is crossed by white line; both have base of bill swollen. Shallow, often reed-fringed, fresh and brackish pools. 18 in. (46 cm.).

RUDDY DUCK *Oxyura jamaicensis*. A North American bird recently established in English West Midlands; smaller than White-headed Duck, with much less white on head of more uniformly chestnut drake. Duck hardly distinguishable except by unswollen base of bill. Fresh water reservoirs and small lakes. 16 in. (41 cm.).   ○R

SAWBILLS, STIFF-TAILS

♂

♀

GOOSANDER

♂

♂

♀

RED-BREASTED MERGANSER

♀

♂

♀

SMEW

♂

♀

HOODED MERGANSER

♀

♂

♂

♀

WHITE-HEADED DUCK

♂

'bubbling'

♂

♀

♀

RUDDY DUCK

67

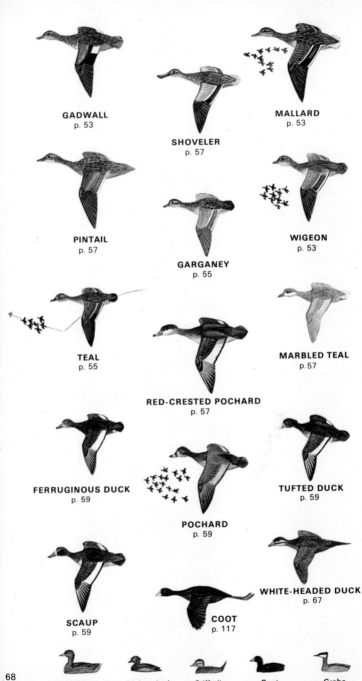

GADWALL
p. 53

SHOVELER
p. 57

MALLARD
p. 53

PINTAIL
p. 57

GARGANEY
p. 55

WIGEON
p. 53

TEAL
p. 55

RED-CRESTED POCHARD
p. 57

MARBLED TEAL
p. 57

FERRUGINOUS DUCK
p. 59

POCHARD
p. 59

TUFTED DUCK
p. 59

SCAUP
p. 59

COOT
p. 117

WHITE-HEADED DUCK
p. 67

Dabbling duck   Diving duck   Stifftail   Coot   Grebe

FEMALE DUCKS IN FLIGHT

Female ducks are often easier to identify in flight than at rest because then the speculum (see p. 50) shows as a wing-bar. Since not all female ducks have a clearly visible wing-bar, e.g. scoters, other points to look for are pointed tail (pintail, white-headed duck), face patches (scoters), and capped or hooded effects (golden eyes, sawbills). Of course female ducks will as often as not be accompanied by the much more easily identifiable males. Beware, however, the eclipse plumages of males, outside the immediate flightless period, which often look so like the female plumage. Immature plumages too are usually very like the adult female.

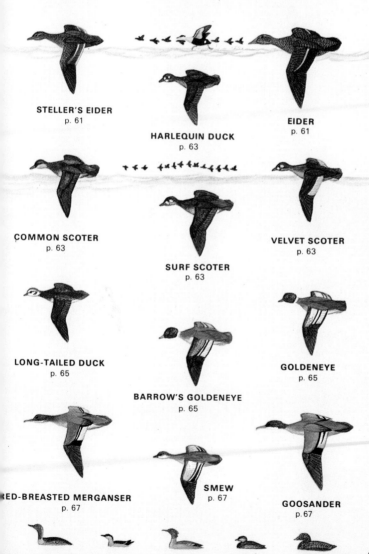

STELLER'S EIDER
p. 61

HARLEQUIN DUCK
p. 63

EIDER
p. 61

COMMON SCOTER
p. 63

SURF SCOTER
p. 63

VELVET SCOTER
p. 63

LONG-TAILED DUCK
p. 65

BARROW'S GOLDENEYE
p. 65

GOLDENEYE
p. 65

RED-BREASTED MERGANSER
p. 67

SMEW
p. 67

GOOSANDER
p. 67

Diver   Auk   Sawbill   Sea duck   Eider

69

● EAGLES, HAWKS AND ALLIES: *Accipitridae.* pp. 71–95.

The diurnal birds of prey are a large, distinctive group of medium to large long-winged birds, adapted to flesh-eating by their hooked bills and powerful talons; their nostrils in a cere at the base of the bill. Females usually larger than males. Immature plumages can be very confusing. Flight powerful, often soaring. Nest in tree or on ledge or ground. The following families occur in the region. Pandionidae (osprey); Accipitridae, comprising the kites, eagles, buzzards, hawks, Old World vultures and harriers; and Falconidae (falcons). 'Hawk' is often used as a general term for smaller birds of prey, as well as more strictly for the genus *Accipiter*. See p. 90 for distinctions of Accipitridae from falcons.

OSPREY *Pandion haliaetus.* Large size, long angled wings, white head and underparts, and habit of fishing by diving from air makes this one of the most distinctive birds of prey; much larger White-tailed Eagle and smaller Marsh Harrier (p. 87), both pale-headed birds seen over water, have dark underparts. Sexes alike. Call a shrill cheeping, suggesting a young game bird. Flight rather slow and flapping, recalling larger gulls, when hunting over water; also soars and hovers. Fond of perching on dead tree or post in water. Breeds in wooded or moorland country with lakes or rivers; in winter frequents large expanses of fresh, brackish and salt water. 20–23 in. (51–58 cm.). ○s**M   Map 50**

WHITE-TAILED EAGLE or SEA EAGLE *Haliaeetus albicilla.* Massive build and wide span of very broad wings distinguished from all other large brown birds of N W Europe except Golden Eagle (p. 79), from which best told at all ages by wedge-shaped, not square, tail and at close range by legs being only half-feathered. Adult White-tailed also differs from immature Golden in lacking black bar at tip of white tail, while immature White-tailed resembles adult Golden in having brown tail, though with base mottled white. Head of adult often pale, sometimes almost white; bill yellow. Sexes alike; tail of immature rather longer. Has various barking calls, the female's deeper. Ponderous, heron-like or vulturine flapping flight, low over water or reed-beds when hunting; also soars and dives from air. Rocky coasts, large lakes and rivers in forested and other wild country. 27–36 in. (69–91 cm.). —**V(b)**

PALLAS'S SEA EAGLE *Haliaeetus leucoryphus.* Smaller than White-tailed Eagle, with smaller dark, not yellow, bill, head always pale, and tail with dark tip like immature Golden Eagle. White on tail very conspicuous in flight. Immatures hard to distinguish, though Pallas's does not have base of tail mottled white. Various barking, neighing and gull-like calls, but rather silent in winter quarters. Inland lakes, swamps and rivers, wintering also on coasts of inland seas, scarcely overlapping White-tailed Eagle. 30–33 in. (76–84 cm.).

OSPREY, SEA EAGLES

adult

imm.

adult

OSPREY

imm.

adult

imm.

adult

WHITE-TAILED EAGLE

imm.

adult

imm.

adult

PALLAS'S SEA EAGLE

Kites: *Milvus.* Large buzzard-like birds of prey with long angular wings, tail forked and sexes alike. Nest in trees. Partly carrion feeders and in S Europe frequent motor roads to feed on animals killed by traffic.

RED KITE *Milvus milvus.* The only large predator of the region with a deeply forked tail, except for the Black Kite. Plumage more rufous and head usually paler than most buzzards, also has pale patch on underwing, which Buzzard may have too, but Black Kite does not. Call a shrill buzzard-like mew. Soars, often with angled wings, but normal flight more buoyant and harrier-like than Black Kite's or Buzzard's. Woodland, mainly deciduous, and areas with scattered trees. 24 in. (61 cm.). ⊙ **R** **Map 51**

BLACK KITE *Milvus migrans.* Tail slightly forked, but fork not always easy to see in flight. Otherwise like a dark Buzzard, (p. 77) but soars less and flaps more with wings held slightly crooked. May also be confused with dark Marsh Harrier (p. 87), but glides with wings level, not canted upwards, and frequently twists tail from side to side. Noisy, with a high-pitched squealing cry. Often gregarious and habitually hunts over water. All types of country except dense woodland, but especially near water; often in towns and villages. Probably the most numerous bird of prey of its size in the world. 22 in. (56 cm.). **—V**

BLACK-SHOULDERED KITE *Elanus caeruleus.* A smallish grey and white bird of prey, easily recognised by its black shoulders and frequent hovering; tail square, eye red. Immatures are browner. Rather silent, but has various weak whistles. Often perches on poles and wires, and may fly at dusk. Open country with scattered trees and woods, often near water; open arid steppes. 13 in. (33 cm.).

SHORT-TOED EAGLE *Circaetus gallicus.* A rather small greyish eagle or very large buzzard, distinguished from all same-sized birds of prey except Osprey (p. 71) by almost completely white underparts, dark only on throat, upper breast and wing-tips, with some dark bars on wings and tail. Head rather rounded, sometimes appearing almost owl-like. Calls mewing, buzzard-like, 'hu-opp' or 'piee-ou'. Soars and often hovers. Open country with scattered woods and trees, in both hills and plains. In S Europe feeds predominantly on snakes, whence sometimes called Snake Eagle. Nest usually on top of low tree. 25–27 in. (63–69 cm.).

Short-toed Eagle   Osprey

KITES, SHORT-TOED EAGLE

imm.

adult

RED KITE

adult

imm.

BLACK KITE

adult

imm.

hunting

BLACK-SHOULDERED KITE

imm.

adult

SHORT-TOED EAGLE

73

Hawks: *Accipiter*. The largest genus of birds of prey in the world includes hawks in the strict sense, recognised by their combination of rather short broad rounded wings and long tail. Female much larger than male. Nest in trees. Specialists in catching smaller birds in woodland and scrub.

SPARROWHAWK *Accipiter nisus*. Differs from smaller falcons (p. 95) in its shortish broad blunt wings, although grey male's are appreciably more pointed than brown female's and may approach shape of female Kestrel or Merlin, especially when these are soaring with outspread wings. Barred underparts also distinctive, rufous in male, grey-brown in female. Chief call a chatter, based on 'kek', 'kew', 'kyow' or 'kiv'. Characteristic flight patterns include: quick dash along a hedgerow, up and over to pounce on prey; fast low flight through wood or across open ground; soaring, often in a circular glide with intermittent spasms of three or four wing-flaps; also a gannet-like downward plummet with closed wings. Wooded country, sometimes penetrating villages and town suburbs. Presence in a wooded area sometimes revealed by plucking posts, with feathers and bones beneath a stump or other perch or even on ground. 11–15 in. (28–38 cm.).
●**Rmw** **Map 52**

Shikra ♂

SHIKRA *Accipiter badius*. Smaller than Levant Sparrowhawk, with pale cheeks, pale tail and brown on neck. Dark throat stripe like immature Levant. Female more like male; underparts variable. S Caspian region only. 12–14 in. (31–36 cm.).

LEVANT SPARROWHAWK *Accipiter brevipes*. Male larger than male Sparrowhawk, with grey not rufous cheeks and paler grey upperparts contrasting more with black wing-tips. Female greyer than female Sparrowhawk. Both have pale underwing, contrasting strongly with black wing-tips, central tail feathers unbarred, and red-brown not yellow eye. Immatures especially may appear strikingly white beneath. Call a distinctive high-pitched 'kewick-kewick'. Flies low over ground or along forest edges. Forests, wooded valleys. 13–15 in. (33–38 cm,).

GOSHAWK *Accipiter gentilis*. An outsize Sparrowhawk readily told from all other buzzard-sized birds of prey by having shorter wings and longer tail than buzzards and eagles, shorter wings and tail than harriers and kites, and broader and blunter wings and longer tail than Peregrine (p. 93). White eyestripe and under tail coverts. In the N, especially N Russia, can be very pale, almost white. Calls a shrill 'ca-ca-ca-ca' or 'qek-qek-qek-qek' and, from female a screaming 'hi-aa, hi-aa'. Has fast low hunting flight, and soars with frequent flaps. Forests, both coniferous and broad-leaved. 19–24 in. (48–61 cm.).
○**Rm**

DARK CHANTING GOSHAWK *Melierax metabates*. Grey, with white-tipped dark tail and barred rump and underparts, and reddish-orange legs and base of bill. Immature mainly brown. Wings broad and rounded like a Goshawk, but flight more harrier-like, quartering the ground; more often seen perched on a tree or post, often in a distinctive horizontal position. Call a series of fluty piping notes, also a shrill whistle. Open dry bush country, 15–19 in. (38–48 cm.).

HAWKS

imm.

♀

♂

♂

♀

Cuckoo
p. 175

SPARROWHAWK

imm.

♀

♂

♀

LEVANT SPARROWHAWK

imm.

adult

adult   northern race

GOSHAWK

adult

adult

imm.

adult

Hen-harrier
p. 87

adult

DARK CHANTING GOSHAWK

75

Buzzard: Colour phases

Buzzards: *Buteo*. Large, short-necked, broad-winged, rather short-tailed birds, much smaller than same-shaped but longer-necked *Aquila* eagles (pp. 79–81) and overlapping with the smaller eagles and the mostly smaller long-winged long-tailed harriers (p. 87). Plumage mainly brown, very variable, of limited identification value except for underwing and tail bars. Flight soaring, on raised, sometimes crooked wings; occasionally hovering. Call based on a mewing 'peeioo'.

BUZZARD *Buteo buteo*. Plumage exceptionally variable from pale to dark; tail barred, often faintly, with obscure dark band at tip; underwing often with large pale patch. Eastern race *vulpinus* often rufous on head and especially on often unbarred tail. Call fairly high-pitched, almost gull-like. Forests and areas with scattered woods; in winter in more open country. 20–22 in. (51–56 cm.). ●Rmw **Map 53**

ROUGH-LEGGED BUZZARD *Buteo lagopus*. Differs from Buzzard in its unbarred tail (white with a dark band near tip), conspicuous black patch at angle of very pale underwing, and usually also by paler head and neck and broad brown breastband. Feathered legs separate it from all other same-sized birds of prey, except smaller eagles. Call louder and less shrill than Buzzard. Hovers more than other buzzards. Open country, tundra, moors, dunes, marshes. 20–24 in. (51–61 cm.). ○W

LONG-LEGGED BUZZARD *Buteo rufinus*. Often very like Buzzard, but larger, rump pale, belly dark and tail always unbarred; may have distinctive white patch on underwing. Rufous phase similar to rufous eastern race of Buzzard *vulpinus*. Immature with barred tail indistinguishable from immature Buzzard. Has a short sharp buzzard-like mew. Plains, semi-deserts, mountains and other treeless country. 20–26 in. (51–66 cm.).

HONEY BUZZARD *Pernis apivorus*. Much the most buzzard-like of the kite group. Best distinction from Buzzard is double broad dark bar near base of tail, which Buzzard lacks, as well as bar at tip, which Buzzard shares. Is also slightly slenderer, with longer, narrower wings and tail and longer neck, accentuating smaller, more 'pigeon-like' head. Normal flight calls, 'puihu' (male) and 'piah' (female), shriller than and quite distinct from Buzzard's; various other calls at or near nest. Often soars on flat wings, sometimes hovers; characteristically droops wings when glides. Spends more time on ground than Buzzard, and has distinctive habit of robbing bees' and wasps' nests. Forested country, mainly deciduous. 20–23 in. (51–58 cm.). ○Sm **Map 54**

BUZZARD

adult

eastern race

ROUGH-LEGGED BUZZARD

adult

N Africa

adult

LONG-LEGGED BUZZARD

imm.

HONEY BUZZARD

77

BONELLI'S EAGLE *Hieraeetus fasciatus*. Intermediate in size between Buzzard (p. 77) and Golden Eagle, and best distinguished from all same-sized birds of prey of the region by contrast between whitish leading edge and dark centre and trailing edge of pointed wing, with conspicuous grey patch at angle. Underparts faintly spotted, but appear white at any distance; legs feathered. Wings longer and narrower than Buzzard; tail longer, with similar dark band at tip. Immature browner with pale chestnut underparts, but *cf* Booted Eagle. Call a rather musical 'klee-klee-klee-klee'. Wooded, often rocky, mountains, in winter in more open country. 26–29 in. (66–74 cm.).

BOOTED EAGLE *Hieraeetus pennatus*. Buzzard-sized, with two plumage phases, the commoner mainly rufous, with white underparts, which contrast strikingly with dark tips and trailing edge of wing from below; tail square, rufous, unbarred, legs feathered. Dark phase rich dark brown with paler tail. Immature more rufous than adult, especially below, paler than immature Bonelli's Eagle. Flight more buoyant than Buzzard (p. 77). Call a shrill 'ki-keee'. Forests, mainly in hill country; in more open country in winter. 18–21 in. (46–53 cm.).

Eagles: *Aquila*. pp. 79–81. Very large birds of prey, with long broad wings, broad tail, legs feathered, and plumage usually some shade of dark brown, the adults darker than the young. Habitually soar. Nest on ledge or in tree, usually inaccessible.

GOLDEN EAGLE *Aquila chrysaetos*. Adult tawny brown, sometimes with pale head; immature distinguished by white base of tail and white patch on spread wing. Differs from White-tailed Eagle (p. 71) in square, not wedge-shaped tail and fully feathered legs; adult has dark tail like immature White-tailed, but immature has much less white on tail than adult White-tailed. For distinctions from other *Aquila* eagles, see below and next page. Rather silent, but has a buzzard-like 'twee-o' and a barking call. Has a majestic soaring and gliding flight, with wing-tips splayed out and upturned, often remaining on the wing for hours at a time. Mainly mountainous country, often treeless. Probably the most numerous eagle of its size in the world. 30–35 in. (75–88 cm.). ⊙ R Map 55

IMPERIAL EAGLE *Aquila heliaca*. Distinguished from other large eagles by white shoulders, especially conspicuous in rare Spanish race *adalberti*, pale patches on nape and tail, becoming paler with age. Immature has distinctive streaky underparts. Rather silent, but has a barking 'owk-owk-owk'. Less often seen on wing than Golden Eagle. Lowland forests, wooded foothills, plains, steppes and marshes with scattered trees. 31–33 in. (78–84 cm.).

imm.

adult

BONELLI'S EAGLE

imm.

adult

rk
ase

adult
pale phase

imm.

dark

pale

BOOTED EAGLE

adult

imm.

1st year

2nd year

GOLDEN EAGLE

imm.

Spanish race adult

eastern race adult

**IMPERIAL
EAGLE**

SPOTTED EAGLE *Aquila clanga*. A medium-sized to large eagle, easily confused with slightly smaller Lesser Spotted Eagle and dark phase of same-sized Tawny Eagle. Adult has less conspicuous whitish patch at base of tail than most Lesser Spotteds (Tawny has none). Immatures of both have distinct whitish V at base of tail, but Spotted has much larger and more conspicuous pale spots on upperparts than Lesser Spotted, which in turn has a distinctive buff patch on nape. Both species are slimmer, broader-winged and squarer-tailed than Tawny Eagle; tail base of Spotted broader than Lesser Spotted. A barking 'kyak, kyak, kyak', like yapping of small dog, less shrill and more resounding than similar call of Lesser Spotted. In flight Spotted Eagle usually holds leading edge of wing straight, but Lesser Spotted flies with wings held slightly forward and so looking more crooked; both species slightly droop wing-tips when gliding. Lowland forests, more often near lakes, rivers or marshes than Lesser Spotted; both species in open country only on migration. 26–29 in. (66–74 cm.). **—V**

LESSER SPOTTED EAGLE *Aquila pomarina*. A buzzard-sized eagle, marginally smaller than Spotted Eagle, for distinctions from which, see above, and from usually larger Tawny Eagle, see below. Habitat similar to Spotted Eagle, but more often seen away from water. 24–26 in. (61–66 cm.).

TAWNY EAGLE and STEPPE EAGLE *Aquila rapax*. A medium-sized eagle exceptionally variable in colour from very dark brown, almost black, to pale brown, nearly white. N African race *belisarius* is never rufous; darker E European race *orientalis* is known as Steppe Eagle. Dark adults best distinguished from Spotted and Lesser Spotted Eagles by broader, more rounded wings, no white above rounded tail, and often a rufous-buff patch on nape; also at close range by oval not rounded nostrils. Immature usually paler than adult, and, especially in Steppe Eagle, may show striking contrast of pale, almost creamy brown upperparts with dark blackish-brown wing-tips and tail, sometimes with white rump patch; shows two pale wing-bars in flight. Call a crow-like barking 'kow-kow-kow'. More often seen perched or flying low than soaring, when wings are held slightly crooked and rather short tail is noticeable. Steppes, plains, savannas, often treeless or bushy. 26–31 in. (66–79 cm.).

VERREAUX'S EAGLE or BLACK EAGLE *Aquila verreauxi*. Rare vagrant to extreme S of region, perhaps breeding in Sinai peninsula. Adults easily told by deep black plumage with conspicuous white patch on rump and pale patch on wing, showing as shoulder patch at rest; wings broader and paler at tip in flight. Immatures paler, larger than Tawny Eagle. Generally silent, but has various barking or crow-like calls. Flight more graceful than most large eagles. Rocky hills. 31–38 in. (79–97 cm.).

EAGLES

adult
pale form

adult

imm.

adult

imm.

SPOTTED EAGLE

adult
Steppe Eagle

imm.

imm.

**LESSER
SPOTTED EAGLE**

adult

adult

imm.

adult
Tawny Eagle

imm.

TAWNY EAGLE

adult

imm.

adult

VERREAUX'S EAGLE

81

Vultures. pp. 83 and 85. Large, short-tailed (except Lammergeier), birds of prey, their long broad wings, with a span of 5–9 ft, highly adapted to soaring. Plumage, except adult Egyptian Vulture, various shades of brown; often with a neck ruff and legs not feathered below 'knee' (except Lammergeier). Sexes alike in plumage and size. Normally rather silent and sluggish birds. Mostly gregarious. Carrion feeders of open country. Vultures soar at great heights, watching not only for carcasses but also for other vultures possibly flying towards carcasses. Once the presence of a carcass has been directly or indirectly detected, they glide down to it rapidly, and large numbers of vultures are thus enabled to assemble in a short time. The order of feeding depends on the stoutness of bill. Only the larger vultures are able to rip open a tough hide and feed, the smaller ones, especially the Egyptian, have to wait their turn.

EGYPTIAN VULTURE *Neophron percnopterus*. A small black and white vulture, with the typical straight-winged soaring outline, but with black-tipped white wings and wedge-shaped tail, longer than typical vultures. Bare yellow skin on head and throat, ruff shaggy, bill much slenderer than other vultures. Immature at first all dark brown, when small size and tail shape and length distinguish from other dark vultures, becoming whiter with each successive moult over five years. Normally silent. Less gregarious than larger vultures. Open country, both mountainous and lowland, a village scavenger in the East and N Africa. Nests on rock ledges. 23–26 in. (58–66 cm.).   **—V**

LAMMERGEIER or BEARDED VULTURE *Gypaetus barbatus*. The largest vulture of the region, with quite different flight outline from the typical vultures, long narrow angled and pointed wings and long diamond-shaped tail, looking almost like a giant Gyrfalcon (p. 91). Mainly dark above, and underparts fulvous; head white with conspicuous black band through eye, terminating in the 'beard'; legs fully feathered. Immature all dark with paler mottlings, underparts gradually becoming paler over five years, but not rufous till adult. Silent except in display, when has high-pitched 'quee-er'. More active than typical vultures. Not gregarious within the region, and does not join other vultures at carcasses. High and usually remote rocky mountains, nesting on rock ledges. Has remarkable habit of dropping bones from a height on to a hard surface to split them so that it can eat the marrow. 40–45 in. (102–114 cm.).

LAPPET-FACED VULTURE *Torgos tracheliotus*. The rarest and one of the largest of the breeding vultures of the region, an all-brown typical broad-winged vulture, readily distinguished at close range by massive bill and bare red skin on head and throat. In flight, pale bar at base of forewing and pale thighs are distinctive; wing span up to 9 ft. Normally silent, but may utter various growling, grunting or yelping sounds. Not usually gregarious in the region. Open plains, savannas and semi-deserts, with scattered trees, in which it nests. 39 in. (100 cm.).

VULTURES

adult

imm.

Griffon

Raven

Kite

adult

sub-adult

imm.

adult

adult

imm.

EGYPTIAN VULTURE

adult

imm.

LAMMERGEIER

adult

LAPPET-FACED VULTURE

83

Black Vulture

White-tailed Eagle
imm.

Lammergeier
imm.

BLACK VULTURE *Aegypius monachus*. The largest Old World vulture, all dark, with outline similar to Griffon, but tail rather longer and usually more wedge-shaped, so that at a great distance can be confused with a sea eagle (p. 71). Seen from above in flight, primaries appear paler than rest of wing. Black down on head and bare blue-grey skin on head and neck, are good distinctions from Lappet-faced Vulture (p. 83). Ruff black. Immature paler beneath. Various croaking, hissing and mewing notes. Less gregarious than most vultures, but will join Griffons at carcasses. Mainly open country, both lowland and mountainous, nesting in trees. Now on the list of endangered European birds. 39–42 in. (99–107 cm.).

GRIFFON VULTURE *Gyps fulvus*. The only large pale-coloured vulture, with dark wing and tail feathers in marked contrast. Head and neck covered with white down, with a creamy-white ruff at the base but this not easily visible in the field. Immature darker and more rufous. Can make a variety of grunting, hissing and whistling sounds of little significance for identification. Usually seen soaring at a considerable height. Flight outline 'like a teatray in the sky', the wings parallel-sided, then broadly rounded with splayed primaries and a horizontal pale mark on underside; tail very short, squared. Rocky mountainous country, breeding on cliff ledges, and generally roosting on rocks or crags. Takes precedence at carcasses over Egyptian Vulture but is dominated by Black Vulture. 38–41 in. (97–104 cm.).   **—V**

RÜPPELL'S VULTURE *Gyps rüppellii*. A wanderer from the south to Egypt and Sinai, rather shorter-winged and darker than Griffon, from which readily distinguished by white-speckled upperparts and three striking broken white horizontal bars on underwing. Immature brown, with white band along leading edge of wing and mottling on underwing more diffuse, confusable with immature African White-backed Vulture *G africanus*, not yet recorded in the region. Voice loud and harsh. Grassy plains and both open and mountainous deserts, gregarious where it is common. 37–42 in. (95–107 cm.).

VULTURES

imm.

adult

BLACK VULTURE

adult

imm.

GRIFFON VULTURE

imm.

adult

imm.

RÜPPELL'S VULTURE

Harriers: *Circus.* Slim medium-sized birds of prey, with long, usually narrow wings and tail, long legs, not very stout bill, and wings pointed (except Marsh Harrier), a ruff of feathers often making the face rounded and owl-like. Males pale grey (except Marsh Harrier), usually smaller than brown females; immatures brown or deep buff. Characteristic hunting technique of gliding low over ground with wings slightly canted upwards. Normally silent out of breeding season.

MARSH HARRIER *Circus aeruginosus.* The largest and most buzzard-like harrier of the region, with broader, more rounded wings and less graceful flight. Male differs from other harriers in its largely brown plumage, grey only on wings and tail; nearer to female in size than other harriers. Female and immature usually easily told from all same-sized birds of prey except Osprey (p. 71), which has white underparts, by pale head. Occasional dark-headed individuals can be told from Black Kite (p. 73) by rounded tail, from buzzards (p. 77) by slenderer build and different flight pattern. Display call disyllabic, female's longer and more drawn-out; alarm call of male 'chuckara, chuckara', of female a shriller 'chinka, chinka'. Marshes, fens, swamps, extensive reed-beds, rice fields. 19–22 in. (48–56 cm.). ⊙**SRm** **Map 56**

HEN-HARRIER *Circus cyaneus.* Male pale grey, with black wing-tips, differing from smaller male Montagu's Harrier in its prominent white rump (instead of white bar at base of tail) and no dark bars on the secondaries or rufous streaks on flanks and underwing. Female brown, with conspicuously barred tail, hard to tell from slenderer female Montagu's except by size, more conspicuous white rump and ruff extending across throat as blackish line. Immature as female, without deep buff underparts of immature Montagu's. *Cf.* Pallid Harrier. Alarm or display call a chattering 'ke-ke-ke' or 'kek-kek-kek'. Moors, grassy steppes, coastal marshes, extensive reed-beds and dunes. 17–20 in. (43–51 cm.). ⊙**RmW** **Map 57**

PALLID HARRIER *Circus macrourus.* Very like both Hen and Montagu's Harriers, male differing from both in paler colour, whiter head and breast, less black on wing-tips and no white on rump, from Montagu's also in no dark bars on secondaries or rufous streaks on underwing. Females and immatures even harder to distinguish, but adult female differs from Hen-Harrier in slenderer build and narrower white rump patch, and from Montagu's in its blackish throat ruff. Immature similar to immature Montagu's. Open grassy plains, savannas and steppes. 17–19 in. (43–48 cm.). **—V**

MONTAGU'S HARRIER *Circus pygargus.* Males especially are appreciably smaller than Hen-Harrier, for differences from which and from Pallid Harrier see above. Immature has distinctive deep rufous buff underparts. A dark melanic form occurs. Call somewhat shriller than Hen-Harrier, 'yick, yick, yick'. More often in marshes, fens and young conifer plantations. 16–18 in. (41–46 cm.). ⊙**Sm** **Map 58**

HARRIERS

♂ ♀

imm.

♂

♀

MARSH HARRIER

♂

♂

♀

HEN-HARRIER

♂

♂

♀

PALLID HARRIER

♂

black phase

♂

♀

MONTAGU'S HARRIER

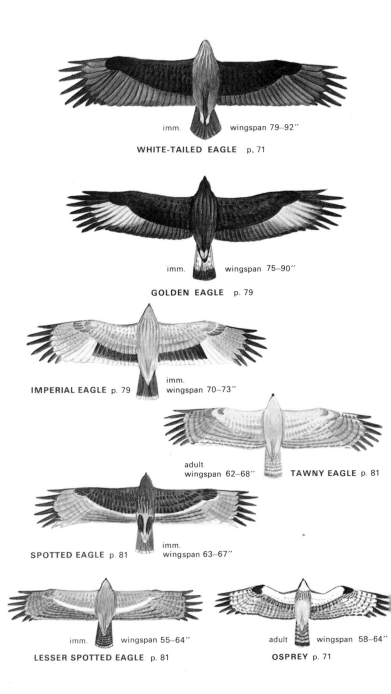

imm.   wingspan 79–92″

WHITE-TAILED EAGLE p. 71

imm.   wingspan 75–90″

GOLDEN EAGLE p. 79

IMPERIAL EAGLE p. 79

imm.
wingspan 70–73″

adult
wingspan 62–68″   **TAWNY EAGLE** p. 81

SPOTTED EAGLE p. 81

imm.
wingspan 63–67″

imm.   wingspan 55–64″

LESSER SPOTTED EAGLE p. 81

adult   wingspan 58–64″

OSPREY p. 71

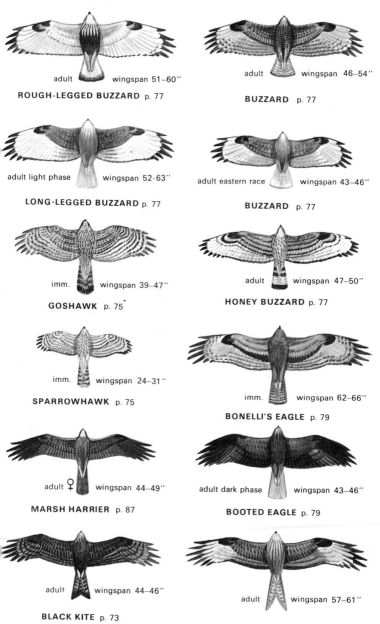

adult   wingspan 51–60″

ROUGH-LEGGED BUZZARD p. 77

adult   wingspan 46–54″

BUZZARD p. 77

adult light phase   wingspan 52-63″

LONG-LEGGED BUZZARD p. 77

adult eastern race   wingspan 43–46″

BUZZARD p. 77

imm.   wingspan 39–47″

GOSHAWK p. 75

adult   wingspan 47–50″

HONEY BUZZARD p. 77

imm.   wingspan 24–31″

SPARROWHAWK p. 75

imm.   wingspan 62–66″

BONELLI'S EAGLE p. 79

adult ♀   wingspan 44–49″

MARSH HARRIER p. 87

adult dark phase   wingspan 43–46″

BOOTED EAGLE p. 79

adult   wingspan 44–46″

BLACK KITE p. 73

adult   wingspan 57–61″

RED KITE p. 73

● FALCONS: *Falconidae.* A very distinct family of diurnal birds of prey (pp. 91–5) characterised by long, pointed scythe-like wings; females often much larger than males. Normally silent, but when alarmed or displaying typical calls are high-pitched and chattering, based on 'gyak', 'kee', 'kee-a' and similar notes. The falcons share with the owls (p. 177) a number of marked behaviour differences from hawks, eagles, buzzards and other members of the Accipitridae (p. 70); their droppings fall straight down from the perch instead of being squirted away; they build no nest of their own; they kill their prey by biting and severing the back of the neck; they hold their food in one claw; the young hiss when afraid or threatening; and they may bob their heads to show curiosity. The larger falcons are among the birds of prey most favoured for the sport of falconry.

GYRFALCON *Falco rusticolus.* The largest falcon of the region, resembling a large stout Peregrine (p. 93) in outline, though with slightly blunter wings with broader bases, and longer tail, but extremely variable in plumage, from almost white with a few dark flecks to almost completely dark grey; most frequent form is like rather pale Peregrine, but lacking the dark moustachial streak. Birds from Greenland and Iceland, known as Greenland Falcon and Iceland Falcon (though separate races are not now recognised by taxonomists) are larger, and white forms, which migrate SE in winter, are most frequent in N Greenland. Immature mainly brown. Flight rather slower than Peregrine, and calls louder, harsher and lower-pitched. Cliffed and rocky sea coasts, mountains, edges of coniferous forest. 20–22 in. (51–56 cm.). **—V**

SAKER FALCON *Falco cherrug.* Resembles a broader-winged longer-tailed Peregrine (p. 93), with upperparts mid-brown like a Buzzard (p. 77), its pale head distinguishing it from both Peregrine and Lanner, though this not always clearly visible; moustachial streak barely perceptible. Spotting rather than barring on tail is a useful pointer, as is contrast between heavily spotted underwing and pale wing tips. Fairly variable, and can be almost as pale as a Gyrfalcon. Immature more streaked. Open country, high plateaux, steppes, plains, semi-deserts, with scattered trees. 18 in. (46 cm.).

LANNER FALCON *Falco biarmicus.* European race *feldeggii* looks smaller and slenderer than Peregrine and differs also in its browner (but not so brown as the Saker) upperparts, pinkish underparts, rufous or buff crown and nape, and much narrower moustachial stripe; also has longer tail and blunter wings. Birds from N Africa and the Middle East, *erlangeri* and *tanypterus*, are paler and much less heavily marked with streaks on crown, bars above and spots below. Saker always has paler crown and is less slender and rakish, but may otherwise be hard to distinguish. Open country, including deserts, usually nesting on cliffs or rocky outcrops, sometimes in ruins. 17 in. (43 cm.).

FALCONS

white phase
adult

grey phase
adult

imm.

Peregrine p. 93

GYRFALCON

imm.

adult

pale form

imm.

SAKER FALCON

imm.

Egypt-Iraq

Europe
adult

N W Africa

LANNER FALCON

91

PEREGRINE *Falco peregrinus*. Readily identified in flight by distinctive anchor-like outline of long wings and rather short tail, and characteristic fast, winnowing wing-beats, followed by a glide; also frequently soars, indulges in aerobatics, and swoops steeply on prey in a power dive. Plumage very variable, from dark to light grey above with buff underparts barred dark grey; black moustachial streak is conspicuous against white chin and cheeks. Northern forms are darkest; pale southern races have some rufous on nape in Mediterranean *(brookei)*. Female much larger than male. Juvenile dark brown above, streaked instead of barred below, and with legs, cere and bare skin round eye blue-grey instead of yellow. Chief call a harsh deep chattering falcon note. Open country, from tundra to semi-deserts, especially with crags or cliffs for breeding, coastal cliffs, occasionally in forests and on tall buildings in towns; in winter frequent on estuaries and flat coast-lines. 15—19 in. (38—48 cm.).

⊙**Rmw   Map 59**

BARBARY FALCON *Falco pelegrinoides*. Like a small pale Peregrine, of which it may be only a race, but much paler and more rufous, with crown and nape very rufous. 15—18 in. (38—45 cm.).

SOOTY FALCON *Falco concolor*. Has two colour phases, one all-grey with black wing-tips, the other almost black. Longer-winged than Kestrel (p. 95). Differs from male Red-footed Falcon (p. 95) in absence of any red or rufous cere, and legs yellow. Smaller than Eleonora's Falcon and grey form much paler. In hobby-like flight can sometimes be distinguished by two central tail feathers protruding. Voice similar to Kestrel. Breeds in open treeless country with rocky outcrops, but winters also in savannas and open woodland. 13—14 in. (32—35 cm.).

ELEONORA'S FALCON *Falco eleonorae*. Intermediate between Peregrine and Hobby (p. 95), slenderer than Peregrine and longer-tailed than both, with wings extending to tip of tail. Plumage varies from pale to dark, but with many intermediates and no two birds exactly the same. Pale form like Hobby but with upperparts more grey-brown and more rufous on heavily streaked underparts. All dark form, blackish-brown like a large Red-footed Falcon (p. 95), but with thighs dark grey instead of rufous and legs, cere and bare skin round eye yellow or blue-grey. Intermediates may include birds pale above and dark below. Sexes nearly same size. Immatures have tail barred, and show barred underwing in flight. More gregarious than most falcons and social breeding, as many as 50 birds sometimes hunting together. Flight patterns resemble Peregrine and Hobby. Chief call note disyllabic. Sea cliffs and rocky islands, breeding in late summer so that young can be fed on birds migrating through the Mediterranean at that time. 15 in. (38 cm.).

FALCONS

imm.

southern race

northern race

PEREGRINE

imm.

adult
light
phase

dark phase

SOOTY FALCON

adult

imm.

adult

BARBARY FALCON

n. light

dark ♀

light ♂

imm. dark

dark ♂

light ♀

ELEONORA'S
FALCON

HOBBY *Falco subbuteo.* Flies like a miniature Peregrine (p. 93), long scythe-like wings with even shorter tail, making outline even more swift-like. Differs in streaked underparts, and rufous thighs and under tail. Females slightly and immatures much browner above, immatures not rufous on thighs. Follows migrating flocks of hirundines and swifts, on which it preys. Open country with scattered trees. Nests in trees. 12–14 in. (30–36 cm.). ⊙**Sm   Map 60**

MERLIN *Falco columbarius.* Smallest and least distinctive small European bird of prey, most easily told by its flight, habitat and general habits. Male differs from male Sparrow-hawk (p. 75) in streaked underparts, and from Hobby in pale thighs, bar at tip of tail, and no moustache or white cheeks. Female differs from both kestrels in brown upperparts. Outline compacter than Hobby, more like Kestrel. Flight more dashing than Kestrel, in pursuit of small birds, though may hover. Hills and moors, often treeless, in winter also often on coastal marshes and dunes. 10½–13 in. (27–33 cm.).
⊙**Rsmw   Map 61**

RED-FOOTED FALCON *Falco vespertinus.* The most gregarious falcon. Male all dark grey with chestnut thighs and under tail coverts, with bright red bill, cere, bare skin round eye and legs. Eastern form with striking white underwing occurs in S Iraq. Female differs from Hobby in rufous crown and nape but not thighs, and red legs. Immature like immature Hobby with pale forehead. Both hovers and glides. Open country with scattered trees and small woods, nesting in trees. 12 in. (30 cm.). —**A**

LESSER KESTREL *Falco naumanni.* Gregarious habits, more active flight, and noisy behaviour are best distinctions from Kestrel, unless male's unspotted mantle can be seen. Also slenderer and has narrower and slightly shorter tail, with underside paler and breast of both sexes sometimes almost unspotted. Female and immature very hard to distinguish except by pale claws. Often in company with Kestrel, hovering (with faster wingbeats) much less often but frequently gliding; wings may appear white beneath. Open country, nesting colonially on inland cliffs and ruined buildings. 12 in. (30 cm.). —**V**

KESTREL *Falco tinnunculus.* Constant hovering is best pointer. In flight, long pointed wings (blunter in female) and long tail look rakish. Sexes same size. No other small bird of prey has male's combination of blue-grey head and tail, spotted chestnut mantle (sparsely spotted in Canary Is) and black tail bar. Barred tail with terminal bar distinguishes female and immature from all other same-sized birds of prey (except Lesser Kestrel). Sparrowhawk (p. 75) has shorter and more rounded wings than female Kestrel, and quite different hunting techniques. Call a loud shrill nuthatch-like 'kee-kee-kee'. Open country, with crags or scattered trees, sea cliffs, towns and villages. Nest on rock-ledge, building or tree. 13½ in. (34 cm.). ●**Rsmw   Map 62**

FALCONS

imm.

adult

HOBBY

imm.

♂

♀

MERLIN

♀

imm.

♂

western race

eastern race

RED-FOOTED FALCON

hovering

♂

♂

♀

KESTREL

♂

♀

J·I·1970

LESSER KESTREL

95

GROUSE: *Tetraonidae.* pp. 97–9. Gamebirds, differing from the pheasants and partridges (Phasianidae p. 100), in their feathered legs and nostrils, and in never having spurs. They do, however, have similar short wings and heavy whirring flight.

WILLOW GROUSE *Lagopus lagopus lagopus.* The varyingly white grouse of northern Europe; birds from coastal Norway are intermediate with the all dark Red Grouse of the British Isles. Males have prominent red wattle over eye. In winter all white, except for black tail, distinguished from slightly smaller Ptarmigan by stouter bill, toes much less heavily feathered, and in males by no black patch between bill and eye. In summer warm brown, although wings and belly still mainly white, especially in flight (Ptarmigan greyer), and in autumn white patches appear (Ptarmigan greyer still). Habitat often best distinction. Calls a loud 'kok-kok-kok' and 'gobak, gobak'. Inhabits, lower levels than Ptarmigan, tundra, arctic prairies with birch and willow scrub, and heather moors and bogs; in winter sometimes descending to farmland. 15–16 in. (38–41 cm.).

RED GROUSE *Lagopus lagopus scoticus.* An all dark race of the Willow Grouse, confined to the British Isles, never turning white in winter. Looks very dark in flight, when lack of wing-bar separates from larger Black Grouse, and dark not rufous tail from partridges (p. 103). Calls and habits as Willow Grouse. Heather moors and bogs, in winter sometimes descends to farmland. 15–16 in. (38–41 cm.).

●R Map 63

PTARMIGAN *Lagopus mutus.* Like closely similar Willow Grouse has three plumages. In winter all white, with toes as well as legs heavily feathered, except for black tail, and in male black patch from bill to eye and red wattle. In summer all upperparts greyish-buff mottled darker in male, more rufous in female, with wings still mainly white, especially in flight. In autumn both sexes, but especially males, turn greyer above. Calls a hoarse croaking 'uk, uk' and a crackling 'karr, ikrikrrikrrrkrrr', also a brief crowing display song. Habitat usually higher than Willow Grouse, mountain tops, tundra, well above tree-line, and in British Isles usually well above 2000 ft. 14 in. (35–36 cm.).

☉R Map 64

HAZELHEN or **HAZEL GROUSE** *Tetrastes bonasia.* A small woodland grouse, both sexes readily identified in flight by black band at tip of grey tail. Plumage greyish-brown, becoming more rufous towards S of range; male with distinctive black-bordered white throat. Call a high-pitched whistle. Flies more readily than other grouse, wings making a distinctive 'rrrrr' sound. Perches in trees. Mainly in mixed woodland, but sometimes in pure broad-leaved or spruce forest, usually with dense shrub layer, often near rivers. 14 in. (35–36 cm.).

Ptarmigan
moulting ♂

Willow Grouse
moulting ♂

♂ Red Grouse

winter ♂

winter ♂

WILLOW GROUSE

imm.

♂ summer

♀

winter

RED GROUSE

♂

d Grouse
rk phase

♀

Willow Grouse
Norwegian coast

♂ summer

♀

HAZELHEN

♀

♂

PTARMIGAN

autumn

♂

♀

northern race

♀

winter

♂

BLACK GROUSE *Lyrurus tetrix.* Intermediate in size between Capercaillie and Red Grouse. Male (Blackcock) is only large black land-bird with white wing-bar and lyre-shaped tail; patch on shoulder and under tail coverts also white. Female (Greyhen) is like a much smaller female Capercaillie with forked tail and narrow pale wing-bar, and no rufous patch on breast or white on flanks. Differs from same-sized Red Grouse (p. 97) in its greyer plumage, darker legs, forked tail and narrow wing-bar. May hybridise with both Capercaillie and Pheasant (p. 107). Call of male a disyllabic sneezing note, of female a pheasant-like 'kok, kok'. Gathers, often in large numbers, at communal display grounds (leks) in spring and autumn. Male display song a medley of cooing, bubbling and crowing notes. Flight as Capercaillie but less noisy; flies higher than Red Grouse. Borders of woodland and moorland, moors, steppes and swampy heaths with scattered trees, especially birches and pines. Male 21 in (53 cm.), female 16 in. (41 cm.).

●R   Map 65

CAUCASIAN BLACKCOCK *Lyrurus mlokosiewiczi.* Smaller than Black Grouse with rather dull greenish, not glossy plumage, relieved only by red wattle and white shoulder patch (i.e. no white wing-bar or under tail), and distinct tail shape, the tips curving downwards rather than outwards. Females more uniformly vermiculated than Greyhen, and have rounded tail. Has similar communal lekking habits. Alpine meadows and scrub in the higher parts of the Caucasus. 20 in. (50 cm.).

CAPERCAILLIE *Tetrao urogallus.* The largest grouse of the region, and only mistakable for an unexpectedly airborne turkey. Male dark grey, with some white on flanks, and conspicuously long broad tail. Female and immature differ from much smaller female Black Grouse by chestnut patch on breast, some white on flanks, rounded tail and no wing-bar. Both sexes may erect hackles on neck when alarmed, to form prominent whiskers. May hybridise with both Black Grouse and Pheasant (p. 107). Call of male, a raucous sound like a man clearing his throat, of female a pheasant-like 'kok, kok'. Remarkable song at communal display ground, starting with a resonant rattle and ending with a sound like drawing a cork and pouring liquid out of a narrow-necked bottle, followed by a crashing sound made by scraping wing quills on the ground. Flight has typical game-bird alternation of quick whirring and gliding on down-turned wings; makes a great clatter when leaving trees, where habitually perches and feeds. Coniferous forest, especially in hills and mountains; in N W Spain in mountain hollywood. Male 34 in. (86 cm.), female 24 in. (62 cm.).   ☉R   Map 66

Red Grouse   Black Grouse   Capercaillie   Hazelhen

GROUSE

♀

BLACK GROUSE

♀ ♂

courtship display

♂

♀

CAUCASIAN
BLACKCOCK

♂

north-eastern race
in courtship display

♀

CAPERCAILLIE

♀

● **PHEASANT FAMILY:** *Phasianidae.* pp. 101–9. Gamebirds with unfeathered, often spurred legs, short rounded wings, heavy whirring direct flight and short thick bill with upper mandible longer. The larger and usually long-tailed ones tend to be called pheasants (pp. 107–109), the medium-sized ones partridges or francolins (pp. 103–105) and the small ones quails (p. 105). Partridges, francolins, snowcocks and quails are often encountered in coveys or small parties up to 12–15

quail, p. 105   partridges, p. 103   snowcocks, p. 101   pheasants, p. 107–9

CASPIAN SNOWCOCK *Tetraogallus caspius.* Larger, darker and much less rufous than Caucasian Snowcock, and distinguished by broader and more conspicuous white wing-bar, giving the impression in flight of a large pale bird with white and grey wings. When flushed either runs uphill or flies downhill, calling vociferously. Most frequent call is a bubbling note very reminiscent of Curlew (p. 139), often uttered with head and neck thrown backwards. Alarm call a repeated 'chok, chok, chok'. High, rocky alpine and sub-alpine meadows in summer generally not below 6000 ft., from the mountains of eastern Turkey (Taurus and Pontus ranges) eastwards; more often in rhododendron scrub than Caucasian Snowcock. 24 in. (61 cm.).

CAUCASIAN SNOWCOCK *Tetraogallus caucasicus.* Like a large rufous and grey domestic fowl or a giant partridge, with whitish cheeks, and distinctive blackish striations on upper breast; the snowcock with least white in its plumage. Sexes alike. Call a melodious and far-carrying whistle, also utters loud squawks and a soft 'tju, tju'. Usually runs uphill, but flies downhill with fast whirring flight. Cliffs, stony slopes and alpine meadows in the high Caucasus, up to the snow line, using its very stout bill for scraping in the ground to uproot plants. 22 in. (56 cm.).

TUFTED GUINEA FOWL *Numida meleagris.* A most distinctive bird, formerly widespread in N Africa, but now confined to a portion of central Morocco between the oueds Bou Regreg and the upper Oum-el-Rbia; also found in S France. A large gamebird, with a conspicuous erect red crest, the origin of the domesticated Guinea-fowl; plumage grey with white spots, head and neck featherless, neck blue-grey, cheeks whitish, wattles red. Gregarious, restless and noisy, with the well known squeaky cackle of the domestic bird. Wooded gullies in hill districts, mainly ground living but roosting in trees. 25 in. (63 cm,).

SNOWCOCKS

CASPIAN
SNOWCOCK

Chukar p. 103

CAUCASIAN
SNOWCOCK

mm.

adult

TUFTED GUINEA
FOWL

101

Partridges: *Alectoris* and *Perdix*. Stoutly built medium-sized brown gamebirds, with rufous tail especially conspicuous in flight. Chukar-type partridges *Alectoris* are longer, more upright and slightly more pheasant-like than smaller *Perdix*, and readily distinguished where they overlap it in W and S Europe by black and white eyestripes, white chin and throat, broad black band extending from eye down neck to form breast-band, conspicuous black and white barring on flanks, and red bill and legs. Sexes alike. Often perching on rocks and other slight elevations. The very similar Chukar, Rock and Red-legged Partridges, separable only at fairly close range, are geographically distinct except in the Balkans (Rock, Chukar).

RED-LEGGED PARTRIDGE *Alectoris rufa*. Best distinguished by black spotting on upper breast below black breast-band; brownish on head and upperparts. Call a loud challenging 'chuka, chuka' or 'chik, chik, chikar', also a sound like whetting a scythe or an old-fashioned steam engine wheezing. Habitat similar to Partridge, but prefers drier and stonier locations. 13½ in. (34 cm.).　　　●R　Map 67

BARBARY PARTRIDGE *Alectoris barbara*. A North African species, the most distinctive of the group, with breast-band chestnut speckled white, chin and throat grey, and stripe behind eye buff. Call like Chukar, also a rapid 'kakelik'. Rocky or stony hillsides and deserts, with scrub or open woodland. 13 in. (33 cm.).

CHUKAR *Alectoris chukar*. Very like Rock Partridge, but with less black between bill and eyes, grey speckling on throat above breast-band, and fewer, larger flank bars. Call distinct, a loud, high-pitched 'chuk, chuk, chuk, chukar', often followed by caccaba, caccaba, caccaba', reminding others of a barnyard fowl. Habitat as Rock Partridge, also in deserts. 13 in. (33 cm.).

ROCK PARTRIDGE *Alectoris graeca*. Distinguished by black breast-band sharply separating unspotted white throat from unspotted grey breast; rather grey on head and upperparts. Calls distinctive, an abrupt quadrisyllabic 'tchertsivit-tchi', a curiously nuthatch-like 'chwit, chwit, chwit', and a sharp 'pitchi-i'. Rocky, stony and thinly grassy hill and mountain slopes; vineyards. 13 in. (33 cm.).

PARTRIDGE *Perdix perdix*. Much the most widespread European partridge, and the only one in Central and Northern Europe. Distinguished from the larger chukar-type partridges by unspotted grey breast, chestnut horseshoe on lower breast, no white about head, less conspicuously barred flanks, greenish bill and grey legs. Juveniles and some hens lack the horseshoe. Cf. Quail (p. 105). Loud high-pitched creaky grating 'keev' or 'keev-it' degenerates into rapid cackling 'it-it-it . . .' when bird flushed. Never perches above ground. Open country, including farmland, especially arable, moorland, downs, steppes, heaths, semi-deserts, shingle tracts, sand dunes. 12 in. (30 cm.).　　　●R　Map 68

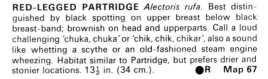

adult

juv.

RED-LEGGED PARTRIDGE

BARBARY PARTRIDGE

Sinai

ROCK PARTRIDGE

CHUKAR

uv. Quail
p. 105

juv.

♂

♀

PARTRIDGE

SAND PARTRIDGE *Ammoperdix heyi* Intermediate between Quail and Partridge (p. 103), having the latter's rufous tail. Cock pinkish-buff with dark grey head, flanks boldly barred rufous and black, white patch behind eye and orange-yellow bill and legs; in Palestine also has white mark in front of eye. Hen browner, vermiculated. Double call resembles two stones grated together; wing quills make a rattling sound in flight. Broken rocky or stony ground with minimal vegetation, but not on open desert sands; usually in pairs. 9½ in. (24 cm.).

SEE-SEE PARTRIDGE *Ammoperdix griseogularis*. Differs from Sand Partridge especially in cock's striking head pattern, white stripe through eye being always flanked by a broad black stripe above and a narrower one below. Double whistling call, 'see-see'; wing quills also whistle in flight. Habitat as Sand Partridge. 9½ in. (24 cm.).

QUAIL *Coturnix coturnix*. Much the smallest European gamebird, and the only migratory one. Distinguished from young Partridge (p. 103) by buff streaks on head, no chestnut in tail and male's blackish (rarely rufous) throat markings; from Andalusian Hemipode (p. 110) by buff not orange breast and flanks streaked not spotted; and from Corncrake (p. 115) in flight by legs not dangling and no chestnut in wings. Cf. Bobwhite (p. 109). Bill grey, unspurred legs pink. Female and juvenile have breast spotted. Typical whirring gamebird in flight, but much more often heard than seen. Chief call an unmistakable far-carrying plangent 'quic-ic-ic' or wet-mi-lips', also a curious growling 'row-ow-ow' only audible at very close quarters and when flushed may call 'crwee-crwee' or 'crucc-crucc'. Farmland, especially among growing crops, open grassland, steppes, semi-deserts. Numbers reaching N W Europe vary greatly from year to year. 7 in. (18 cm.).   ○S   **Map 69**

BLACK FRANCOLIN or BLACK PARTRIDGE *Francolinus francolinus*. Spurred cock is one of the most distinctive medium-sized gamebirds, with black face, throat and underparts, chestnut collar, white face patch and flanks strongly spotted white. Spurless hen resembles many other speckled brown gamebirds, but can be told by chestnut patch on nape. As often heard as seen; characteristic loud far-reaching, gratingly high-pitched call is variously rendered 'che-chirree, chik, chiree' and 'chik-cheek-cheek-keraykek'. Areas of fairly dense vegetation, such as tall grasslands and crops, scrub, especially tamarisk, and marshes. 13 in. (34 cm.).

DOUBLE-SPURRED FRANCOLIN *Francolinus bicalcaratus*. A partridge-sized gamebird, only in Morocco. Spurred cock has black, white and chestnut head pattern and underparts strongly streaked with same colours; spurless hen similar but duller. Chief call a loud deep repeated 'quair, quair' or 'coak, coak'; also 'cocoi'. Open woods and scrub, palm groves, cultivation clearings. 12½ in. (32 cm.).

PARTRIDGES, FRANCOLINS

SEE-SEE
PARTRIDGE

SAND PARTRIDGE

with brown throat

QUAIL

juv. Andalusian Hemipode p. 110

BLACK FRANCOLIN

DOUBLE-SPURRED FRANCOLIN

PHEASANT *Phasianus colchicus*. The most widespread gamebird in the world, native in Eurasia, but introduced in W Europe, N Africa, N America and elsewhere. General appearance of both sexes too familiar to need detailed description; head and neck of male usually metallic green.

Juvenile pheasants while still growing their long tails need to be distinguished from partridges (p. 103) unless accompanied by adults. Occasionally hybridises with Capercaillie (p. 99), Black Grouse (p. 99) and other species of introduced pheasant (p. 109). Cock crows with a loud harsh 'kor-kok', often stimulated by distant explosions or thunder, at close quarters a whirring from the wings can be heard before and after this. Both sexes also cackle and chuckle, e.g. 'kuttuc, kuttuc' when flushed. Juveniles have a curious double bullfinch-like pipe followed by a creaking third note. Flight whirring; can rocket upwards with remarkable acceleration when startled, though often prefer to run. Open country, with scattered woods, copses or riverine belts of trees or shrubs, marshes, extensive reed-beds, rarely in large gardens, often feeding on cultivated land.

Native birds of region, from Caucasus and SW Asia, all belong to black-necked *colchicus* type, with rather dark and purplish plumage, lower back and rump mainly rufous, and no neck ring; these were first introduced in W Europe and in Britain, where they have been present for at least 900 years, used to be known as the 'Old English' type. Later various Far Eastern forms with a more or less conspicuous white neck ring and lower back and rump mainly green, *torquatus* group, (2) were introduced, and these have interbred not only with *colchicus* type but with other subspecies introduced from time to time, till the British Isles and much of W Europe are occupied by an indescribable amalgam of pheasant forms from all over Asia. Forms containing features of the following races may also be seen: *principalis* (1) (from Transcaspia and Turkestan) with some white on the wing coverts and upper parts yellowish or orange red, *mongolicus* (4) (from Turkestan, not Mongolia) with white on the wing and partial white collar and upperparts coppery-red glossed with green and the blue-rumped *formosanus* (3) from Taiwan. Two very distinct varieties are the so-called 'melanistic mutant', (6) dark in both sexes (cock deep blue and green, hen very dark brown), and the flavistic Bohemian pheasant (5) buff or cream-coloured with blackish markings and dark head. Male 30–35 in. (66–89 cm.), female 21–25 in. (53–63 cm.).
●R   Map 70

JAPANESE PHEASANT or GREEN PHEASANT *Phasianus versicolor*. Introduced in W Europe; closely resembles dark 'melanistic mutant' form of Pheasant, but cock can be distinguished by dark green instead of blackish-brown and coppery-red underparts, pale instead of dark rump, and blue wing-coverts. Hens cannot be separated in the field. Hybridisation also confuses the issue. Habits and habitats as Pheasant. Male *c* 25 in. (63 cm.), female *c* 22 in. (56 cm.).

PHEASANTS

Partridge p. 103

juv.

imm.

♂

♂

♀

PHEASANT

1

2

3

4

5

6

♀

♂

JAPANESE PHEASANT

107

LADY AMHERST'S PHEASANT *Chrysolophus amherstiae*
Female differs from female Golden in horn-coloured, not greenish bill, blue-grey legs and bare skin; round eye blue-green, not red. Call indistinguishable from Golden England. ○▶

GOLDEN PHEASANT *Chrysolophus pictus*. Female has longer and more strongly barred tail than female Pheasant (p. 107); Call more rasping and higher-pitched. Cf. Lady Amherst's. Much prefers running to flying. Britain. ○**R**

SILVER PHEASANT *Lop nycthemera*. Female has blac brown crest and black and in tail. Male has shrill wh female a repeated deep 'wl Germany.

REEVES'S PHEASANT *Syrmaticus reevesii*. Male has tail up to 6 ft. Calls a twittering chuckle and a musical pipe. Scotland, France, Germany. ○**R**

INTRODUCED GAME BIRDS:
Among numerous species of game birds from Asia and North America which have been introduced into the region from time to time, these have established themselves in at least one area, the pheasants in woodlands.

CALIFORNIA QUAIL *Lophortyx californicus*. Like a small Partridge or large Quail, greyish, with a distinctive short curved black plume on the crown; male also has black and white pattern on face and throat. Call a trisyllabic 'qua-quer-go'. Open country or scrub. Germany.

BOBWHITE *Colinus virginianus*. Smaller than California Quail, rufous, male with dark brown and white eyestripes and white throat; white areas buff in female. Call a loud double whistle 'bob-white'. Open and cultivated country and scrub. England, Germany. ○R

WILD TURKEY *Meleagris gallopavo*. Unmistakably a rather slimmer version of the farmyard turkey, but with no white tip to tail. Male 'gobbles'; alarm note 'pit' or 'put-put'. Mainly woodland. Germany.

CRANES: *Gruidae.* Large, long-legged, long-winged, long-necked but rather short-tailed land and marsh birds, with stout straight bills, fairly long but shorter than herons (p. 35) and storks (p. 43). Plumage usually a combination of grey, black and white. In slow, strong but direct flight, both neck and legs are stretched out, a good distinction from herons but not from storks. Voice loud, clanging or trumpeting. Many species have remarkable dancing displays.

Crane   Heron   Goose

CRANE *Grus grus.* Grey, with black head and wing-tips, conspicuous white stripe from cheek down neck, red crown (not visible at a distance) and a large tuft of plumes obscuring the tail. Juvenile darker, with brownish head and neck. Flight attitude, head pattern, plumes all separate crane from Grey Heron (p. 35), but beware habit in some country districts of Britain of still calling herons 'cranes'. Beware Sarus Crane *Grus antigone*, a not infrequent escape from wildfowl collections, which is much larger (60 in., [156 cm.]) and differs in having bare red skin on head and upper neck, grey crown, white tips to plumes and reddish legs. Call a harsh clanging 'krooh' or 'krr'. Flies in V-formation or lines on migration. Extensive marshes, bogs and wet heathland or tundra, in winter also in drier open country. 45 in. (114 cm.).   **—A**

SIBERIAN CRANE *Grus leucogeranus.* A large white crane with black wing-tips and conspicuous white plumes; legs, bill and bare skin on face red. Has shorter bill than White Stork (p. 43), and shows no black at all when at rest. Immature tinged buff, almost rufous on feathered head and neck. Voice softer and more musical than Crane, 'krouk, krouk'. Very local and now much decreased in marshes in the extreme E of the region. 55 in. (140 cm.).

DEMOISELLE CRANE *Anthropoides virgo.* Nearly a foot shorter than Crane, from which it also differs in its conspicuous white ear-tufts, black lower neck and breast, terminating in a plume, much less conspicuous wing plumes, lack of red on head, and higher-pitched voice. Immature grey on head and neck with smaller grey ear tufts. Marshes and marshy river valleys; in N Africa on high plateaux. 38 in. (96 cm.).

ANDALUSIAN HEMIPODE *Turnix sylvatica* (Turnicidae). A small quail-like bird but with rufous breast, and black spots on flanks. Very shy and hard to flush, often zigzags, frequently only detectable by distinctive low mooing or crooning note; When does fly skims low and drops down, hardly ever rising again. Sandy plains and dry grassland with cover typically in dwarf palmetto vegetation. 6 in. (15 cm.).

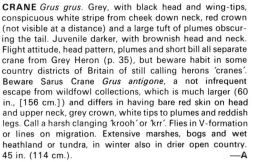

Andalusian Hemipode ♀

CRANES

on migration

adult

CRANE

adult

juv.

SIBERIAN CRANE

adult

DEMOISELLE CRANE

adult

adult

juv.

111

● **BUSTARDS**: *Otididae*. Medium-large to very large, rather long-necked and long-legged land birds; bill stout, somewhat flattened. Normal gait a sedate walk, with head erect, but usually either crouching with neck extended or running when alarmed. Flight strong, with broad wings, legs and neck extended, like cranes (p. 111) and storks (p. 43). Open treeless country.

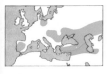

GREAT BUSTARD *Otis tarda*. One of the largest land birds of the region, showing much white on black-tipped wings in flight. Male, substantially larger than female, has long moustachial bristles and rufous chestnut breast band. Rather silent, but has a low bark or grunt. Gregarious, in small flocks. Treeless plains, steppes and extensive cultivations. Male 40 in. (102 cm.), female 30 in. (76 cm.). —V(b)

♀	♂	♂	♂
adult	1 year	3–6 years	over 6 years

LITTLE BUSTARD *Otis tetrax*. Suggests a large long-legged gamebird and though mainly brown at rest shows a striking contrast in flight, with almost as much white as a flying Shelduck (p. 51). Breeding male has conspicuously horizontal head and neck pattern of grey, black and white. Flight note, a short 'dahg'; display note a far-carrying snorting 'ptrr'. Flight intermediate between duck and gamebird, with quivering and whistling wing quills; less given to crouching and running than other bustards. Grassy and cultivated plains, sometimes with scattered trees and bushes. 17 in. (43 cm.). —V

HOUBARA BUSTARD *Chlamydotis undulata*. Easily told in breeding plumage by conspicuous vertical black and white frill or skirt on neck, as well as backward-pointing black and white crest, less conspicuous than Arabian Bustard's. In winter neck grey in front with dark streaks down side. When crouching blends perfectly with sandy background. Much less white in wings than other bustards of region. A silent bird. Flight fairly fast though with seemingly slow wing beats, but more often runs. Dry open plains, semi-desert and desert, usually with little or no scrub. 25 in. (64 cm.). —V

ARABIAN BUSTARD *Ardeotis arabs*. A large bustard whose backward-pointing crest gives it an outline more like the African Kori Bustard *A. kori* than the Great Bustard, like which it shows white on the wings in flight. Otherwise more uniform in plumage. Calls a rasping croak and a drawn-out fluty whistle. Dry grassy plains or open scrub, semi-deserts. Male 35 in. (90 cm.), female 29 in (74 cm.).

BUSTARDS

courtship display

♀

♂

GREAT BUSTARD

♀

♂

LITTLE BUSTARD

♀

♂

winter

HOUBARA BUSTARD

ARABIAN BUSTARD 113

RAILS and CRAKES: *Rallidae.* Small to medium, shy, ground-dwelling birds; legs and toes fairly long, wings and tail rather short. Gait jerky, with tail often flirted, legs dangling in flight. Marsh dwellers (except Corncrake) inhabiting densely vegetated wetlands, swamps, bogs, fens, marshes, reed-beds and fresh-water margins. Rarely seen in the open, either on ground or in flight.

WATER RAIL *Rallus aquaticus.* Like a small Moorhen (p. 117) with a long red bill, which also distinguishes it from all the smaller crakes; most often seen in rear view, as it dashes back into cover, when barred flanks and greyer under tail coverts distinguish from Moorhen. Much more often heard than seen, uttering various clucking, grunting and miaouing notes, a singular loud harsh call beginning as a grunt and ending as a squeal, and several repeated monosyllables. Most often in the open in hard weather, feeding on unfrozen patches. 11 in. (28 cm.). ⊙ **RmW Map 71**

SPOTTED CRAKE *Porzana porzana.* Even more skulking than Water Rail. White-spotted upperparts and buff under tail coverts. In flight shows large pale patches on short, rounded dark brown wings. Most likely to be seen at dusk feeding on mud at edge of thick swampy cover. Has a rhythmical snipe-like 'tic-toc' and a loud 'h'wit, h'wit', like a whiplash. 9 in. (23 cm.). ○**SMw Map 72**

LITTLE CRAKE *Porzana parva.* Like a miniature short-billed Water Rail, with unspotted underparts, barred under tail coverts and green bill. Male differs from both sexes of Baillon's Crake in its olive-brown upperparts, unstreaked wing coverts, unbarred flanks, red base of bill and green legs. Female and juvenile have distinctive buff face and underparts. Call a reiterated monosyllable ending in an almost yapping trill; also an explosive double note. 7½ in. (19 cm.). **—V**

BAILLON'S CRAKE *Porzana pusilla.* Both sexes differ from male Little Crake in having rufous upperparts, white streaks on wing coverts, flanks barred, bill all green and legs greyish-pink. Voice perhaps similar to Little Crake, with which it has been thoroughly confused. 7 in. (18 cm.). **—V(b)**

STRIPED CRAKE *Porzana marginalis.* The smallest crake of the region, very rare in N Africa, streaked above, but differing from both Baillon's and Little Crake in its paler flanks and rufous under tail coverts. Voice not known. 6¾ in. (17 cm.).

SORA RAIL *Porzana carolina.* A vagrant from America, very like Spotted Crake, but with white under tail coverts and in adults (not immatures) a black face patch. 9 in. (23 cm.). **—V**

CORNCRAKE *Crex crex.* A bird whose loud rasping song, recalling a grated comb, 'crex, crex', is much more often heard than its slim brown form is seen. When flushed, chestnut wings and dangling legs separate it at once from Quail (p. 105) and young Partridges (p. 103). Rough grassland, hayfields. 10½ in. (27 cm.). ⊙ **Sm Map 73**

Corncrake

RAILS, CRAKES

adult

imm.

WATER RAIL

♀

♂

♀

SPOTTED CRAKE

imm.

imm.

♂

♀

LITTLE CRAKE

♂

BAILLON'S CRAKE

STRIPED CRAKE

SORA RAIL

Quail p. 105

CORNCRAKE

115

MOORHEN *Gallinula chloropus*. The only waterfowl with both red forehead and habit of constantly flirting white under tail coverts. This, together with white line along flank and lack of white wingbar in flight, distinguish it from coots. Legs green with red garter, bill red with yellow tip. More olive-brown juveniles differ from both young coots and adult winter Dabchick (p. 23) in their white under tail coverts, and have much less white on throat than young coots. Chief call notes are loud but rather liquid disyllabic croaks, 'curruc' and 'kittic' and a 'kaak'. Flight weak, laboured and pattering take-off from water and legs trailing down first, later straight out behind. Habitually swims, with jerky forward movement; sometimes dives. Fresh water with thick marginal cover, swamps, sometimes plentiful in town parks; often feeds on grassland, usually near water. 13 in. (33 cm.).

⬤**RW   Map 74**

ALLEN'S GALLINULE *Porphyrula alleni*. Vagrant from southern Africa. Back and wings green, legs red, forehead pale blue; juvenile has rufous underparts. Calls croaking and shrieking. 9½ in. (24 cm.).

AMERICAN PURPLE GALLINULE *Porphyrula martinica*. Rare transatlantic vagrant. Purple and bronze-green plumage, pale blue forehead and yellow legs. Immature like pale brown young Moorhen with more white under tail. 12–14 in. (30–36 cm.)   **—V**

PURPLE GALLINULE or GREEN-BACKED GALLINULE *Porphyrio porphyrio*. An outsize dark bluish-purple Moorhen, with no white line on flank, longer red legs and very large stout all-red bill; juvenile greyer. Form breeding in Egypt (*aegyptiacus*) has green back, juvenile with whitish underparts. Calls include many loud hooting, cackling, clucking and hoarse rippling notes, and a softer 'chuck-chuck' contact note. Shy where persecuted; elsewhere comes out into open, often flirting tail, and climbs reed stems; flight as Moorhen. Swamps, reed-beds, freshwater margins with thick cover. 19 in. (48 cm.).

COOT *Fulica atra*. Coots are the only all-black waterfowl with a conspicuous white forehead and bill, dumpier than most ducks; legs green. In laboured moorhen-like flight shows white wing-bar. Juvenile has no distinctive features except for all-dark upperparts and all whitish underparts. Downy young have rufous head and neck (Moorhens are all dark). Calls distinctive loud high-pitched 'kowk', 'kewk', and 'cut'. Gregarious; large flocks make remarkable roaring sound on surface of water when disturbed by birds of prey. Much given to quarrelsome chases, habitually dives and has pattering take-off. Fresh water, usually with vegetated margins, sometimes in town parks. 15 in. (38 cm.).   ⬤**RW   Map 75**

CRESTED COOT *Fulica cristata*. Only distinguishable from Coot by lack of white wing-bar, hooting call-note, and, at close range blunter angle of black between forehead and upper mandible, two red knobs on forehead and bluish feet. Reed marshes with patches of open water. 16 in. (41 cm.).

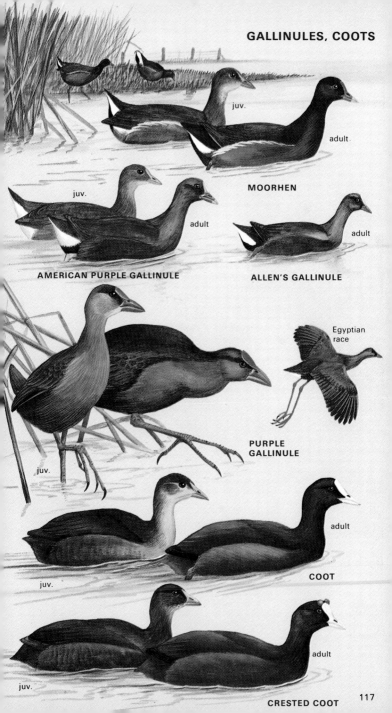

GALLINULES, COOTS

juv.

adult

adult

MOORHEN

juv.

adult

AMERICAN PURPLE GALLINULE

adult

ALLEN'S GALLINULE

Egyptian race

juv.

PURPLE GALLINULE

juv.

adult

COOT

juv.

adult

CRESTED COOT

117

WADERS pp. 119–43. Nine families of mainly long-legged, long-necked and (except for the plovers, pp. 121–5) long-billed, gregarious marsh or waterside birds, breeding in marshy tundra, taiga, moorland, or grassland, and wintering on estuaries and muddy or sandy seashores, occurring at freshwater margins chiefly on migration. Wing-bars and call-notes important in identification. Sexes usually more or less alike. Song usually delivered in aerial display. In autumn and winter flocks often perform tight-packed aerial evolutions. The two principal families are the plovers (pp. 121–5) and the sandpipers and snipes and their allies (pp. 127–41). We start with three families of large black and white waders.

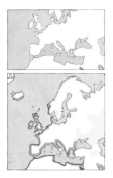

CRAB PLOVER *Dromas ardeola* (Dromadidae). A large black and white wader, mantle and wing-tips grey in immature. Noisy goose-like honking. Long neck hunched at rest, outstretched in flight. Feeds mainly on crabs. Occasional, sandy shores, coastal lagoons in Egypt. 14 in. (35 cm.).

OYSTERCATCHER *Haematopus ostralegus* (Haematopodidae). Differs from all other large pied shore birds by long orange bill and longish pink legs; throat black in summer, white in winter; white wing-bar shows in flight. Juveniles have dark tip to bill. Normal call a shrill penetrating 'kleeep', also a shorter 'pic, pic', and a loud communal piping display. Seashores; also inland in river valleys in hill districts, by salt lakes and on sand steppes. 17 in. (43 cm.).
●RsmW Map 76

AFRICAN BLACK OYSTERCATCHER *Haematopus moquini*. An all-black oystercatcher, except for white patch on wing, recently seen again in Canary Is., its only locality in region, where believed extinct since 1913. 16 in. (41 cm.).

BLACK-WINGED STILT *Himantopus himantopus* (Recurvirostridae). Fantastically long pink legs; long straight black bill also distinctive. Male has crown and nape black in summer, white in winter; female as male winter but with browner mantle. Juvenile like female but with greyish head and neck. Wings black beneath. Call a rather coot-like 'kik-kik-kik'. In flight legs trail out behind, making bird appear unexpectedly long. Fresh and brackish marshes and pools, also in saltmarshes and on shore. 15 in. (38 cm.). —A(b)

AVOCET *Recurvirostra avosetta*. Another unmistakable bird, with its strikingly upcurved bill, used with a side-to-side sweeping motion in feeding, and blue-grey legs. Juvenile browner. Swims readily and up-ends. Main call 'klooit', also a soft grunting flight note, and loud yelping cries when nest or young endangered. Salt and brackish marshes and pools, both coastal and inland, estuaries, less often by fresh water. 17 in. (43 cm.). ☉ Srm Map 77

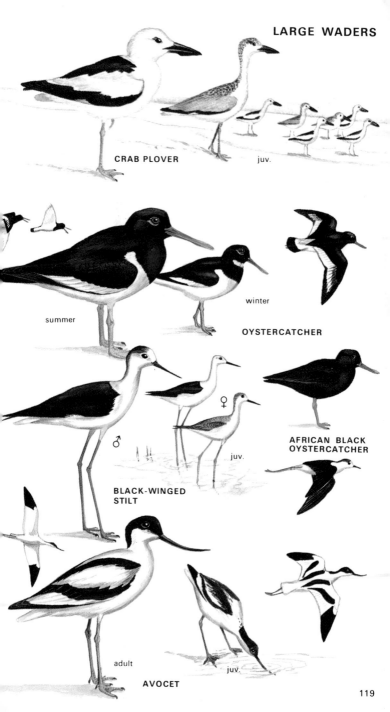

LARGE WADERS

CRAB PLOVER

juv.

summer

winter

OYSTERCATCHER

AFRICAN BLACK OYSTERCATCHER

♂

♀

juv.

BLACK-WINGED STILT

adult

juv.

AVOCET

PLOVERS: *Charadriidae.* pp. 121–5. Short-billed, small to medium-sized waders. When feeding characteristically run a little way and then stop, often bobbing head nervously; head held up as if listening, not down like Knot (p. 129) or Dunlin (p. 127). *Charadrius* plovers are small to medium-sized, usually sandy or greyish-brown above, many with striking patterns of black and white bands on head and neck.

RINGED PLOVER *Charadrius hiaticula.* One of the commonest northern shore birds, with distinctive pied head and breast pattern, prominent pale wing-bar, and orange-yellow legs. Immature has no black on head and often incomplete brownish breast-band. Calls a liquid musical 'too-i' and 'queep' or 'queec'; latter forming basis of plangent song, delivered in bat-like display flight. Sandy and shingly seashores, less often similar fresh and brackish water shores, rarely sandy flats inland; in winter also muddy seashores and estuaries. 7½ in. (19 cm.). ●RMW **Map 78**

LITTLE RINGED PLOVER *Charadrius dubius.* Best distinction from Ringed Plover is no wing-bar in flight, also white line above black forehead, bill yellow only at base of lower mandible, pink to yellowish-green legs and yellow orbital ring. Call also diagnostic, 'pee-oo', 'pip-pip. . .' and a reedy note resembling Little Tern (p. 161); song a trilling elaboration of calls. Not very gregarious. Sand or shingle by *fresh* water. 6 in. (15 cm.). ☉S **Map 79**

KENTISH PLOVER *Charadrius alexandrinus.* Smaller, slimmer and paler than Ringed Plover, with rufous crown, less black on cheeks and only incomplete black breast-band; bill black, legs blackish. White wing-bar separates from Little Ringed Plover. Calls distinct from both ringed plovers, 'wit', 'wee-it' and 'prr-ip', with a trilling song. Sand and shingle, mainly coastal. 6¼ in. (16 cm.). ○M(b) **Map 80**

GREATER SANDPLOVER *Charadrius leschenaultii.* A large heavy-billed pale grey-brown plover, black stripe through eye, grey patches at sides of breast, breeding male with a chestnut breast-band. Has a clear one or two-note whistle. Salt and fresh water margins. 10 in. (25 cm.).

LESSER SANDPLOVER or **MONGOLIAN PLOVER** *Charadrius mongolus.* Much rarer than Greater Sandplover, from which distinguishable in winter only by size, darker plumage, shorter, less stout bill and more gregarious habits; in summer both sexes as male Greater Sandplover but with breast warm buff. Cf. Caspian Plover (p. 123). 8 in. (20 cm.).

KILLDEER *Charadrius vociferus.* Transatlantic vagrant. A large ringed plover recognisable by double breast-band and loud 'kill-dee' call, frequenting grassland rather than watersides. 10 in. (25 cm.). —V

KITTLITZ'S SANDPLOVER *Charadrius pecuarius.* Like a small Kentish Plover, with longer bill, sandy crown, white nape, no dark band on pale rufous breast, and dark line backward from eye. Call a clear plaintive 'pipip'. Freshwater and coastal margins, sand or mud flats. 5¼ in. (13 cm.).

ummer

winter

RINGED PLOVER

summer

winter

LITTLE RINGED PLOVER

adult

♂

♀

KENTISH PLOVER

summer

♂

winter

GREATER SANDPLOVER

summer

♂

winter

LESSER SANDPLOVER

KILLDEER

adult

imm.

KITTLITZ'S SANDPLOVER

CASPIAN PLOVER *Charadrius asiaticus.* Vagrant from C Asia, in winter like yellowish-buff Lesser Sandplover (p. 121) but frequenting grassy plains and semi-deserts. In summer has chestnut breast-band with black mark beneath. Call a low double or treble whistle. 7½ in. (19 cm.). —V

Golden Plovers: *Pluvialis.* Upperparts spangled with grey or yellowish or black; no white on nape; underparts in breeding plumage largely black.

GOLDEN PLOVER *Pluvialis apricaria.* A large plover, with yellow-brown upperparts, white axillaries and underwing, and in summer black cheeks, throat and underparts, bordered in northern breeding birds conspicuously with white. Call a liquid piping 'tlui'; mournful trilling song. Gregarious, and easily told from Lapwing (p. 125) in mixed flocks by pointed wings; much given to aerial manoeuvres. Moors, tundra marshes, arctic heaths; in winter on farmland, estuaries, muddy seashores. 11 in. (28 cm.). ●RMW Map 81

LESSER GOLDEN PLOVER *Pluvialis dominica.* Vagrant from arctic Asia and America, smaller than Golden Plover, with longish legs, greyish-buff underwings and axillaries, and more white but less white on face and underparts. Calls a whistling 'teeh' and a high-pitched 'tu-ee' or 'tee-tew', like a Greenshank (p. 131) but richer. 10 in. (25 cm.). —V

GREY PLOVER *Pluvialis squatarola.* Plumper than Golden Plover, and distinguished especially by black axillaries, showing in flight, whitish rump and greyish upperparts. Striking black and white breeding plumage. Triple call-note, 'tee-oo-ee' sounds like boy wolf-whistling, with middle syllable lower than other two. Individuals usually more widely scattered over shore than Golden Plovers, and less given to manoeuvres in close flocks. Breeds on tundra; in winter on estuaries and muddy and sandy seashores, and uncommon inland. 11 in. (28 cm.). ⊙ MW Map 82

DOTTEREL *Eudromias morinellus.* White eyestripes meeting in V on nape, chestnut lower breast and black belly are best field marks, all much fainter in winter. Chief call a sweet twittering or trilling 'wit-e-wee, wit-e-wee, wit-e-wee', also a soft 'peep, peep', a sharp 'ting' and a brief song uttered on the ground. Mountain tops, tundra, and recently on arable in Netherlands; migration in open country inland, and in winter mainly on sandy and muddy shores. 8½ in. (22 cm.).
○SM Map 83

TURNSTONE *Arenaria interpres.* The only small short-billed wader looking black and white both at rest and in flight; legs orange. In summer tortoiseshell appearance of upperparts also distinctive. Calls a twittering, 'kititit', a clear 'keeoo, keeoo' and a grunting 'tuk-a-tuk'. Turns over small stones and weed in search of food. Breeds on tundra and adjacent coasts, also on small islands in Baltic; in winter mainly on rocky and weedy shores, often with Purple Sandpipers (p. 129). 9 in. (23 cm.). ●MW Map 84

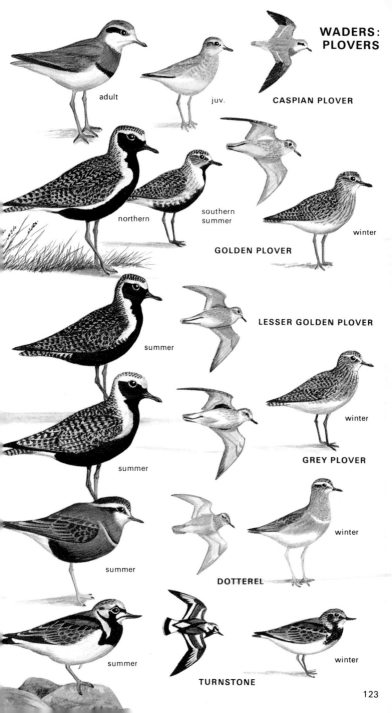

WADERS: PLOVERS

adult

juv.

CASPIAN PLOVER

northern

southern summer

winter

GOLDEN PLOVER

summer

LESSER GOLDEN PLOVER

summer

winter

GREY PLOVER

summer

winter

DOTTEREL

summer

winter

TURNSTONE

LAPWINGS: *Vanellus.* A distinct genus of plovers, whose wing-tips are always black and usually have a broad white bar, and whose tail is always white at the base and usually black at the tip. Rather noisy, especially in breeding season.

LAPWING *Vanellus vanellus.* The most distinctive plover of the region, the commonest inland over the greater part of it, and the only *Vanellus* breeding over most of Europe. Easily recognised by generally black and white appearance, upper-parts showing green in bright sunlight, by crest, and in flight by conspicuously broad rounded wings; throat black in summer, white in winter. Calls and song all variations on 'pee-wit' theme (Peewit is a vernacular English name), usual ground call being 'peeet', flight call 'pee-wit' and song, delivered in striking aerobatic display, 'p'weet, pee-wit, pee-wit'. In display flight wings make loud throbbing or 'lapping' sound, origin of standard English name. Highly gregarious. Farmland, grassland with short turf, marshy fields, moors, heaths, bogs; in winter also at freshwater margins and on estuaries and coastal mud and sandflats. 12 in. (30 cm.). ●**RSMW   Map 85**

RED-WATTLED PLOVER *Vanellus indicus.* A large black, white and brownish plover, with long yellow legs and distinctive black and white head pattern with a bright red wattle around and in front of each eye. Loud shrieking call rendered did ye do it?' or monotonously iterated single note. Slow deliberate flight. Not very gregarious. Open country near fresh water. 13 in. (33 cm.).

WHITE-TAILED PLOVER *Vanellus leucurus.* Brown and white, with long yellow legs; most easily recognised in flight, which reveals pure white rump and tail and strikingly black and white wing pattern. Loud double call like Lapwing but less high-pitched. Marshes and freshwater margins; resident in S Iraq, rare vagrant elsewhere in S of region. 11 in. (28 cm.).

SPUR-WINGED PLOVER *Vanellus spinosus.* Predominantly black and white, black on crown, throat and underparts, white on sides of face, throat and breast, and typical black and white *Vanellus* wing and tail pattern; slightly crested, small spur at angle of wing. Voice not unlike Red-wattled Plover but higher-pitched 'zit-zeet-zeet'. Flies slowly, stands in hunched position. Open country near flowing fresh and salt water. 10½ in. (27 cm.).

SOCIABLE PLOVER *Vanellus gregarius.* Another rather large grey-brown plover, with distinctive black crown, encircled by white lines meeting on forehead and nape, and typical black and white *Vanellus* wing and tail pattern. Belly dark chestnut in summer, giving impression at any distance of a pale bird with dark crown and belly. Calls a short high-pitched whistle and a harsh grating note. Breeds on dry steppes, wintering in dry open country and farmland as well as at freshwater margins. 11½ in. (29 cm.). **—V**

adult

imm.

LAPWING

WHITE-TAILED
PLOVER

winter

RED-WATTLED
PLOVER
legs usually yellow

SPUR-WINGED PLOVER

summer

winter

SOCIABLE PLOVER

SANDPIPERS and SNIPE: *Scolopacidae.* pp. 127–41. Long-billed, small to large waders. STINT-TYPE SANDPIPERS: *Calidris* and *Limicola*, pp. 127–9. Mostly rather small waders, the smallest called stints (peeps in N America), with only moderately long bill and legs and shortish wings and neck. Usually rather subdued piping or twittering calls, flocks often keeping up a conversational twitter. Breeding on tundra and moors, wintering mainly on coasts.

BROAD-BILLED SANDPIPER *Limicola falcinellus.* Resembles a rather small dark long-billed short-legged winter Dunlin, with distinctive snipe-like markings on mantle and two white lines down each side; coppery edges of secondaries show at close quarters. Conspicuous white eyestripe forks behind eye; throat white, bill distinctly decurved at tip. Flight call a low-pitched trilling 'chr-r-eek'; also a double note and a trilling song in breeding season. Rather solitary. 6½ in. (16·5 cm.). —V

CURLEW-SANDPIPER *Calidris ferruginea.* In flight house-martin-like white rump distinguishes at all times from all small waders, except White-rumped (p. 136), Green and Wood Sandpipers (p. 134), all of which have straight bills. Markedly curved bill is other good field mark at all times. In summer rufous plumage distinguishes from all except larger Knot and white-bellied Sanderling (p. 129), both also straight-billed. Immature has buffish tinge. In winter like Dunlin, but larger, slimmer, with longer legs and longer, curved bill. Flight note a soft 'chirrup'. 7½ in. (19 cm.). ⊙ **M Map 86**

DUNLIN *Calidris alpina.* Generally the commonest small wader of the shore, very variable in size, northern breeding birds larger than southern ones. In summer is only small wader with black lower breast and belly. In winter, when breast greyish, differs from Sanderling (p. 129) in contrast between grey-brown upperparts and whiter underparts and no black shoulder spot, from much larger and greyer Knot (p. 129) by white sides of rump and tail. Bill slightly decurved, especially in northern birds. Juvenile has smudgy mark on sides of lower breast. Flight-note a rather weak 'treep' or 'teerp'; trilling song. Breeds also on wet heaths and coastal marshes. 6½–7½ in. (17–19 cm.). ● **rsMW Map 87**

TEMMINCK'S STINT *Calidris temminckii.* Differs from Little Stint in appearing more like a miniature Common Sandpiper (p. 133), and in having white outer tail feathers and greenish-yellow legs. Voice, a shrill spluttering 'pt-r-r-r-r' and habit of towering when flushed, also distinct from Little Stint. On passage mainly at freshwater margins, with vegetation cover. 5½ in. (14 cm.). ◯ **M(b) Map 88**

LITTLE STINT *Calidris minuta.* The smallest breeding wader of the region, like a miniature straight-billed Dunlin with white sides to rump but no white in tail. Upperparts boldly patterned, with white belly in summer and pure white breast in winter; legs black, cf. Temminck's Stint. Immature shows two distinctive white V's on back. Flight note 'chik' sometimes prolonged to a short trill. 5¼ in. (13 cm.). ⊙ **Mw Map 89**

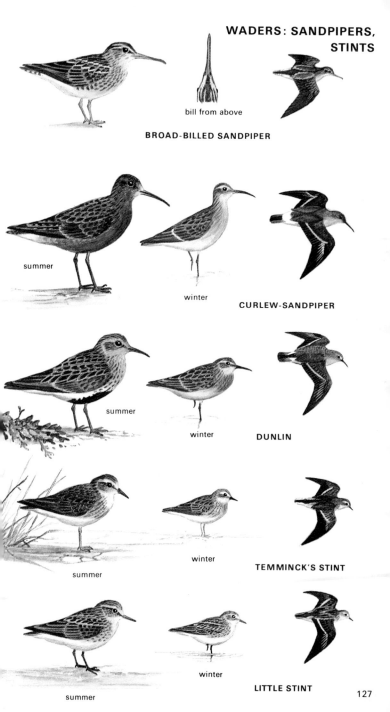

WADERS: SANDPIPERS, STINTS

bill from above

BROAD-BILLED SANDPIPER

summer

winter

CURLEW-SANDPIPER

summer

winter

DUNLIN

winter

TEMMINCK'S STINT

summer

winter

LITTLE STINT

summer

127

KNOT *Calidris canutus*. A dumpy wader, grey in winter, rufous in summer, intermediate in size between Redshank (p. 131) and Dunlin (p. 127). In winter differs from smaller Dunlin and Sanderling in uniform grey tail, from larger Redshank in no white on wings, and from larger, less gregarious Grey Plover (p. 123) in longer bill and no black under wings. Summer plumage distinctive, except from white-bellied Sanderling and white-rumped Curlew Sandpiper (p. 127). Call a low 'knut'. Highly gregarious in winter, flocks appearing tightly packed at a distance, feeding with their heads well down. 10 in. (25 cm.).　●**MW　Map 90**

SANDERLING *Calidris alba*. Slightly larger than Dunlin (p. 127) and in winter easily told from all other same-sized birds on shore by almost white appearance with blackish shoulder spot. In summer rufous above and on breast, white belly distinguishing from both Dunlin and larger Knot; more conspicuous white wing-bar separates from Dunlin at all times. Flight note 'twick, twick'. Patters fast and restlessly along edge of tide, preferring to run rather than fly when approached. Almost confined to sandy shores. 8 in. (20 cm.).　●**MW　Map 91**

PURPLE SANDPIPER *Calidris maritima*. Slightly larger than Dunlin (p. 127), and the only small dark wader with yellow legs likely to be met with on rocky shores. White wing-bar, round-shouldered appearance and frequent association with Turnstones (p. 123) are other useful pointers. Summer adult and juvenile speckled paler; purple gloss on mantle only visible in very good light. Call a low 'weet-wit', also a piping note. Not very gregarious. In winter on rocky shores, reefs, weed-covered groynes, breakwaters and patches of stones. 8¼ in. (21 cm.).　☉ **MW　Map 92**

● **PHALAROPES**: *Phalaropodidae*. Small, rather tame and confiding aquatic waders, much the smallest birds likely to be seen swimming, except for a few all-dark petrels. Winter plumage grey and white, the two common species with a wing-bar; feet lobed. Males smaller, duller than females. Flight rather weak, but buoyant swimmers, like tiny gulls, often spinning round in circles and picking insects off surface. Pelagic in winter.

GREY PHALAROPE *Phalaropus fulicarius*. In summer has reddish throat and underparts; always differs from Red-necked Phalarope in shorter stouter bill yellow at tip (male) or base (female) and in winter has rather more uniform grey back. Call a low 'twit'. 8 in. (20·5 cm.).　☉ **Mw　Map 93**

Grey　Red-necked

RED-NECKED PHALAROPE *Phalaropus lobatus*. In summer orange patches on sides of neck and throat are diagnostic; bill blackish, thin, almost needle-like. Calls 'twit', 'tirric, tirric' and a curious little pre-flight grunt. Flight graceful and rather swallow-like, faster than Grey Phalarope. 7 in. (18 cm.).　○**sm　Map 94**

WILSON'S PHALAROPE *Phalaropus tricolor*. A transatlantic vagrant, larger, longer-billed, much more prone to run on land, white rump, no wing-bar. 9 in. (23 cm.).　**—A**

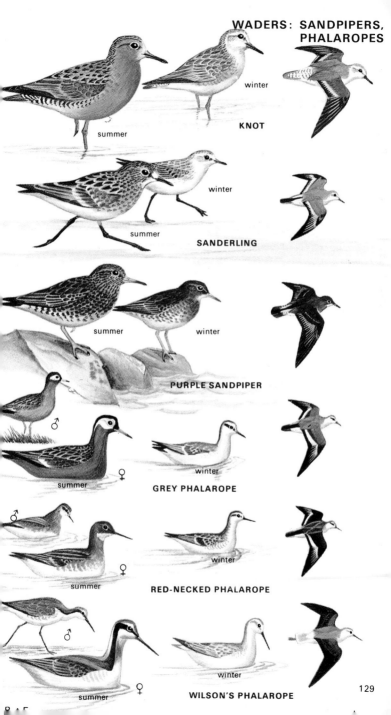

WADERS: SANDPIPERS, PHALAROPES

winter

summer

KNOT

winter

summer

SANDERLING

summer

winter

PURPLE SANDPIPER

♂

♀

summer

winter

GREY PHALAROPE

♂

♀

summer

winter

RED-NECKED PHALAROPE

♂

♀

summer

winter

WILSON'S PHALAROPE

129

Shanks and Sandpipers: *Tringa.* pp. 131–3. Fairly long-legged and long-billed small to medium waders, less gregarious than *Calidris* (pp. 127–9), and with conspicuous white marks on wings or rump and loud piping calls. In winter by shallow fresh and salt water.

TEREK SANDPIPER *Tringa cinereus.* Rather like a small Redshank, especially in flight, but with long upcurved bill, less white on open wing and rump, and shorter yellow legs; two black stripes down back. Has trilling call, based on 'du', also disyllabic alarm note and whimbrel-like call. Song varied and musical. On the ground bobs head and resembles Common Sandpiper (p. 133) in other ways. Breeds by fresh water in forest and scrub. 9 in. (23 cm.).   —**V**

REDSHANK *Tringa totanus.* The only wader with a broad white hindwing, which with equally conspicuous white rump makes striking contrast in flight. At rest grey-brown plumage relieved only by orange-red bill and legs. Various loud yelping but fairly musical cries, mainly elaborations of 'tu' note; also a loud clamorous cry when startled and a scolding 'teuk-teuk-teuk' or 'chip-chip-chip' when alarmed. Yodelling song based on more musical call-notes. Fast direct flight with quick clipped wing-beats; at rest bobs head when suspicious. Grassy fresh and coastal marshes, damp grassland, wet heaths. 11 in. (28 cm.).   ●**RMW   Map 95**

SPOTTED REDSHANK *Tringa erythropus.* In summer the only all-dark wader with a wedge-shaped white rump. Long, almost snipe-like red-based bill always distinguishes from other 'shanks. In winter from Redshank also by dark wings, white underparts and longer legs, trailing well behind in flight, and from Greenshank by darker upper parts and red legs. Call note diagnostic, a clear disyllabic 'too-it' or 'tchu-eet', quite distinct from normal call of both the others; also a scolding 'chick-chick-chick'. Breeds in swampy places in forest, heath and tundra; in winter mainly at brackish and salt water margins. 12 in. (30 cm.).   ●**Mw   Map 96**

GREENSHANK *Tringa nebularia.* Larger and paler than Redshank, with no white on wings but a larger wedge of white on black, grey-blue bill, very slightly upcurved, and pale olive-green legs. In winter upper parts much paler and greyer. Flight note, nearly always uttered when flushed, a clear far-carrying 'chu-chu-chu'; also an insistent redshank-like 'chip' note and more rarely a disyllabic call not unlike Spotted Redshank. Song a fluty repeated 'ru-tu'. Not gregarious. Marshes, bogs, moors, swampy clearings in forests. 12 in. (30·5 cm.).   ●**sMw   Map 97**

MARSH SANDPIPER *Tringa stagnatilis.* A miniature Greenshank, but more graceful, with thinner straight bill, white forehead and face, and longer legs, which project further beyond tail. In summer upperparts appear spotted darker. In winter greyer, with distinct dark shoulder. White on rump more elongated than in Wood and Green Sandpipers (p. 133). Calls 'teu', 'teeoo', 'chik', etc., not so loud as other shanks, also a liquid twittering trill. Marshy freshwater margins. 9 in. (23 cm.).   —**V**

WADERS: SANDPIPERS, SHANKS

TEREK SANDPIPER

REDSHANK

summer   winter

SPOTTED REDSHANK

GREENSHANK

summer   winter

MARSH SANDPIPER

131

COMMON SANDPIPER *Tringa hypoleucos.* A small grey-brown wader with white underparts, sides to rump and tail and wing-bar, best distinguished from other similar waders, e.g. winter Dunlin (p. 127), by characteristic flight and call-note and generally solitary habits. Typically flies low over water, with shrill 'twee-wee-wee' call and flickering wings, appearing distinctly bowed when held momentarily at the downward stroke. Also has a circular display flight (song an elaboration of the call-note); does not tower when flushed; often perches on low objects, bobbing head and tail. Breeds by freshwater streams and lakes and sheltered inlets of the sea; in winter mainly by fresh water. Cf. Spotted Sandpiper (p. 136). 7¾ in. (20 cm.). ●Smw **Map 98**

WOOD SANDPIPER *Tringa glareola.* Intermediate between Common and Green Sandpipers, differing from both in voice and in legs projecting beyond tail in flight, from Common in its white rump and different flight pattern, and from Green in its much less strongly contrasted dark and light appearance, greyish underwing and barred tail. Usual flight note a rather flat triple 'wee-wee-wee' or 'wit-wit-wit', also a more musical greenshank-like 'chew-ew' and a shrill alarm note 'chip-chip-chip'; song, liquid and musical, recalling Redshank. Towers when flushed. Breeds in swampy bogs, scrub and woodlands; winters mainly at freshwater margins. 8 in. (20 cm.). ⊙sM **Map 99**

GREEN SANDPIPER *Tringa ochropus.* Larger than Wood Sandpiper, and differing especially in its conspicuous white rump contrasting strongly with dark upperparts and barred tip of tail, but much smaller than Greenshank (p. 131), which is paler above. Cf. Marsh Sandpiper. When flushed dashes up and towers with a shrill 'weet-a-weet' note, much louder than Wood Sandpiper, before flying off with a rather snipe-like flight. Song liquid and musical. Breeds in swampy woodlands, the nest placed in old nest of another bird; in winter mainly by fresh water. 9 in. (23 cm.). ●Mw(b) **Map 100**

RUFF and REEVE *Philomachus pugnax.* Male (Ruff) in summer with ruff and ear tufts quite unmistakable; whole plumage very variable, almost any combination of black, white, rufous brown and buff with bars and streaks, ruff usually differing from ear tufts. Bill and leg colour also variable, bill red, yellow, brown or blackish, legs green, yellow, orange or flesh. Winter male can be told from Redshank (p. 131) by thicker neck, dark wings, dark centre of rump, distinctive hen-pheasant-like pattern on back, and sometimes by bill and leg colour. Female (Reeve) and immature are both markedly smaller, and thinner-necked. Any puzzling ruff-sized wader is much more likely to be a Ruff than an American vagrant. Rather silent, but has flight note 'too-i' and in spring a deep 'uk'. Not very gregarious. Marshes, swamps, damp meadows; in winter at shallow margins of fresh and salt water. Male 11½ in. (29 cm.), female 9 in. (23 cm.). ⊙sMw **Map 101**

WADERS: SANDPIPERS, RUFF

COMMON SANDPIPER

WOOD SANDPIPER

GREEN SANDPIPER

♂
winter

♀

RUFF

Ruffs in summer plumage

133

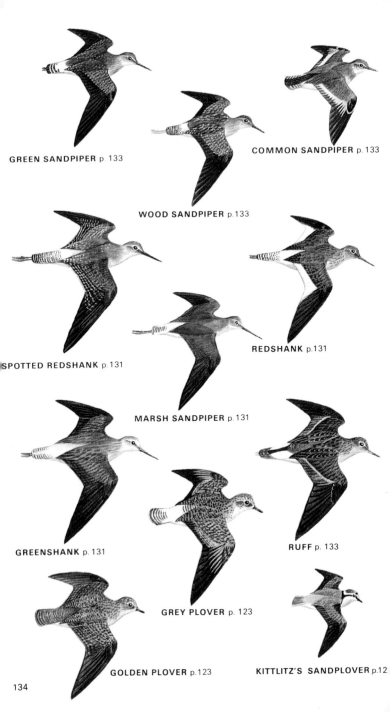

GREEN SANDPIPER p. 133

COMMON SANDPIPER p. 133

WOOD SANDPIPER p.133

SPOTTED REDSHANK p.131

REDSHANK p.131

MARSH SANDPIPER p.131

GREENSHANK p.131

RUFF p. 133

GREY PLOVER p.123

GOLDEN PLOVER p.123

KITTLITZ'S SANDPLOVER p.12

134

DUNLIN p. 127

TEMMINCK'S STINT p. 127

LITTLE STINT p. 127

CURLEW SANDPIPER p. 127

KNOT p. 129

SANDERLING p. 129

TURNSTONE
p. 123

RED-NECKED PHALAROPE
p. 129

PURPLE SANDPIPER
p. 129

ITTLE RINGED PLOVER
p. 121

RINGED PLOVER
p. 121

KENTISH PLOVER
p. 121

**WHITE-RUMPED SAND-
PIPER** *Calidris fuscicollis.*
Curved white patch on rump
narrower than Curlew Sandpiper's. Characteristic 'jeet'
note. **—A**

**SEMIPALMATED SAND-
PIPER** *Calidris pusillus.*
Greyer, less rufous and with
shorter call-note than Least
Sandpiper, with stouter bill.
Legs dark. **—V**

LEAST SANDPIPER *Calidris minutilla.* Smaller, darker and less rufous than
Little Stint (p. 127), but with
paler legs. Cf. also Semipalmated Sandpiper. **—V**

PECTORAL SANDPIPER
Calidris melanotos. Much the
commonest transatlantic vagrant; larger than Dunlin
(p. 127). Sharp division
between streaked breast and
white belly. **—A**

**SHARP-TAILED SAND-
PIPER** *Calidris acuminata.*
Differs from Pectoral Sandpiper by rufous crown and in
summer lack of clear-cut
breast-band. (Siberia) **—V**

BAIRD'S SANDPIPER
Calidris bairdii. Buff head
and breast, wings longer
than tail at rest, no white
sides to tail. **—V**

winter

summer

SPOTTED SANDPIPER *Tringa
macularia.* In winter very like Common
Sandpiper (p. 133), in summer distinguished by black spots and breast
and dark-tipped yellow bill. **—A**

BUFF-BREASTED SANDPIPER
Tryngites subruficollis. The only small
wader with whole underparts buff,
like a small long-necked Reeve (p.
133), with small roundish head, short
bill and bright yellow legs. May occur
in dry country. **—A**

WESTERN SANDPIPER *Calidris
mauri.* Longish, slightly decurved bill, obscure pale
wing-bar, rufous upperparts in summer, legs
black. Call a thin 'jeet'. **—V**

VAGRANT WADERS FROM NORTH AMERICA

SOLITARY SANDPIPER *Tringa solitaria.* Like a small Green Sandpiper (p. 133) with black rump but white sides to tail. —V

STILT-SANDPIPER *Micropalama himantopus.* Long bill, long legs projecting well beyond tail in flight, white rump, no wing-bar, barred underparts in summer. —V

GREATER YELLOWLEGS *Tringa melanoleuca.* Like a large yellow-legged Greenshank (p. 131) with white on rump and tail only. Call louder than Yellowlegs. —V

YELLOWLEGS *Tringa flavipes.* Like slender Redshank (p. 131) with yellow legs; in flight white only on rump and tail. Call 'yew' or 'yew-yew'. —A

LONG-BILLED

SHORT-BILLED

UPLAND SANDPIPER *Bartramia longicauda.* A slender sandpiper with plover-like habits; small head, short bill, longish rufous tail and barred undersides showing when wings characteristically held upright on alighting. May fly like Common Sandpiper (p. 133), often perches on posts. Dry open country. —V

LONG-BILLED DOWITCHER *Limnodromus scolopaceus.* Like a large Snipe (p. 141) with white lower back and rump; flanks barred. Call 'keek' or 'keek-keek-keek', higher pitched than Short-billed Dowitcher. —A

SHORT-BILLED DOWITCHER *Limnodromus griseus.* Bill shorter than Long-billed Dowitcher, wings project beyond tail at rest and flanks spotted. Call 'tu-tu-tu'. —V

137

Curlews: *Numenius.* Large, long-legged, white-rumped waders, appearing uniformly brown at rest. Long curved bill and legs projecting beyond tail distinguish them at once from otherwise not dissimilar immature gulls in flight.

CURLEW *Numenius arquata.* The largest and generally the commonest white-rumped brown wader, very variable in size. Varied repertoire of calls includes characteristic loud 'quee, quee, quee' and 'cooorwee, cooorwee' notes, and a rarely heard whimbrel-like titter. Loud musical bubbling song, delivered on wing, starts with plangent version of 'quee' note. Moors, bogs, wet heaths, sand dunes, moist grassland and other open damp country. 21–23 in. (53–58 cm.).　●RsmW　Map 102

SLENDER-BILLED CURLEW *Numenius tenuirostris.* Differs from Whimbrel in lacking stripes on head, and from both Curlew and Whimbrel in large dark spots on flanks and purer white rump and belly. Call note briefer and higher-pitched than Curlew; alarm note 'kew-ee'. Winter visitor·from Asian steppes. 16 in. (41 cm.).

WHIMBREL *Numenius phaeopus.* Markedly smaller than smallest Curlews, from which also distinguished by faster wing-beats, distinctive tittering trill and at close range by two dark and one pale stripes on head. Curved bill separates from godwits, whose rufous plumage is also distinctive in summer. Song resembles Curlew. High northern, sub-Arctic and Arctic moors and tundra. 16 in. (41 cm.).　●sMw　Map 103

Godwits: *Limosa.* Fairly large waders, rather variable in size, distinguished from all three curlews by their straight bills and in summer also by their handsome rufous plumage.

BLACK-TAILED GODWIT *Limosa limosa.* Easily told from both curlews and Bar-tailed Godwit by conspicuous white bar on wing, also by black and white tail, giving an almost oystercatcher-like appearance in flight. Flight call 'wicka, wicka, wicka', and on breeding grounds also a lapwing-like 'pee-oo-ee' and a greenshank-like 'wik-ik-ik'. Song a repetition of 'crweetuu'. Less given to aerobatics than Bar-tailed Godwit. Breeds in damp grassland and on wet heaths. 16 in. (41 cm.).　⊙ sMW　Map 104

BAR-TAILED GODWIT *Limosa lapponica.* In winter like a straight-billed Whimbrel, in summer reddish plumage precludes confusion. Differs from Black-tailed Godwit at all times in having no white on wings, in feet scarcely projecting beyond tail in flight and in summer in having reddish vent. Legs somewhat shorter than both curlews and Black-tailed Godwit; bill slightly curved upwards at tip. Flight notes 'kirruc, kirruc' and 'wik-wik-wik-wik-wik'. Fast direct flight, flocks sometimes performing aerobatics, like Knot (p. 129) and Dunlin (p. 127). Breeds on marshy parts of the tundra. 15 in. (38 cm.).　●MW　Map 105

CURLEW

SLENDER-BILLED CURLEW

WHIMBREL

summer

winter

BLACK-TAILED GODWIT

summer

winter

BAR-TAILED GODWIT

WOODCOCK *Scolopax rusticola*. Most often seen either as a long-winged rufous bird flying fast and twistingly out of sight among the trees, or in unmistakable territorial flight ('roding'). Roding male flies a circuit at dusk and dawn, with an owlish flight and interrupted wing-beats, uttering two distinct notes, a rather sibilant 'twisick' and a frog-like croak or grunting growl. Not gregarious. Forests, heathland with scattered trees, feeding on marshy and swampy ground; on passage also in more open country. 13½ in. (34 cm.).

●RmW   Map 106

Snipe: *Gallinago*. Medium-sized brown waders, with long bill and short legs, breeding in marshes, bogs, damp meadows, wet moors and heaths; in winter at freshwater margins with fairly thick vegetation.

GREAT SNIPE *Gallinago media*. Only slightly larger than Snipe, differing chiefly in adult's more conspicuous white at sides and tip of tail, also on wing, especially at trailing edge. Bill somewhat shorter, underparts more heavily marked, and in flight appears darker and heavier, with slower, more direct flight. Croaks when flushed; collective bubbling song on display grounds. Sometimes on drier ground, especially in winter. 11 in. (28 cm.).   —A

JACK SNIPE *Lymnocryptes minimus*. Like a small Snipe with a much shorter bill, two narrow instead of one broad pale streaks on crown, and slower and less erratic flight, dropping down much sooner into cover. No white in tail. Often silent when flushed, or utters a low weak call. Drums like Snipe, but in display hovers and bobs up and down like a marionette, making note likened to distant galloping horse. Breeds in wet swamps and bogs; in winter more often in dry places. 7½ in. (19 cm.).   ●MW   Map 107

SNIPE *Gallinago gallinago*. Has proportionately the longest bill of any bird in the region, which together with its zigzag flight and loud harsh 'creech' when flushed and remarkable 'drumming' or 'bleating' display flight, diving at an angle of 45°, are its best field marks. Will perch on low objects, often when uttering an insistent 'chip-per', 'chip-per'. Often in small parties ('wisps') which perform aerial evolutions. 10½ in. (27 cm.).   ●RmW   Map 108

PIN-TAILED SNIPE *Gallinago stenura*. Very like Snipe, but slightly darker and heavier in flight, axillaries and under wing coverts more heavily and darkly barred; bill shorter; more often on drier ground. 10½ in. (27 cm.).

PAINTED SNIPE *Rostratula benghalensis* (Rostratulidae). Strikingly patterned, longer-legged than Snipe, with shorter bill turned down at tip. Female brighter with rufous neck and upper breast, where male grey-brown. Male has squeaky trill, female wheezy hiss and repeated 'ook' in display, also low croak. In flight legs dangle, and rounded wing-tips show large round buff spots. Secretive, hard to flush, remaining motionless for long periods. Swamps, densely vegetated freshwater margins. Egypt only. 10 in. (25 cm.).

WOODCOCK

GREAT SNIPE

JACK SNIPE

SNIPE

♂

♀ PAINTED SNIPE

PIN-TAILED SNIPE 141

STONE CURLEW *Burhinus oedicnemus* (Burhinidae). Easily told from Curlew (p. 139) by short straight bill (black tip, yellow at base), large round head, yellow legs, whitish bar on closed wing, and at close quarters by staring yellow eye. In rather slow, direct flight, with legs trailing behind, also easily recognised by two white and one black bars on wing. Call more curlew-like than appearance, a wild shrill wailing 'coo-leee', often heard at night. Sometimes in large flocks in autumn. Open dry, usually stony country, heaths, semi-deserts, farmland. 16 in. (41 cm.). ⊙**S Map 109**

SENEGAL THICK-KNEE *Burhinus senegalensis*. A smaller version of the Stone Curlew, only in Egypt and distinguishable in flight by having only one white wing bar, not visible at rest. Call more nasal or metallic. Sandy river beds, orchards, gardens. 15 in. (38 cm.).

● **PRATINCOLES and COURSERS:** *Glareolidae.* Smallish plover-like birds, with fairly long legs and pointed bills. Sexes similar. Habit of appearing to stand on tiptoe, stretching the neck. The Pratincoles *Pratincola* are plover-like on the ground, but swallow-like or tern-like in flight, with long pointed wings, black and white forked tail, legs short; bill short, black with a red base.

BLACK-WINGED PRATINCOLE *Glareola nordmanni*. An E European bird, only vagrant in N Africa, best distinguishable from Collared Pratincole when lifts wings at rest to reveal black underwing but also lacks white-edged secondaries. 10 in. (25 cm.). —V

COLLARED PRATINCOLE *Glareola pratincola*. Brown, with creamy throat bordered black; distinctive chestnut underwing shows best when bird raises wings ar rest; in flight may look black. White rump and black tail also conspicuous in flight. Immature has blackish streaks on throat, broader but incomplete black collar. Gregarious, flocks often hawking for flying insects and spiralling up to perform aerobatics. Flocks noisy, with tern-like chattering. Sometimes crepuscular. Open steppes and savannas, sun-baked mudflats, bare freshwater margins. 10 in. (25 cm.). —V

CREAM-COLOURED COURSER *Cursorius cursor*. Like a small slim sandy Golden Plover (p. 123), with grey nape, and black and white eyestripes and curved bill. In jerky flight looks long-winged, with black wing-tips and axillaries conspicuous, but more often alternately runs and crouches. immature has brown-speckled upperparts. Rather silent, but has a 'praak-praak' call-note on the wing. Deserts and semi-deserts. 9 in. (23 cm.). —V

EGYPTIAN PLOVER *Pluvianus aegyptius*. A strikingly plumaged, rather short-legged, very tame wader, with conspicuous white eyestripe and greenish black breast-band. Immature lacks greenish tinge and has some rufous on shoulder. Call a weak 'tsi-tsi-tsi' or 'teep-teep-teep'. Freshwater margins, occasionally in nearby villages, in Egypt only, now rare. 8 in. (20 cm.).

WADERS: THICK-KNEES, PRATINCOLES

desert form

STONE CURLEW

SENEGAL THICK-KNEE

BLACK-WINGED PRATINCOLE

adult

juv.

COLLARED PRATINCOLE

adult

juv.

CREAM-COLOURED COURSER

EGYPTIAN PLOVER

143

SKUAS: *Stercorariidae*. Dark gull-like seabirds, called Jaegers in North America, noted for their piratical methods of feeding, by pursuing other seabirds, especially gulls and terns, to make them disgorge their last catch. The persistence with which they fly down their victims is quite distinct from the desultory mutual robbery of immature gulls. Further distinguished from immature gulls by white wing patch (but beware occasional immature gull with pale wing patch), and by holding their wings more angled at the carpal joint. Adults (except Great Skua) have two distinct plumage phases, dark and light, and the middle feathers of the tail elongated; in immatures these feathers project scarcely at all. Bill slightly hooked. Breeding on barren moorlands and tundra; passing along coasts on passage, but well out to sea in winter, and rare inland after breeding. Nest on ground, adults often persistently attacking and even buffeting humans and animals who come too close.

GREAT SKUA *Stercorarius skua*. Superficially like an immature Herring Gull (p. 151), but with shorter wings and tail; larger, heavier than other skuas, the white wing-flashes more marked. Calls 'a-er' in flight and a deep 'tuk, tuk' in defence of its nest. Flight appreciably heavier than a gull but less so than a buzzard, and remarkably agile when chasing other birds; will pursue even Gannets. Also has a harrier-like display flight, with wings raised. 23 in. (58 cm.).
⊙ **Sm   Map 110**

ARCTIC SKUA *Stercorarius parasiticus*. Generally the commonest skua, the size of a Common Gull (p. 153). Many puzzling intermediates between dark and pale phases, ranging from all dark to cheeks, neck and underparts creamy white, the cheeks and neck being barred brown in winter. Two common intermediates are brown with distinct dark cap and paler cheeks, and brown with yellow neck ring. Generally appears much darker than any immature gull, from which adults readily distinguished by central pointed tail feathers projecting 3–4 in; in immature these scarcely project. On breeding grounds has a wailing 'ka-aaow' and a deeper 'tuk-tuk'. Flight graceful, buoyant and rather hawk-like. 18 in. (46 cm.).
● **Sm   Map 111**

POMARINE SKUA *Stercorarius pomarinus*. Larger than Arctic Skua, from which adult best told by blunt and twisted central tail feathers, but immature separable only by larger size. Pale forms much more frequent than dark. Call a sharp 'which-yew' and other, more gull-like notes. Flight heavier than Arctic Skua. 20 in. (51 cm.).
○ **M**

LONG-TAILED SKUA *Stercorarius longicaudus*. Adult is the most distinctive skua and the smallest in bulk, easily told by the pointed central tail feathers extending from 5 to 10 in. beyond the rest of the tail. Legs grey, bill black. Dark form now extremely rare. Pale forms usually lack breast band found in other skuas. Immature distinguishable from other immature skuas by small size, smaller bill and much less white in wings. A high-pitched 'kreee' at breeding grounds, otherwise silent. Flight more graceful than Arctic Skua. 20–22 in. (51–56 cm.).
○ **M**

SKUAS

GREAT SKUA

ARCTIC SKUA

light phase

dark phase

imm.

POMARINE SKUA

light phase

dark phase

imm.

LONG-TAILED SKUA

adult

145

GULLS and TERNS: *Laridae.* pp. 147–63. Gregarious long-winged web-footed seabirds, some species also occurring inland, divided into the larger, stouter Gulls and the smaller, slenderer Terns (pp. 159–63). GULLS: Larinae. Adults have white underparts, grey to black upperparts, head generally white, tail generally square-ended, bill and legs red, pink or yellow; for winter plumages, see pp. 154–5. Immatures (see pp. 156–7) start brown and gradually develop adult plumage, over 3–4 years in the larger species. Wings broader and blunter than Terns, and flight heavier, often soaring; legs longer. Gulls rarely dive. Many are scavengers; others rarely come to land except to breed. Colonial nesting, often very noisy on nesting grounds on cliffs or flat ground by the sea, some also inland by fresh water.

AUDOUIN'S GULL *Larus audouinii.* The rarest breeding gull of the region, intermediate between Common (p. 153) and Herring Gulls (p. 151) in size, differing from both in narrower wings; red rim round eye; blackish-green legs; and red bill with a black band near the yellow tip, which looks all black at a distance. Immature pale brown, with grey crown and neck. Calls a hoarse 'kiaou' and a quieter 'crick-crick'; alarm call a goose-like 'guggugguggugg'. Flight buoyant, like a Gannet (p. 31). Breeds on rocky islands, otherwise mainly at sea. 19½ in. (50 cm.)

SLENDER-BILLED GULL *Larus genei.* Like a largish winter Black-headed Gull (p. 149), sharing its white forewing blaze, but with longer neck and longer, stouter, much darker red bill (yellow in winter). In breeding plumage white of body suffused pink. Immature, see p. 157; legs yellow. Calls varied, some resembling Gull-billed Tern (p. 159), others more laughing and gull-like, 'kau-kau'. Breeds by fresh and brackish lakes and coastal lagoons, wintering mainly in coastal waters. 17 in. (43 cm.). **—V**

SOOTY GULL *Larus hemprichii.* A dark brown gull, with back of neck, tail and belly white; bill greenish-yellow, with black and red tip; legs olive-green; eyes dark. Immature has tail brown but throat white, with most of bill slate blue. Call a mewing whistle. Prefers perching on rocks or buoys to resting on water; piratical in habits, like skuas (pp. 145). 16½ in. (42 cm.).

WHITE-EYED GULL *Larus leucophthalmus.* Differs from the slightly larger Sooty Gull, with which it hardly overlaps, in its black head and throat, white ring round white eye, paler breast, longer and slenderer black-tipped red bill and yellow legs. Immature differs from immature Sooty Gull in blackish red bill tipped red. Call similar. 16 in. (41 cm.).

GREAT BLACK-HEADED GULL *Larus ichthyaetus.* In summer the only large gull with dark hood; has white mark around bright red eye-rim. In winter resembles large Herring Gull (p. 151) with dark smudges on head and whiter axillaries and upper tail coverts. At all times has distinctive tricoloured bill and greenish legs. Immatures best told from other large immature gulls by distinctive shape of bill, heavy and appearing to droop at tip. Breeding call a laughing 'kyauu-kyauu-kyau,' otherwise a loud harsh croaking 'kraapa'. Flight graceful, often sailing with outstretched wings for long periods; indulges in piracy against smaller gulls. Breeds by salt or brackish water, wintering in coastal waters; by fresh water only on passage. 26 in. (66 cm.). **—V**

GULLS

juv

adult

AUDOUIN'S GULL

adult summer

SLENDER-BILLED GULL

summer

SOOTY GULL

summer

WHITE-EYED GULL

adult winter

summer

GREAT BLACK-HEADED GULL

147

BLACK-HEADED GULL *Larus ridibundus*. The smallest common breeding gull of the region; like Little and Mediterranean Gulls has red bill and legs. In summer, has conspicuous *chocolate-brown* hood, not extending on to nape, turning white with dark smudges in winter. In winter easily distinguished by conspicuous white forewing, black only at the tip. Most frequent call a raucous 'kraah' and other harsh cries. Flight strong and buoyant over long distances, more wavering and almost tern-like at other times. Breeds on bogs, marshes, islands in lakes, dunes and shingle; in winter widespread inland on farmland, short turf, and waste ground, and by fresh water, as well as on coasts and estuaries, a typical urban bird in N W Europe. 14–15 in. (35–38 cm.).
●RsmW   **Map 112**

LITTLE GULL *Larus minutus*. The smallest and most tern-like gull of the region. From Black-headed Gull differs in summer by *black* hood extending over nape on to upper neck, in winter by blackish bill and at all times by smoky grey underwing and no black on wing-tips. Differs from marsh terns in winter by square white tail, smoky underwing and no sharply defined white shoulder. Diagonal wing-bar separates cleft-tailed immature (p. 156) from all except larger immature Kittiwake (p. 156). Calls a rather harsh, sharp 'kek-kek-kek' and 'ka-ka-ka'. Flight graceful and wavering, recalling marsh terns. Breeds by fresh water pools, bogs and marshes; on passage at coastal and fresh waters; in winter at sea. 11 in. (28 cm.).   ☉Mw   **Map 113**

MEDITERRANEAN GULL *Larus melanocephalus*. More like Common than Black-headed Gull, to which *black* head of adult in summer is only real likeness. Stockier build than Common Gull (p. 153) with white wing-tips, heavy red bill appearing to droop at tip, and longer red legs, while winter and immature birds usually have dark smudge through eye. Second-year birds have black wing-tips, but without white spots. Calls higher-pitched than Common but deeper than Black-headed: 'kau-kau-kyau', 'kee-er' or 'kek-ke-ke'. Flight rather jerky, with shallower wing-beats than Common. on grassy coastal marshes and flats; otherwise frequents coastal waters. 15 in. (39 cm.).   ○MW(b)

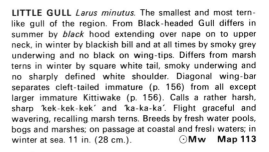

imm.

Sabine's Gull

BONAPARTE'S GULL *Larus philadelphia*. A vagrant from North America, differing from Black-headed Gull in its shorter slenderer black bill, dark *slate-grey* hood in summer, orange legs of adult, under surface of primaries white, and more buoyant tern-like flight. 12–14 in. (30–35 cm.)   —V

SABINE'S GULL *Larus sabini*. A small tern-like gull, the only one in the region with a markedly forked tail; forewings strikingly black, with trailing edge contrastingly white. Adult in summer is only gull with grey hood, extending over nape. Immature, with grey nape and black-tipped tail, lacks diagonal dark wing-bar of immature Kittiwake and Little Gull. Harsh grating cry resembles Arctic Tern (p. 161), but briefer. Flight buoyant, feeding off surface of water. Breeds on marshy tundras by fresh or coastal waters, winters at sea. 13 in. (33 cm.).   ○Mw

BLACK-HEADED GULL

adult
summer

adult
winter

LITTLE GULL

adult
summer

adult
winter

MEDITERRANEAN GULL

adult
summer

adult winter

BONAPARTE'S GULL

adult
summer

adult
winter

SABINE'S GULL

adult
summer

adult winter

149

HERRING GULL *Larus argentatus*. The commonest and most widespread of the larger gulls, very variable in size; males average larger than females. Variable also in mantle colour from silver grey to slate grey; the British and Western European *argentatus* the palest, but other races, notably *heuglini* (N W Russia) and *atlantis* (Atlantic Islands) almost as dark as Lesser Black-back. Since all except pink-legged *argentatus* and W Scandinavian *omissus* are yellow-legged, considerable confusion with Lesser Black-back is possible, though Herring Gull generally larger with stouter bill. Has many wailing, chuckling and yelping notes, commonest being 'kee-yow' and in spring a loud echoing 'gah-gah-gah'. Flight strong, deliberate, frequently soaring and gliding. Breeds on sea cliffs, dunes, shingle and marine islands, more rarely inland, even on buildings. In winter widespread both on coasts and inland, also feeding on rubbish dumps and short turf. 22–26 in. (56–66 cm.). ●RW **Map 114**

LESSER BLACK-BACK *Larus fuscus*. Great and Lesser Black-backs are the only two gulls which are all white except for dark grey to black mantle and wings. Lesser is always markedly smaller than Great, with less stout bill and yellow legs (but sub-adult and winter Lessers may still have pink legs). British and W European race of Lesser *graellsii* has much paler mantle than Great, with contrasting black wing-tips, but in Scandinavian race *fuscus* mantle often as dark as Great. Cf. also yellow-legged races of Herring Gull. Calls (rather gruffer), similar to Herring Gull, but migratory in N of range. 21–22 in. (53–56 cm.). ●Srm **Map 115**

GREAT BLACK-BACK *Larus marinus*. A larger edition of Lesser Black-back; upperparts almost black and legs pink at all times. Flight even more ponderous than Herring Gull, and voice similar but deeper and more raucous, with a deep goblin-like chuckle in nesting territory. Breeds mainly on sea cliffs or marine islands, more rarely on flat shores and inland. In winter more confined to coast than Herring and Lesser Black-back. 25–31 in. (64–79 cm.). ●RW **Map 116**

GLAUCOUS GULL *Larus hyperboreus*. Glaucous and Iceland Gulls are like all-pale Great and Lesser Black-backs, their pale silver-grey mantle and wings unrelieved by any black at the tip. Glaucous has a larger head and neck and heavier bill, recalling Great Black-back, whereas the Iceland's are notably smaller and slenderer. Glaucous extremely variable in size, from Herring to Great Black-back. At very close range the colour of the orbital ring round the adult's eye (yellow in Glaucous brick-red in Iceland) is decisive. In flight the ponderous wing-beats of the Glaucous contrast with the quick, almost kittiwake-like flight of the Iceland. Breeds on cliffed and rocky coasts visiting flat coasts and harbours in winter, but rare inland. Hybrids with Herring Gull frequent in Iceland. 25–32 in. (64–81 cm.). ☉W **Map 117**

ICELAND GULL *Larus glaucoides*. A small version of Glaucous Gull, with smaller head and less stout bill, recalling Common Gull (p. 153), and much more buoyant flight, but voice, habits and habitat similar. Cf. Ivory Gull (p. 153). 22–26 in. (56–66 cm.). ○W **Map 118**

GULLS

HERRING GULL

adult

adult

adult

adult

LESSER BLACK-BACK

adult

adult

GREAT BLACK-BACK

adult

adult

adult

adult

GLAUCOUS GULL

adult

adult

ICELAND GULL

COMMON GULL *Larus canus*. Like a small Herring Gull (p. 151), but adult easily separated by yellow-green legs and bill; bill much less stout and with no red spot near tip. From winter Black-headed Gull (p. 154) also differs in bill and leg colour, as well as white spots on blunter black wing-tips and no white blaze on forewing. Cf. Kittiwake and Mediterranean Gull (p. 149). Winter adults have heads streaked ash-brown like Herring Gull, not smudged darker, like Black-headed. Most frequent call resembles a rather feeble but high-pitched Herring, 'kee-ya', also has a gobbling 'kak-kak-kak', often heard from flocks on migration in spring. Flight more graceful than Herring but less so than Black-headed. Breeds on rocky, sandy and shingly coasts and marine islands, also by fresh water inland. In winter widespread on coasts, estuaries and farmland; in some regions an increasing urban bird. 16 in. (41 cm.)

●RmW   Map 119

KITTIWAKE *Rissa tridactyla*. Adult like a rather daintier Common Gull but with no white spots on black wingtips, black legs and in winter uniform grey head and nape. Immatures ('tarrocks') (p. 156) have strikingly different wing-pattern, with black bar across forewing and another diagonally from 'elbow' on to hind wing, but cf. Little Gull (p. 156), which also has a slightly cleft tail, with a dark bar at the tip; cf. also Sabine's gull (p. 149). At breeding colonies air is filled with deafening cries of 'kitt-ee-wayke'; also has a low 'uk-uk-uk' and a wailing note. Flight as graceful and buoyant as Black-headed Gull; habitually follows ships. Breeds on ledges on sea cliffs and in sea caves, exceptionally also on buildings, shingle or dunes by the sea; in winter mainly well out at sea, though flocks occasionally visit coast. 16 in. (41 cm.)   ●RSmw   Map 120

IVORY GULL *Pagophila eburnea*. Adult is only pure white medium-sized seabird of region, having no darker streaks or smudges on head in winter; breast faintly suffused pink. Bill yellow tipped red, legs short, black; vermilion orbital ring round eye. Immature (p. 156) has unique plumage among seabirds of region, with grey face and throat, dark spots on upperparts, and wing-tips and tail-bar black; bill grey with whitish tip. Harsh 'krii-krii', 'keer' and 'karr' notes resemble Arctic Tern. Buoyant, tern-like flight; not often seen on surface of water. Nests on cliffs and rocky ground near sea, wintering at sea mainly at the edge of the pack ice. 17½ in. (44 cm.).   —V

ROSS'S GULL *Rhodostethia rosea*. The second smallest gull of the region, breeding adult has distinctive combination of narrow black collar, whole plumage except mantle and wings strongly suffused pink, markedly long wedge-shaped tail, short thin black bill and red legs. In winter (p. 154) black collar goes, pink fades and creamy white head, tail and body contrast with pale grey upperparts. Note also small bill and lack of dark wing-tips. Immature resembles immature Sabine's Gull but with wedge-shaped tail. Voice higher-pitched than other gulls, with wide vocabulary, most frequent note 'e-vu, e-vu'. Flight agile, tern-like with long, pointed wings, angled like a tern's. Breeds grassy, wooded tundra; in winter on Arctic coasts and at sea. 12½ in. (32 cm.).

—V

GULLS

adult

adult

COMMON GULL

adult

adult

KITTIWAKE

adult

adult

IVORY GULL

adult

adult

ROSS'S GULL

21·VII·1970

153

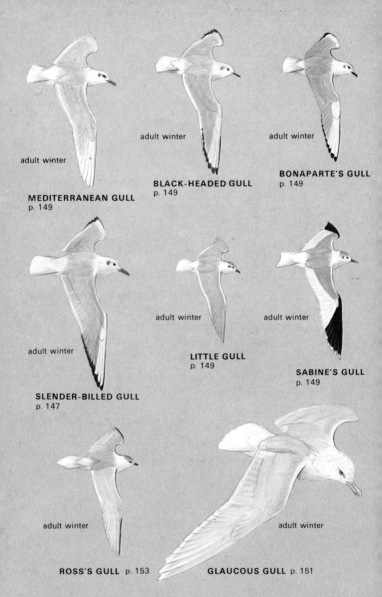

adult winter

MEDITERRANEAN GULL
p. 149

adult winter

BLACK-HEADED GULL
p. 149

adult winter

BONAPARTE'S GULL
p. 149

adult winter

adult winter

LITTLE GULL
p. 149

adult winter

SABINE'S GULL
p. 149

adult winter

SLENDER-BILLED GULL
p. 147

adult winter

ROSS'S GULL   p. 153

adult winter

GLAUCOUS GULL   p. 151

WINTER GULLS:

All the adult gulls with black or brown hoods in the breeding season (Black-headed, Little, Mediterranean, Great Black-headed, and the rare Sabine's, Bonaparte's and Laughing) lose them in winter and are then best distinguished from other same-sized gulls by the dark smudges instead of faint streaks on their heads. (Adult winter

GULLS
winter plumages of adults and
second year birds

2nd winter

GREAT BLACK-BACK
p. 151

winter

HERRING GULL
p. 151

2nd winter

LESSER BLACK-BACK p. 151

adult winter

GREAT BLACK-HEADED GULL
p. 147

2nd winter

GLAUCOUS GULL
p. 151

2nd winter

ICELAND GULL
p. 151

Great Black-headed has both smudges and streaks). Of the smudge-headed winter
gulls, the Mediterranean and Little have no black at the wing-tips, and the Black-
headed and rare Bonaparte's have a distinctive white blaze on the forewing. Sabine's
is unique with its broad black forewing. Of the streak-headed group, Glaucous and
Iceland are the two which have no black at the wing-tips.

MEDITERRANEAN GULL
p. 149

BLACK-HEADED GULL
p. 149

BONAPARTE'S GULL
p. 149

COMMON GULL
p. 153

LITTLE GULL
p. 149

SLENDER-BILLED GULL
p. 147

IVORY GULL
p. 153

ROSS'S GULL
p. 153

KITTIWAKE
p. 153

IMMATURE GULLS start brown, usually with a dark tail-bar, and gradually develop adult plumage. Identifying them is one of the more difficult exercises in bird-watching. The smaller gulls take two years to assume full adult plumage, the larger ones four. Herring and Lesser Black-backed Gulls are virtually identical as juveniles and hardly distinguishable in first-winter plumage, but by the second winter (p. 155) the typical mantle colour which distinguishes the adults begins to

GREAT BLACK-BACK
p. 151

HERRING GULL
p. 151

LESSER BLACK-BACK p. 151

GREAT BLACK-
HEADED GULL
p. 147

GLAUCOUS GULL p. 151

ICELAND GULL p. 151

appear. Immature Great Black-back differs from both by larger size, heavier bill and generally darker head and underparts. Immature Common Gull usually whiter than immature Herring, especially on tail. Immature Glaucous and Iceland can appear whiter than any other gulls except adult Ivory (p. 153). Immature Kittiwake and Little Gull both have prominent diagonal dark bar across hindwing.

TERNS : *Sterninae.* pp. 159–63. Most terns resemble graceful small gulls, with longer wings, deeply forked tail, and thinner, more pointed bills, often carried almost vertically downwards in their buoyant flight, as they hover and plunge into the water after their small fish prey. The commoner Sea Terns (*Sterna, Gelochelidon, Hydroprogne*) of the region are all grey and white with white wing-tips and black head and nape, the forehead turning white in winter. Size, bill colour and calls are the best field marks. Juveniles have upperparts speckled brown. Summer visitors, colonial nesting, very noisy at breeding colonies; nest always on flat ground usually sand, shingle or rocky marine islands.

GULL-BILLED TERN *Gelochelidon nilotica.* Very similar to Sandwich Tern, but has much shorter, stouter all-black bill, grey rump and tail and black soles to feet; also broader-winged and heavier-bodied. At rest in mixed flocks legs show longer. Head of winter adult whiter than most other terns. Immatures have paler markings on upperparts, white forehead and reddish legs. Calls quite distinct, 'quac-quac-quac' and 'cher-wuc'. Flight rather heavier and more gull-like. 15 in. (38 cm.).　　　　　　　　　　**—A(b)**

CASPIAN TERN *Hydroprogne tschegrava.* The largest tern of the region, like small black-capped Herring Gull (p. 151), but with very stout red bill and forked tail. Streaked white forehead and dark undersides of primaries separate from Royal Tern in winter, when Caspian's bill may also be orange-yellow. Immature like winter adult with dark marks on upperparts and black-tipped tail. Call a rather gruff 'kaah' 'kaa-uh'. Flight gull-like rather than tern-like. Mainly coastal. 21 in. (53 cm.).　　　　　　　　　　**—A**

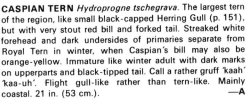

ROYAL TERN *Sterna maxima.* Almost as large and heavily built as Caspian Tern, but in summer has orange-yellow bill and more distinct crest, in winter (but not during the moult) has unstreaked white forehead, and at all times has more deeply forked tail, paler undersides of primaries, and higher-pitched call, a trilling 'kir'. Only likely off N W Africa. 20 in. (50 cm.).　　　　　　　　　　**—V**

SWIFT TERN *Sterna bergii.* Appreciably larger than Sandwich Tern; adult distinguishable from Lesser Crested only by size, heavier and yellower bill and darker grey plumage, but immature apparently lacks black wing-bar. 19 in. (48 cm.).

LESSER CRESTED TERN *Sterna bengalensis.* Best told from Sandwich and Gull-billed Terns by smaller size, orange-yellow bill and narrow white band on forehead even in breeding plumage; from Gull-billed also by longer bill and yellow soles of feet. Immature differs from immature Sandwich in blackish bar along shoulder of wing and black outer tail feathers. Cf. Swift Tern. 14 in. (36 cm.).

SANDWICH TERN *Sterna sandvicensis.* A larger tern than any on p. 161, though less stout, further differing from Common Tern in its white upperparts, yellow-tipped black bill, yellow-soled black feet, less deeply forked tail, crested appearance of elongated nape feathers in a wind, heavier flight and distinctive call-note, a rather harsh 'kirrick' or 'kirr-whit'. Immature brown on head and nape, and tail tipped blackish. Almost exclusively coastal. 16 in. (41 cm.). ● **Sm　Map 121**

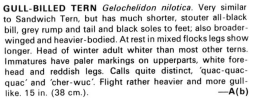

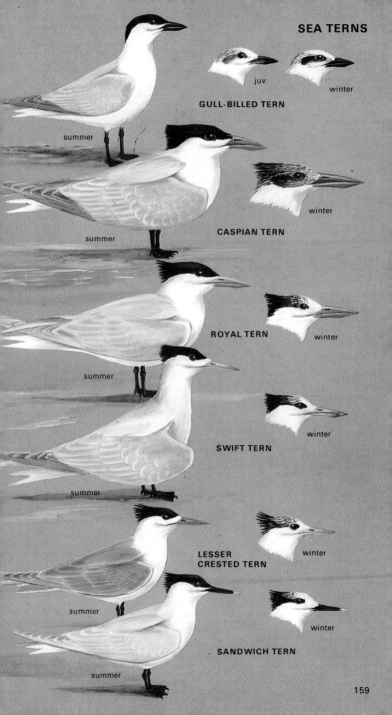

SEA TERNS

juv.
winter

GULL-BILLED TERN

summer

winter

summer

CASPIAN TERN

winter

ROYAL TERN

summer

winter

summer

SWIFT TERN

winter

**LESSER
CRESTED TERN**

summer

winter

summer

SANDWICH TERN

summer

COMMON TERN *Sterna hirundo*. Generally the commonest and most widespread tern of the region, extremely like Arctic Tern. Two of the safest field marks are bill colour (vermilion Common, blood-red Arctic) and leg length (much shorter in Arctic, which at rest may almost appear legless). In full breeding plumage Common normally has dark tip to bill, but Arctic normally does not; in winter both have blackish bills. In flight all Arctic's primaries, seen against light, appear translucent and silvery, but Common has only innermost four primaries making a pale translucent patch. Most Commons have much whiter breast and underparts than most Arctics, contrasting strongly with their mantles. Juvenile Common best distinguished from juvenile Arctic by pale flesh-pink (not black) basal half of bill, brownish tinge (which Arctic lacks) on head and mantle, much more conspicuous black shoulder at rest and bar on forewing in flight, and a broad dusky (not narrow black) band on trailing edge of wing seen from beneath. Main calls, strident and high-pitched, are 'keeerree', 'keeyah' and 'kik-kik-kik.' Breeds by fresh water, on moor and on coast. In winter on S coasts and at sea. 14 in. (35 cm.). ●SM Map 122

ARCTIC TERN *Sterna paradisaea*. Very similar to Common Tern, q.v. for distinctions. Some Arctics are so grey on the face that a white streak appears to separate the face from the black crown, a feature never seen in the Common; but cf. White-cheeked Tern. Often breeds in same colonies, but generally more northerly, and not inland except on the tundra. 14 in. (35 cm.). ●SM Map 123

ROSEATE TERN *Sterna dougallii*. Longer tail streamers, extending far beyond wing-tips at rest (Arctic's extend a little beyond, Common's not at all) account for greater length. Otherwise best distinguished from Common and Arctic by all black bill (except from midsummer to early autumn, when base becomes red), and distinctive harsh, grating 'aach, aach' call note. Field marks include longer legs and pinkish flush on breast in summer, but Common has breast tinged pale mauve. At any distance can sometimes be picked out by generally whiter appearance. Juvenile differs from juvenile Common in its all-black bill, black legs, all dark head, virtual lack of dark shoulder mark at rest and white band on trailing edge of underside of wing. Mostly on marine islands; rare at fresh water, even on migration. 15 in. (38 cm.). ⊙ Sm Map 124

WHITE-CHEEKED TERN *Sterna repressa*. Much darker grey than Common Tern, both above and below, so white cheeks stand out very conspicuously; differing also in winter in its blackish-red bill and more uniformly grey tail. More deeply forked tail and longer thinner bill separate from Whiskered Tern (p. 163) in summer. 13 in. (33 cm.).

LITTLE TERN *Sterna albifrons*. Much the smallest sea tern, and readily told by its always white forehead, its black-tipped yellow bill, its orange-yellow legs and its quicker, jerkier flight, hovering like a marionette. Chief calls 'kik-kik', 'pee-e-eer' and trills. 9½ in. (24 cm.). ●SM Map 125

SEA TERNS

summer

winter

COMMON TERN

summer

winter

ARCTIC TERN

summer

winter

ROSEATE TERN

summer

winter

WHITE-CHEEKED TERN

summer

juv.

winter

LITTLE TERN

161

BRIDLED TERN *Sterna anaethetus*. A sea tern (p. 158) with all dark upperparts, except for a white collar, confusable only with Sooty Tern. Forehead white with white eyebrows extending back beyond eye, bill black, white-tipped tail deeply forked. In winter head mottled with white, eye-stripe indistinct and upperparts sparingly marked white. Immature similar, but with whole upperparts mottled buff. Flight graceful, rather slow, with the body appearing to move up and down with each rather exaggerated wing-beat; may soar high. Call 'kirk'. Coastal and maritime. 14 in. (35 cm.). —**V**

SOOTY TERN *Sterna fuscata*. Rare vagrant to E Atlantic seas and coasts from Western Approaches to Canaries, a larger version of Bridled Tern, with darker upperparts, no white collar, white of forehead not extending back beyond eye, and outer tail feathers not wholly white at tip. Immature all sooty black with white speckles on upperparts. Flight less buoyant. Oceanic. 16 in. (40 cm.). —**V**

MARSH TERNS: *Chlidonias*. Smaller than any sea terns, except Little Tern; in winter with same general pattern of pale grey above and white below, with white forehead, but tail less forked and bill rather slender. Cf. Little Gull (p. 149). Most distinctive feature is graceful dipping flight, often stooping to surface of water to pick up insects, but very rarely diving in. Breed exclusively by fresh and brackish water and marshes; often in coastal waters on migration.

BLACK TERN *Chlidonias niger*. Generally the commonest marsh tern and the only water bird that has whole head and body black or greyish black, relieved only by white of under tail coverts; bill black, legs reddish. Female has greyer throat and underparts. Wings show paler underneath. In winter differs from all sea terns by more sharply defined white shoulder patch, variable but distinctive black spot on side of breast and black bill, as well as by less deeply forked tail. Immature resembles winter adult but with darker mantle. Large flocks have a collective reedy cry; also occasionally calls 'kik, kik', 'keek' or 'krew'. Nest floating on vegetation in shallow water. 9½ in. (24 cm.). ⊙ **sM (b)**   **Map 126**

WHITE-WINGED BLACK TERN *Chlidonias leucopterus*. In summer readily distinguished from Black Tern by conspicuous white forewing, rump and tail, shorter stouter reddish-brown bill, but in winter hard to separate except by lack of dark spot on side of breast, paler rump or brighter red legs. Complete white collar, paler rump and less forked tail are best distinctions from winter Whiskered Tern. Immature has contrasting dark mantle and grey wings. Calls hoarser, on passage sometimes a guttural 'kerr'. Habitat similar but breeds in somewhat drier marshes. 9¼ in. (24 cm.). —**A**

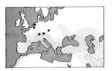

WHISKERED TERN *Chlidonias hybrida*. In summer like a sea tern with black cap, grey underparts, white cheeks and red bill, white underwing and under tail coverts conspicuous in flight. In winter pale on upperparts and very like Common Tern (p. 161). Immature differs from both black terns in its mottled mantle, and has darker rump than White-winged. Very noisy at breeding colonies; double flight-note alternates a rasping note like a Corncrake with a shrill cheep like a domestic chick. 9¼ in. (24 cm.). —**V**

SEA TERNS, MARSH TERNS

imm.

adult

BRIDLED TERN

imm.

adult

SOOTY TERN

moulting

summer

summer

winter

juv.

BLACK TERN

summer

summer

winter

WHITE-WINGED BLACK TERN

summer

juv.

winter

summer

WHISKERED TERN

163

● **AUKS**: *Alcidae*. Short-necked, short-tailed black and white diving seabirds; sexes alike. Wings rather short and narrow, legs set well back, giving upright stance at rest. Voice a harsh growling 'arrrr' or 'karrrr'. Flight whirring, fast and direct, low over water, legs and feet often outstretched. Auks swim and dive readily and constantly, but on land can only shuffle awkwardly. In winter at sea.

RAZORBILL *Alca torda*. Easily told from all other seabirds by unique bill, flattened in vertical plane, and from Guillemot also by white line on bill and in summer also on face. White wing-bar shows in flight. Winter adult and immature also have white cheeks and throat, immature's bill much less stout. Breeds in loose colonies, usually higher up cliff than Guillemots, with the single egg (oval, not pear-shaped) more often sheltered than in the open. 16 in. (41 cm.).
●Rsw   Map 127

GUILLEMOT *Uria aalge*. Generally the commonest auk, with a long straight unmarked bill. In good light brown plumage of southern *albionis* form (chocolate in summer, greyish in winter) should also be evident; northern birds *aalge* have upperparts black though head always browner. Striking bridled variety, more frequent in north, has narrow white ring round and line back from eye. Juvenile has a shrill whistle. Breeds in close-packed colonies on inaccessible open cliff ledges; single egg markedly pear-shaped. 16½ in. (42 cm.).
●Rsw   Map 128

BRÜNNICH'S GUILLEMOT *Uria lomvia*. Virtually impossible to distinguish from northern Guillemots at any distance, but has darker head, shorter and stouter bill with thin pale line along base of upper mandible, and in winter also by black of crown extending well below eye, with no dark stripe on face. 16½ in. (42 cm.).   —V

PUFFIN *Fratercula arctica*. The smallest breeding auk south of the Arctic, unmistakable in summer, with its grotesque bill and face ornamentation, giving it a solemn clown-like mien, and even in winter when bill smaller and mainly yellow; no white wing-bar. Cheeks and throat-band grey in winter. Juvenile has plaintive 'chip-chip-chip' call. Breeds in often huge colonies in burrows, usually in turf on islands. 12 in. (30 cm.).   ⊙rSw   Map 129

BLACK GUILLEMOT *Cepphus grylle*. In summer the only seabird all black with a large white wing-patch and in winter the only one with barred black and white upperparts; legs red. Immature like winter adult but browner. Call a rather feeble high-pitched whistle or whine. The least sociable auk, breeding in very loose colonies, in crevices of cliffs and rocks. Shallower seas, much further up inlets than other auks. 13½ in. (34 cm.).   ⊙R   Map 130

LITTLE AUK *Alle alle*. Much the smallest and shortest-billed auk, also the smallest diving seabird. Beware small-billed juveniles of other auks, though only young Puffin (which has grey cheeks and no wing-bar) is as tiny, and none have white of cheeks extending back almost across nape. 8 in. (20 cm.).   ⊙W   Map 131

AUKS

summer

RAZORBILL

imm.

winter

bridled form

summer

GUILLEMOT

winter

summer

BRÜNNICH'S
GUILLEMOT

winter

imm.

PUFFIN

winter

BLACK
GUILLEMOT

winter

summer

summer

LITTLE AUK

winter

summer

165

● **SANDGROUSE**: *Pteroclidae.* pp. 167-9. Mainly sandy coloured terrestrial birds, hard to see when at rest in their desert environment, when they resemble small long-tailed partridges; in flight more like plump parakeets or long-tailed pigeons or golden plover. Neck very short; legs short, legs and toes feathered in front (all round in Pallas's Sandgrouse). Flight fast, flocks performing aerial evolutions recalling golden plover, and undertaking long, often noisy daily journeys – up to 40 miles and back – to and from water to drink either at dawn or dusk. Gait pigeon-like, rather tripping, with short waddling steps. Most sandgrouse are liable to flock with other species. Deserts, semi-deserts, and other dry stony ground, nesting on ground. Voice is one of the best clues to sandgrouse identification.

SPOTTED SANDGROUSE *Pterocles senegallus.* A rather small pale sandgrouse, with elongated needle-like tail feathers and much less black on the belly than the short-tailed Black-bellied (p. 169). Male has largely uniform upperparts, yellow throat and blue-grey band through eye; female markedly spotted, with much whiter throat. Cf. Chestnut-bellied Sandgrouse (p. 169). Distinctive liquid musical call, variously rendered 'cuito, cuito', 'wittoo, wittoo' and 'waku, waku'. Goes in smaller flocks than most species, and inhabits wide range of dry open country from desert to fairly thick bush, coming to water both quite late in the morning (after 0800) and in hot weather sometimes again in the evening. 13 in. (33 cm.).

CROWNED SANDGROUSE *Pterocles coronatus.* A small sandgrouse of the shorter-tailed group, both sexes also lacking the dark line on the breast possessed by all other breeding sandgrouse of the region except the long-tailed Spotted and the short-tailed female Lichtenstein's. Black chin and black mark between bill and eye distinguish male from males of both Spotted and Lichtenstein's. Female differs from female Spotted by much yellower throat and less distinctly spotted appearance, from female Lichtenstein's by yellow instead of speckled throat. Call higher-pitched than other sandgrouse, and rising in pitch, 'cla-cla-cla' or 'chachagarra'. Stony deserts and mountainsides, much more widespread than Lichtenstein's. Flies very fast to water, mainly in early morning; will drink quite brackish water. 11 in. (28 cm.).

LICHTENSTEIN'S SANDGROUSE *Pterocles lichtensteinii.* The smallest sandgrouse of the region, looking rather dark from its close barring, and one of the shorter-tailed group. Male has distinctive black and white markings on crown and forehead, and yellow breast with three black lines. Female is only completely uniformly barred sandgrouse, lacking any distinctive markings. Cf. Crowned Sandgrouse (above). Call a wigeon-like double whistle, 'whittou', but often flies silently, and so escapes detection when flighting to water as it usually does, after dark and before dawn. Has singular habit of descending into wells to drink, when arrival and departure have been compared to those of wasps at a hole nest. Less gregarious than other sandgrouse, frequenting rocky and bushy desert areas. 10 in. (25 cm.).

SANDGROUSE

♀

♂

SPOTTED SANDGROUSE

♂

Palestine
Sinai

♀

♂

CROWNED SANDGROUSE

♀

♂

LICHTENSTEIN'S SANDGROUSE

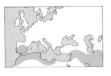

PIN-TAILED SANDGROUSE *Pterocles alchata*. The only breeding sandgrouse of the region with a white belly, and the most distinctive of the four species with needle-like elongated tail feathers; the other three are the Spotted (p. 167), the Chestnut-bellied and Pallas's. Male's rufous breast and female's pure white throat are both unique features, while male is only sandgrouse with both chin and throat black — Crowned (p. 167) has black chin and Black-bellied has black throat, but both are shorter-tailed. In flight Pin-tailed shows distinctive white wing-bar and white underwing with black tip. Call, a loud ringing 'kata, kata', frequently uttered in flight, can be very puzzling when light too bright to see birds overhead. Highly gregarious. Avoids open desert; sometimes nests in loose colonies. 14½ in. (37 cm.)

CHESTNUT-BELLIED SANDGROUSE *Pterocles exustus*. The most local breeding sandgrouse of the region (Egypt only), the smallest of the three with needle-like elongated tail feathers. Male is only one of three with whole belly appearing dark (actually very dark chestnut), while female's dark belly barred pale is unique among the six species. Differs from Spotted in having a black line on the breast; male has distinctive yellow head and wings, while female lacks Spotted's spotted appearance. Harmonious deep-toned call 'gouta, gouta'. Very gregarious, gathering in huge flocks to water between 0700 and 0900 hours, and in hot weather again in evening. A bird of the open desert. 12½ in. (32 cm.).

BLACK-BELLIED SANDGROUSE *Pterocles orientalis*. The largest breeding sandgrouse of the region, and the only one with whole belly black, though dark chestnut belly of long-tailed male Chestnut-bellied often looks almost black. In fact no other sandgrouse with any black on belly at all has a short tail. At rest male's yellow wings and in flight white underwing contrasting strongly with black belly are useful pointers. Male is only sandgrouse with throat but not chin black. Call rather gruff, variously rendered 'churr-rur-rur' or 'tchourou'. Avoids open desert. 13½ in. (34 cm.).

PALLAS'S SANDGROUSE *Syrrhaptes paradoxus*. The only sandgrouse likely to be seen north of the Mediterranean region, and then only when one of its now very infrequent irruptions (none on a large scale since 1908) from Central Asia occurs. Tail feathers more elongated than any of the N African sandgrouse, with a conspicuous black patch towards the front of the belly, very noticeable in flight, when wings are held rather curved, like a partridge, and quills may hum or whistle. Finer details of plumage only visible at close range. Voice variously described as 'chack, chack', 'köcki, köcki' or 'köckerik, köckerik'. During irruptions frequents dunes, arable fields and other open habitats. 14—16 in. (35—41 cm.).   —V(b)

SANDGROUSE

PIN-TAILED SANDGROUSE

♂ ♀

CHESTNUT-BELLIED
SANDGROUSE

♂ ♀

BLACK-BELLIED SANDGROUSE

♂ ♀

♂ ♀

PALLAS'S SANDGROUSE

169

● PIGEONS and DOVES: *Columbidae.* pp. 171–3. Pigeons tend to be larger and doves to be smaller, but no real distinction. Soberly coloured, in pastel shades of grey or brown, with smallish heads, short bills, longish tails and crooning or cooing voices. Gait a walk. Tree or ledge nesters.

ROCK DOVE and FERAL PIGEON *Columba livia.* The wild Rock Dove is the ancestor of the Domestic Pigeon, with its varied plumages. Has general outline of Stock Dove, from which always differs in its grey wing-tips, and except in Middle East in its white rump. Feral Pigeons in towns have wide range of plumages based on black, white, blue-grey and reddish cinnamon, but blue rock type almost identical with wild Rock Dove. Blue-chequer variant also occurs in quite wild Rock Dove populations. Display flight as Stock Dove. Voice the familiar coo of the Domestic Pigeon, 'coo-roo-coo'. Rock Dove on cliffs and rocks, mainly by the sea in the W, but on mountain and hillsides also in the E; nest in a rock crevice or cave ledge. Feral Pigeon in towns, especially ports, also on inland and sea cliffs; nests on ledges of buildings and cliffs. 13 in. (33 cm.).   ⊙/●R   **Map 132**

STOCK DOVE *Columba oenas.* Smaller and shorter-tailed than Woodpigeon, with no white patches, but has black wing-tips and two short black bars on wing. Black wing-tips and lack of pale or white rump are best distinctions from Rock Dove. Call a grunting double coo, with accent on second syllable. Display flight circular, sometimes gliding with raised wings. Woodland and country with scattered trees, also on cliffs and sometimes in towns. Nests in holes. 13 in. (33 cm.).   ●Rw   **Map 133**

WOODPIGEON *Columba palumbus.* The largest pigeon of the region, easily told by the prominent white patches on neck and wings; dark tail-bar also conspicuous in flight. Young are darker and have no white on neck. Voice a soothing 'coo-coo-coo, coo-coo'. Flight fast and direct; makes a noisy clatter when flushed from cover. In distinctive display flight flaps upwards at a steep angle and then glides down with wings scarcely upraised. Wooded country, feeding both in the trees and on adjacent farmland; also among scattered trees, and in W Europe regularly in town parks and squares and large gardens. Nests in trees. 16 in. (41 cm.).   ●Rw   **Map 134**

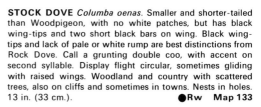

LONG-TOED PIGEON *Columba trocaz.* Like a Woodpigeon without any white wing patches. On Madeira has a silvery neck patch, but not in Canaries, where dark bar at end of tail distinguishes from Laurel Pigeon on Palma and Gomera. Cooing voice and display flight as Woodpigeon. Woodland. 15–16 in. (38–40 cm.).

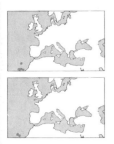

LAUREL PIGEON *Columba junoniae.* Like a slender Woodpigeon, with brown upperparts, vinous underparts, a green patch on the side of the neck and no white patches at all. Cf. Long-toed Pigeon. Has a distinctive soft flapping flight. Laurel forests, now very rare. 15 in. (38 cm.).

Feral pigeons

Sinai, Canary Is.

ROCK DOVE

STOCK DOVE

WOODPIGEON

LONG-TOED PIGEON

LAUREL PIGEON

DOVES: *Streptopelia*. Smaller and slimmer than the *Columba* doves; tail pattern often an important field mark. Most have much faster, more clipped flight, wings being brought in and out again in quick jerks, and also a wing-clapping and gliding display flight. Tree nesters.

COLLARED DOVE *Streptopelia decaocto*. The largest and palest of the wild *Streptopelia* doves, stock-dove-size, with generally rather dull ash-brown plumage, readily distinguished from Turtle Dove by blackish wing-tips, black base to *underside* of tail, and black half-collars. Half-collars obscure in juveniles. Song a persistent triple 'coo-cooo-cuh', accent on middle syllable and final one somewhat truncated. Flight more direct, less clipped, than Turtle Dove. In the E, areas with scattered trees and bushes, from palm groves and oases to villages and towns; in the W, as a very recent colonist, mainly since 1950, almost a commensal of man, especially in towns and villages, and where grain is fed to other birds. 12½ in. (32 cm.) ●R   **Map 135**

BARBARY DOVE *Streptopelia risoria*. A favourite cage bird, often escaping and occasionally breeding in the wild. Markedly smaller and creamier than Collared Dove, but with no dark wing-tips, and no blue-grey in tail. Call distinct, 'koo-krr-oo'. 10 in. (25 cm.).

TURTLE DOVE *Streptopelia turtur*. Generally darker than Collared Dove, with chestnut upperparts, and black and white patch on either side of neck. In flight much the best distinction is tail, mainly black with conspicuous white edge above and beneath. Juvenile browner, with no neck patches. Call a soothing 'turrr, turrr'. Wide range of country with open woodland or scattered trees, including palm groves, large gardens, heaths and parks, often feeding in farmland. 11 in. (27 cm.). ●Sm   **Map 136**

RUFOUS TURTLE DOVE *Streptopelia orientalis*. A rare vagrant from C Asia, larger, darker and more pigeon-like than Turtle Dove, with more heavily spotted, richer chestnut upperparts, darker underparts and blue-grey instead of white neck patch. Song a soporific 'cooo-cooo-kakoor'. 13 in. (33 cm.). —V

PALM DOVE or LAUGHING DOVE *Streptopelia senegalensis*. Smaller than Turtle Dove with similar tail pattern, but readily distinguished by black spots on the front of lower neck, and in flight by more conspicuous blue-grey forewing. Very distinctive rising and falling song: 'oh-cook-cook-oo-oo'. Common in towns, villages, and oases. 10¼ in. (26 cm.).

NAMAQUA DOVE *Oena capensis*. The smallest and only long-tailed dove of the region. Morocco only, rare. Rather like a large long-tailed sparrow or lark, the tail and the black of the male's face and throat being unmistakable. Call a weak 'koo, koo'. Flight fast and direct, showing much chestnut. Open bush country, palm groves. 11 in. (28 cm.).

DOVES

COLLARED DOVE

BARBARY DOVE

desert form

adult

imm.

TURTLE DOVE

Feral pigeon

RUFOUS TURTLE DOVE

PALM DOVE

♂

♀

NAMAQUA DOVE

173

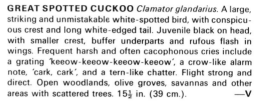

CUCKOOS: *Cuculidae.* Medium to large, rather slender, solitary arboreal birds, with tail long and graduated, and bill slightly decurved. All species in region (except Senegal Coucal) laying their eggs in other birds' nests.

GREAT SPOTTED CUCKOO *Clamator glandarius.* A large, striking and unmistakable white-spotted bird, with conspicuous crest and long white-edged tail. Juvenile black on head, with smaller crest, buffer underparts and rufous flash in wings. Frequent harsh and often cacophonous cries include a grating 'keeow-keeow-keeow-keeow', a crow-like alarm note, 'cark, cark', and a tern-like chatter. Flight strong and direct. Open woodlands, olive groves, savannas and other areas with scattered trees. 15½ in. (39 cm.).   **—V**

CUCKOO *Cuculus canorus.* Grey adult rather like a bird of prey, but can always be told by graduated tail, with white spots and tips, and non-hooked bill, and from male Sparrowhawk (p. 75) in particular by pointed wings. Rare hepatic form of adult female is rufous brown. Juvenile can be either grey or red-brown, with conspicuous white patch on nape and at first appears very round-winged. Well known 'coocooo' song of male has variants such as 'cooc-cooc-ooo'; hen has a 'water-bubbling' trill. Both make coughing and choking notes when excited. In distinctive low-wing flight wings are hardly raised above horizontal plane and depressed far down below body at bottom of downstroke. Very catholic in choice of habitat, from tundra, moors, heaths and forests to farmland, town parks, dunes and coastal marshes. 13 in. (33 cm.).   **●Sm   Map 137**

ORIENTAL CUCKOO or **MUTED CUCKOO** *Cuculus saturatus.* Slightly smaller but otherwise hardly distinguishable in field from Cuckoo, except by pale rufous underwing and call, a muffled hoopoe-like 'du-du, du-du', repeated six or eight times in succession, preceded by a more rapidly uttered quadrisyllabic version of the same notes. A shy skulking bird, especially in breeding season, when keeps to tree tops. In forested regions, especially dense pine and spruce forests. 12 in. (31 cm.).

YELLOW-BILLED CUCKOO *Coccyzus americanus.* A North American vagrant slenderer than Cuckoo, with conspicuous rufous flash in open wings and bold white spots on tail. Might utter a single 'coo'. 11–12½ in. (28–32 cm.).   **—V**

BLACK-BILLED CUCKOO *Coccyzus erythrophthalmus.* Another transatlantic vagrant, with less rufous in wings, smaller tail spots and all-black bill. 11–12 in. (28–31 cm.).   **—V**

SENEGAL COUCAL *Centropus senegalensis.* A very distinctive species, with its conspicuous rufous wings. Has a characteristic song, with a series of cooing or bubbling notes that run down and then up the scale. Shy and secretive, with a slow, rather clumsy flight, usually in thick cover in marshes or by rivers or streams; spends much time on ground. 16 in. (41 cm.).

CUCKOOS

agpie as host

imm.

GREAT SPOTTED
CUCKOO

Wren as host

CUCKOO

brown phase

ORIENTAL
CUCKOO

brown phase

YELLOW-BILLED
CUCKOO

BLACK-BILLED
CUCKOO

SENEGAL COUCAL

OWLS: *Tytonidae (Barn owl) and Strigidae (the rest)*.

pp. 177–83. Nocturnal birds of prey, though some species also hunt by day, with long rounded wings, short tail and feathered legs and feet. Head large, with large eyes facing forwards and set in a flattened facial disc, whose feathers usually conceal the short hooked bill. The ear tufts of a few species do not represent true ears. Plumage usually some shade of brown or white, with darker markings; sexes alike, except Snowy Owl. Flight of larger owls slow and flapping, of smaller ones quicker and markedly bounding. Stance upright. Nest in hole, in old nest of other bird, or on ground.

BARN OWL *Tyto alba.* White-breasted race *alba* is the only owl which is golden-buff above and white below, though most often seen ghost-like in the dusk, or caught in the headlights of a car, when it appears all-white. Dark-breasted race *guttata,* deep buff below and strongly marked grey-blue above, can be told from Tawny Owl (p. 183) in flight by its longer wings and at rest by its longer legs. Call a prolonged, strangled, almost blood-curdling screech; also hisses, snores and barks. Farmland and other open, often arid country, with scattered trees, feeding mainly on small rodents, frequently nesting in barns, churches and other old buildings. 13½ in. (34 cm.). ●R Map 138

SNOWY OWL *Nyctea scandiaca.* Huge size and predominantly white plumage make this an unmistakable owl; female appreciably larger than male, and with much more numerous blackish or brownish bars on upperparts. Usually silent away from breeding grounds, where male has a loud harsh bark and a deep hoot, and female a higher-pitched bark. Flight more buzzard-like than owl-like, often gliding. Frequently alights on ground. Tundra and high northern moorland, feeding mainly on lemmings and birds the size of Ptarmigan and Oystercatcher. Irruptions to S and W linked with fluctuations in lemming stocks. 21–26 in. (53–66 cm.). **ORw**

EAGLE OWL *Bubo bubo.* One of the two largest owls of the region, an enormous, almost eagle-sized bird, the prominent ear-tufts and facial disc distinguishing it from all diurnal birds of prey. Eyes large, orange. Cf. Great Grey Owl (p. 183). Song a deep 'oo-hu'; other calls include a harsh 'kveck, kveck'. Dense forests, coniferous and broad-leaved, also rocky gorges on mountains and in deserts, hunting at dawn and dusk for mammals as large as roe deer and birds as large as Capercaillie. 26–28 in. (66–71 cm.).   **—V**

BROWN FISH OWL *Ketupa zeylonensis.* Distinguished from Eagle Owl, by its much shorter ear tufts, unfeathered tarsi and feet, and more uniform plumage. Song a rather dismal moaning 'oomp-ooo-oo', with accent on middle syllable, also a single hoot. Forests, near water, feeding mainly on fish; spends much time on ground, even trampling out trails along stream banks. More strictly nocturnal than Eagle Owl. 22 in. (56 cm.).

white-breasted races

OWLS

BARN OWL

dark-breasted races

♂

♀

SNOWY OWL

N Africa

EAGLE OWL

BROWN FISH OWL

LONG-EARED OWL *Asio otus.* A medium-sized brown owl, the only one with long ear tufts, noticeably longer than Short-eared Owl's. Slimmer and with more elongated face than both Short-eared and Tawny Owls; further distinguished from Tawny (p. 183) by longer wings and orange-yellow eyes, and from Short-eared by lack of dark patch on upper wing. Has a more long-drawn-out, moaning hoot than Tawny Owl; young birds have a similar unoiled-hinge hunger cry. Forests, especially coniferous, areas with scattered trees and clumps, heaths, marshes, dunes, even large gardens; hunts mainly over open country. Nest usually in old nest of other bird. 14 in. (36 cm.).

⊙**Rmw   Map 139**

SHORT-EARED OWL *Asio flammeus.* Much the most likely medium-sized brown owl to be seen by day; ear-tufts rarely visible in field. Has conspicuously long wings, with which it soars, wheels and glides like a harrier, in addition to normal slow, flapping owl-like flight, and wing-clapping circular display flight. In flight shows blackish patch on both upper and under surface of wing at 'elbow'. Cf. Long-eared Owl and Tawny Owl (p. 183). Has a harsh barking flight note; song, a deep triple hoot, usually uttered in display flight. Open plains, moors, downs, rough hillsides, heaths, marshes, dunes. 15 in. (38 cm.).

●**RsmW   Map 140**

AFRICAN MARSH OWL *Asio capensis.* Smaller than Short-eared Owl, with longer ear-tufts, more uniformly brown upperparts, darker face, and brown eyes. Has a hoarse croak. Hunts, sometimes by day but regularly in dusk, usually in small parties, often flying close to an observer, normally quartering ground like a harrier. Marshes and swamps, feeding mainly on large insects. 12 in. (30 cm.).

SCOPS OWL *Otus scops.* In Europe the only small owl with ear-tufts, though these are not always very conspicuous, and unfeathered toes. Often adopts slim elongated posture. Most often detected by rather monotonous 'piu' call, not unlike single note of Redshank, repeated at short intervals, usually at night. Flight less markedly bounding than Little Owl (p. 181). Areas with scattered broad-leaved trees, open woodland, orchards, farmland, palm groves, parks, ruins, villages, small towns; feeding mainly on large insects. Largely nocturnal. 7½ in. (19 cm.).   —**V**

BRUCE'S SCOPS OWL or STRIATED SCOPS OWL *Otus brucei.* A paler eastern version of Scops Owl, with two distinct plumage phases, one basically yellow, the other basically grey-brown, and various intermediates. Some calls distinctive from Scops, the song 'ukh-ukh' and a warbling 'tsirr-va-vaa', but others identical. Habitat similar to Scops, in S Russia especially in cultivated countryside; often in semi-deserts. 8¼ in. (21 cm.).

OWLS

tree nester

LONG-EARED OWL

ground nester

SHORT-EARED OWL

AFRICAN MARSH OWL

brown phase

grey phase   SCOPS OWL

BRUCE'S SCOPS OWL

179

HAWK OWL *Surnia ulula.* The longest-tailed medium-sized owl of the region, the most hawk-like in appearance and habits, and the only one with barred underparts. Pale facial disc distinctively edged black, forming sideburns. Short wings, more pointed than other owls, combine with long tail to give hawk-like silhouette. Call, a chattering 'ki-ki-ki' also more hawk-like than owl-like. Habitually appears by day, perching, often conspicuously in inclined hawk-like attitude, flying low with final upward sweep to perch and sometimes hovering. Coniferous forests of northern taiga and mountains, also in other woods and thickets, especially on tundra. 14–16 in. (36–40 cm.). **—V**

PYGMY OWL *Glaucidium passerinum.* The smallest owl of the region. Relatively small head and less well marked facial disc than other owls are its best field marks, together with distinctive habit of flicking tail. Calls a whistling 'tyu-tyu-tyu' and 'kuvitt'; song more like Bullfinch's pipe than other owls' hoots. Hunts down small birds both by day and night. Coniferous forests, often dense, in taiga and on mountains, less often in other woods. Nests mainly in old woodpecker holes. 6½ in. (16·5 cm.).

TENGMALM'S OWL *Aegolius funereus.* The largest of the five smaller owls of the region, fully nocturnal, except in the Arctic. Only confusable with Little Owl, but is brown rather than grey-brown, with more fully feathered feet, adopts more upright stance, and has quite distinct facial expression. Where Little Owl has low-browed, frowning mien, Tengmalm's brows appear to be raised, as if slightly surprised, accentuated by blacker edge of facial disc and broader white eyebrows. Juvenile Tengmalm's uniformly rufous, including most of facial disc, except for eyebrows. Song a hoopoe-like succession of hoots, rising at first and falling at the end, sometimes in the form of a trill. Usually roosts in dense tree. Coniferous forests in hill districts and in the taiga, more rarely in mixed or deciduous woods. 10 in. (25 cm.). **—V**

Spotted Little Owl

SPOTTED LITTLE OWL *Athene brama.* Very like Little Owl, but underparts barred not spotted and white spots on head smaller. S Iraq. 8½ in. (22 cm.).

LITTLE OWL *Athene noctua.* Its partly diurnal habits make this the most familiar of the six smaller owls of the region, short tail and conspicuously bounding flight. Cf. Tengmalm's Owl (above). Call a loud ringing 'kiew, kiew', habitually uttered by day; song remarkably like opening sequence of Curlew's (p. 139) song. Juvenile has a shrill persistent wheeze. Often perches on posts and other prominent lookouts; bobs, waggles head, and may turn it through 180° when curious or suspicious. Often flies by night, and hovers for insects in dusk. Farmland and open country with scattered trees, open woodland, orchards, palm groves, dunes, semi-deserts, also marine islands and other treeless but rocky places. 8½ in. (22 cm.). **●R Map 141**

HAWK OWL

juv.

PYGMY OWL

juv.

TENGMALM'S OWL

Sinai
Palestine

LITTLE OWL

181

TAWNY OWL *Strix aluco.* Generally the commonest medium-sized brown owl; predominantly nocturnal and most often detected in daytime hunched up in its tree roost, being mobbed by smaller birds, when can be distinguished from Barn Owl by dark brown face and underparts and from Long-eared and Short-eared Owls (p. 179) by black eyes and lack of ear-tufts. When seen by day, it appears shorter-winged than these three, and larger and stouter in build than Barn and Long-eared. Very variable in ground colour, from rich chestnut tawny through various shades of buff, brown and grey-brown to greyish-white; juvenile barred. Most familiar note is long quavering hoot, but equally often heard, especially from young birds in late summer and autumn, is a sharp 'ke-wick'. (These two notes are origin of traditional 'tu-whit, tu-whoo'). Juveniles in or just out of nest may make a sound remarkably like a gate on an unoiled hinge. Open, mainly deciduous, woodland, parkland, large gardens and other areas with scattered trees, not uncommon in villages, towns and some cities. Nest usually in tree holes. Feeds mainly on small birds and rodents. 15 in. (38 cm.).

●R   Map 142

HUME'S TAWNY OWL *Strix butleri.* One of the least known owls in the world, very rarely reliably observed in the field; upperparts buff with greyer wings and distinct golden collar; Tawny Owl can be so pale that unfeathered toes of Hume's are only really good distinction; perhaps black-tipped crown feathers would show a darker crown in the field. Flight direct but laboured. Song a clear drawn-out 'huu', also a more quavering hoot. Among rocks and in palm groves near rocks. In our region only known from four or five localities. 15 in. (38 cm.).

GREAT GREY OWL *Strix nebulosa.* One of the giant owls of the region, about the size of an Eagle Owl (p. 177), but with longer tail, rounder head and no ear tufts, smaller yellow eyes set in a facial disc with concentric dark rings, and a black patch on the chin. Cf. Ural Owl. Song and calls both resemble Tawny Owl, but hoot much deeper. Coniferous forests, often hunting by day for mammals as large as squirrels and lemmings. Nest usually in old nest of other bird. 27 in. (69 cm.).

URAL OWL *Strix uralensis.* Only a little smaller than Great Grey Owl, from which it differs chiefly in dark eyes, unlined facial disc, and no black patch on chin. From paler forms of much smaller Tawny Owl, differs also in its long tail, which hangs down in flight, and relatively smaller eyes. Hoot more muffled than Tawny's, also a barking 'khau, khau' and a harsher version of Tawny's 'ke-wick'. Forests, coniferous, deciduous and mixed, sometimes in villages and large cities, often hunting by day for mammals up to the size of a red squirrel and birds up to the size of a Hazelhen. 24 in. (61 cm.).

OWLS

grey phase

brown phase

TAWNY OWL

HUME'S TAWNY OWL

GREAT GREY OWL

URAL OWL

NIGHTJARS: *Caprimulgidae*. Exclusively nocturnal birds, well adapted by their long wings and tail, large eyes and gape, and small bill and feet, to catch moths, beetles and other flying insect prey by night; seen by day only when flushed from the ground or perched on a branch (normally horizontally along it), being well camouflaged by their mottled brown plumage. Sexes more or less alike. Flight silent, and very agile, gliding and wheeling, with sudden darts after prey. Southern species often sit in dirt roads or sandy tracks and appear in car headlights. Eggs laid on bare ground.

NIGHTJAR *Caprimulgus europaeus*. The only widespread nightjar of the region, most often detected by its song, a far-carrying churr, sustained but with occasional abrupt changes of pitch, not usually heard till 45–60 minutes after sunset. When flushed, appears a long-winged, long-tailed, hawk-like bird, readily told from all birds of prey by its very short, straight bill, and from juvenile Cuckoo (p. 175) by unbarred underparts and no white patch on nape. Male has white tips to outer tail feathers and three white spots on outer wing quills. Call a soft but insistent 'cu-ic', also makes a whip-crack sound by clapping wings together. Open woodlands, forest edges, patches of felled woodland, heaths, low moors, open country with scattered trees, semi-deserts. 10½ in. (27 cm.).   ⊙**Sm   Map 143**

RED-NECKED NIGHTJAR *Caprimulgus ruficollis*. Larger and paler than Nightjar, with a conspicuous rufous collar and white throat patch, and more conspicuous white wing and tail spots, the female also having pale spots. Song quite distinct, a rapid loud echoing repetition of 'kutuk'. Dry open country and semi-deserts, with scattered trees and shrubs. 12 in. (31 cm.).   **—V**

NUBIAN NIGHTJAR *Caprimulgus nubicus*. A small pale greyish nightjar with a rufous collar and very conspicuous white tips to outer tail feathers, male also with white spots on wing tips. Tamarisk, thorn and other scrub, desert edges, roosting by day in shade of rocks or bushes. 8½ in. (22 cm.).

EGYPTIAN NIGHTJAR *Caprimulgus aegyptius*. Like a pale, sandy Nightjar, with a conspicuous white throat patch, but the white tail and wing spots obscure or non-existent. Song very variously described, 'tukl-tukl', 'kre-kre-kre', at times turning to clear 'u' or 'o' with metallic timbre, and nightjar-like churr. Deserts and semi-deserts, often hunting close to bedouin and other nomad encampments. In Iraq is sometimes forced to move in daytime when ground gets too hot for it to rest on. 10 in. (25 cm.)   **—V**

AMERICAN NIGHTHAWK *Chordeiles minor*. A rare transatlantic vagrant, easily distinguished from all nightjars of the region by conspicuous white wing patches; also has white chin and in male, white bar near end of tail. Call a nasal 'peent' or 'peeik'. 8½–10 in. (22–25 cm.)   **—V**

NIGHTJARS

NIGHTJAR

RED-NECKED NIGHTJAR

NUBIAN NIGHTJAR

EGYPTIAN NIGHTJAR

AMERICAN NIGHTHAWK

I·VIII·70

185

SWIFTS: *Apodidae.* The most aerial of all birds, superficially resembling swallows and martins, feeding on flying insects. Plumage brown or blackish, sometimes with white patches. Sexes alike. Narrow, scythe-like wings, short usually forked tail adapted to very fast flight. Short legs for clinging on vertical surfaces; very rarely on ground. Nest in hole or crevice of natural or artificial cliff, often in towns and villages, the material being glued together with saliva.

SWIFT *Apus apus.* Easily told from the swallow tribe by short tail and long curved wings, as well as by all dark plumage, apart from whitish throat, rather more obvious in juvenile which also has pale tips to wing feathers. Cf. Pallid Swift and Plain Swift. Has vigorous dashing flight, wheeling and gliding, and excited squealing parties chase each other round the houses in towns and villages. Normal cry a harsh scream. Feeds over fresh water, open country and built-up areas. 6½ in. (16·5 cm.). ●**Sm   Map 144**

PALLID SWIFT *Apus pallidus.* Very hard to separate from Swift, even in good light, but is distinctly paler brown and has more conspicuous white throat patch, rather paler forehead and slight contrast between paler secondaries and rest of wing; also slightly different outline, especially broader head, and slower wing-beats. Cf. Plain Swift. Spends longer at breeding colonies, but otherwise as Swift, with which often flies. 6½ in. (16·5 cm.).

ALPINE SWIFT *Apus melba.* The largest swift of the region, with a 21-inch wing-span, easily told by its pale brown plumage, with white underparts crossed by brown breastband. Parties utter a loud trilling whistle, rising and falling in pitch. Flight even more vigorous and powerful than Swift. 8½ in. (22 cm.).   **—A**

WHITE-RUMPED SWIFT *Apus caffer.* Larger and rather more uniformly dark than Little Swift, and with a markedly narrower white rump and distinctly forked tail. Has a more guttural twittering call, and is less noisy. Uses old nests of Red-rumped and other swallows. 5½ in. (14 cm.).

LITTLE SWIFT or HOUSE SWIFT *Apus affinis.* Much the smallest swift of the region, distinguished by short square tail, and from all except White-rumped Swift by conspicuous broad white rump; throat whitish. Cf. House Martin. Call a high-pitched twittering trill. 4¾ in. (12 cm.).   **—V**

PLAIN SWIFT *Apus unicolor.* Rather smaller and darker than Swift and Pallid Swift, differing especially in its dark throat and faster flight. Screams and has a rapid trill. Canaries and Madeira only. 6 in. (15 cm.).

NEEDLE-TAILED SWIFT *Hirundapus caudacutus.* A rare vagrant from E Asia. Very short square tail and conspicuous white horseshoe on adult underparts. 7½ in. (19 cm.).   **—V**

Needle-tailed
Swift

Plain Swift

186

SWIFTS

SWIFT

PALLID
SWIFT

ALPINE
SWIFT

WHITE-RUMPED
SWIFT

LITTLE SWIFT

PLAIN SWIFT

187

BEE-EATERS: *Meropidae.*

Gregarious brightly coloured long-winged, long-tailed, terres.ial birds, with sexes more or less alike; bill long, slightly curved. Perching on wires or bush tops on look out for bees, wasps and other flying insects; flight swallow-like, with long glides on triangular wings and tremendous acceleration to capture prey, after which they return to perch with a graceful upward sweep and batter it to death before swallowing it. Open country with scattered trees and bushes, often near rivers, in whose sandy banks and in the sides of sand and gravel pits they dig their usually colonial nest holes.

BEE-EATER *Merops apiaster.* The most widespread bee-eater of the region, and the only bird with harlequin plumage and central tail feathers slightly projecting likely to be seen over the greater part of it. Mainly blue-green, with chestnut head and mantle, yellow rump and throat, and black breast-band and stripe through eye. Yellow rump and pale chestnut underwing with black trailing edge especially noticeable in flight. Flight-note a distinctive, constantly uttered liquid 'quilp', also a throaty 'kroop, kroop'. 11 in. (28 cm.) **—A(b)**

BLUE-CHEEKED BEE-EATER *Merops superciliosus.* Looks much greener than Bee-eater, and has much longer central tail feathers, blue cheeks, chestnut throat, and no black breast-band. Call hardly distinguishable, but tends to be shriller and less loud. 12 in. (31 cm.). **—V**

LITTLE GREEN BEE-EATER *Merops orientalis.* Predominantly green, and differing from Blue-cheeked Bee-eater, with which it overlaps in Egypt and the Middle East, in its markedly smaller size, green throat with black breast band, and much less blue on face, head and neck being tinged red-brown. Call a chattering 'tit, tit' or 'tree-tree-tree'. 10 in. (25 cm.).

ROLLERS: *Coraciidae.*

Brightly coloured crow-like terrestrial birds, with sexes more or less alike, named from their somersaulting habits in courtship display. Bill stout, slightly hooked. Often perch conspicuously on posts, wires or bush tops, flying down to capture beetles, lizards and other small animals on ground. Hole nesters.

ROLLER *Coracias garrulus.* Over most of the region, the only crow-sized bird, apart from Jay (p. 305), to show a bright blue wing-patch in flight, but a much larger blue patch than Jay, wings appearing blue with black tips and edges. At rest resembles a smallish blue-green crow with a chestnut back. Flight direct, woodpigeon-like. Call a harsh, rather crow-like 'rack, kack', kacker'. All kinds of open country with scattered trees, scrub, parkland, open woods, tree-lined roads. 12 in. (31 cm.). **—A**

INDIAN ROLLER or BLUE JAY *Coracias benghalensis.* Differs from Roller in its chestnut breast as well as mantle. Voice croaking and heron-like, a loud quacking clatter and a staccato 'k'yow, k'yow'. S Iraq only. 13 in. (33 cm.).

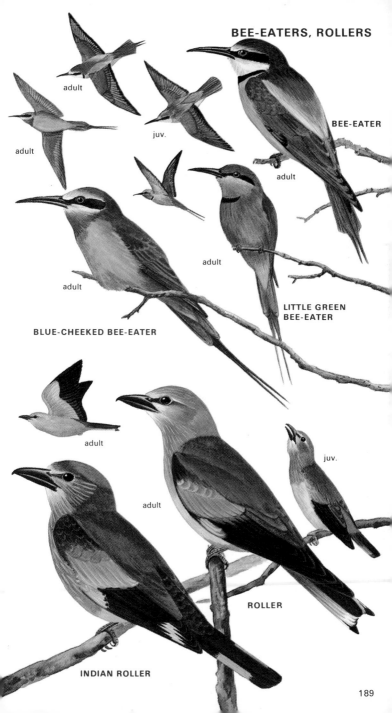

BEE-EATERS, ROLLERS

adult

adult

juv.

BEE-EATER

adult

adult

adult

**LITTLE GREEN
BEE-EATER**

adult

BLUE-CHEEKED BEE-EATER

adult

adult

juv.

adult

ROLLER

INDIAN ROLLER

RING-NECKED PARAKEET *Psittacula krameri* (Psittacidae). The only parrot of the region, conspicuously long-tailed, green, with hooked red bill, male with black throat and narrow rose-pink collar on hind neck. Flies with fast clipped wingbeats, always uttering its shrill, monosyllabic screech. Gregarious, frequenting areas with trees; a hole-nester. 16 in. (41 cm.) (including tail 10 in. [25 cm.]).

● **KINGFISHERS:** *Alcedinidae.* Medium-sized birds with short legs, long stout bill, brightly coloured plumage and habit of perching upright. Sexes alike. Not all feeding on fish. Hole nesters.

KINGFISHER *Alcedo atthis.* One of the most brilliantly coloured birds of the region, the only one with plumage all blue-green above and all rich chestnut below; tail short, bill black, base reddish in female, legs red. Call a loud shrill penetrating 'cheee' or 'chikeee'; song, rarely heard, a whistling trill. Lowland fresh water of all kinds, in winter also on estuaries and sea coast; dives either from a perch or while hovering to catch fish. 6½ in. (16·5 cm.).   ●R **Map 145**

SMYRNA KINGFISHER *Halcyon smyrnensis.* Striking and unmistakable, with contrast of chestnut, bright blue and white; feet and massive bill red. In flight white bar shows on underwing. Very vocal, with a loud laughing cry. Cultivated land, gardens, open plains, forests, fresh water, sea coast. 10½ in. (27 cm.).

LESSER PIED KINGFISHER *Ceryle rudis.* Equally striking and unmistakable with its all black and white plumage, but always associated with water. Male has two black bands on breast, female only one; head crested. Call a sharp penetrating 'keek, keek'; also a whistling note; small parties often collectively noisy. Fresh water, except in forests or high on mountains, and estuaries; characteristically fishes by hovering with beating wings, then plummeting into water. 10 in. (25 cm.).

BELTED KINGFISHER *Ceryle alcyon.* Rare vagrant from N America, with dark head and crest, grey back and breast-band, chestnut breast-band and flanks (in female only) and white throat, neck and underparts. 11–14 in. (28–35 cm.).

HOOPOE *Upupa epops* (Upupidae). Quite unmistakable, with long curved dark bill and prominent black-tipped crest, either folded down or erected fan-wise. Plumage pinkish-cinnamon; tail and rounded wings strongly barred black and white so that in flight looks like huge round-winged black and white moth. Chief call a rapid far-carrying clipped 'hoo-hoo-hoo', less musical than Cuckoo (p. 175) and less drawn-out and quavering than Tawny Owl (p. 183). Grassy and wooded plains, farmland, orchards, vineyards, parks and gardens; a hole nester. 11 in. (28 cm.). ○M(b) **Map 146**

PARAKEETS, KINGFISHERS, HOOPOE

KINGFISHER

♂

♀

RING-NECKED PARAKEET

LESSER PIED
KINGFISHER

♂

♀

SMYRNA
KINGFISHER

HOOPOE

♂

BELTED KINGFISHER

191

Terrestrial birds highly adapted to climbing about trees, extracting insect prey from their bark and rotten wood, and also excavating nest holes: tail stiff (except in Wryneck), to act as support against vertical surfaces, with zygodactyl feet (two toes pointing forwards, two backwards) but one toe vestigial; legs short, bill stout (except Wryneck), and tongue very long. Tail square, but may appear forked when pressed against tree trunk. Male usually with red patch on head. Flight markedly undulating or dipping; gait a hop. Most species of region drum in spring, a mechanical sound made by resonance of dead branches under rapid blows from bill, and resembling sound of small metal clappers on wooden sounding board, or creaking of dead branch. Always associated with trees, though some species regularly feed on ground. Nest in hole in tree; no nest material.

BLACK WOODPECKER *Dryocopus martius*. Much the largest woodpecker of the region, and the most distinctive, male being the only large all-black land bird with red crown and crest; female and juvenile browner, female with red on nape only. Has a distinctly angular way of holding its neck, which alone should suffice to distinguish from any other woodpecker seen against the light. Flight very markedly undulating. Far-carrying voice a loud, clear, vibrant, fluty string of double notes; also a single repeated musical yelp. Drums, with appreciably longer phrase than Great Spotted Woodpecker (p. 195). Coniferous forests, also mixed and sometimes beech woodland. 18 in. (46 cm.).

GREY-HEADED WOODPECKER *Picus canus*. Superficially like a small Green Woodpecker, but head and underparts predominantly grey, male has red on forehead only, female has no red at all, and black moustachial streaks are much narrower. Juvenile browner, with barred flanks. Call like Green Woodpecker, but more musical, slower and falling away at the end. Habitat similar. 10 in. (25 cm.).

GREEN WOODPECKER *Picus viridis*. Readily distinguished from all other birds of region, except Grey-headed Woodpecker, by combination of green plumage, conspicuous yellow-green rump in flight, and red on head. Both sexes have red crown and black moustachial stripe, male has red moustachial stripe also. Juvenile paler but speckled darker. Spanish race *sharpei* has grey cheeks with narrower black moustaches; North African race *levaillanti*, treated by some as a species, similar, but male lacks red moustache and female has red only on nape or back of crown (fortunately Grey-headed Woodpecker does not extend S of the Loire). Spring call a loud, ringing, far-carrying 'plue-plue-plue', at other times various loud yelping cries. Exceptionally drums, with a light rattling sound. Broad-leaved and mixed forests, and all kinds of well timbered country, including parks, large gardens, and roadside trees. Also feeds on ground, especially on lawns and at anthills. 12½ in. (32 cm.). ●R   **Map 147**

WOODPECKERS

Crow

♀

♂

BLACK WOODPECKER

♀

GREY-HEADED WOODPECKER

♀

juv.

Green
Iberian
Peninsula

♂

Green
N W Africa

♂

♂

♂

♀

GREEN WOODPECKER

193

Spotted Woodpeckers: *Dendrocopos.* pp. 195–97. Black and white woodpeckers, distinguished from each other and from the Three-toed Woodpecker (p. 197) as follows:

Red on crown: Syrian juv., Great Spotted juv., White-backed male and (faint) juv., Middle Spotted adult and juv., Lesser Spotted male and juv.; *on nape:* Great Spotted male, Syrian male; *on breast:* N. African Great Spotted male; *under tail coverts:* Great spotted adult and juv., Syrian adult and juv., White-backed adult and juv., Middle Spotted adult and juv.

Yellow on crown: Three-toed male.

Large white patch on wing: Great Spotted adult and juv., Syrian adult and juv., Middle Spotted adult and juv.

Wings mainly barred: White-backed adult and juv., Lesser Spotted adult and juv.; *mainly black:* Three-toed.

SYRIAN WOODPECKER *Dendrocopos syriacus.* Very similar to Great Spotted, and chiefly distinguished by white face due to absence of black bar on side of neck; from Middle Spotted and White-backed distinguished by lack of red crown, and from White-backed also by large white wing patch. Juvenile further distinguished from Middle Spotted by moustachial streak reaching bill, and obscure reddish breast band. Voice similar to Great Spotted, also has a liquid moorhen-like note. Habitat as Great Spotted, which within range of Syrian is largely confined to mountain forests; steadily spreading into Europe from the south-east. 9 in. (23 cm.).

GREAT SPOTTED WOODPECKER or PIED WOOD-PECKER *Dendrocopos major.* Over most of the region the commonest black and white woodpecker, with prominent white patch on each wing and red under tail coverts; male with black crown and red nape, and juvenile with both crown and nape red. Male of N African race *numidus* has red on breast. Flight conspicuously bounding, wings being folded against body at bottom of each bound. Usual call note a sharp 'tchick', also various trills and titters and a harsh mistle-thrush-like churring note when excited. Drums frequently in spring, with 8–10 blows lasting for one second only. Coniferous, broad-leaved and mixed forests, areas with scattered trees, parks, orchards, large gardens. 9 in. (23 cm.).
●Rmw **Map 148**

MIDDLE SPOTTED WOODPECKER *Dendrocopos medius.* The smallest of the three spotted woodpeckers that have a conspicuous white patch on each wing, a feature at once distinguishing it from the three on p. 197, while its red crown separates it from adult Great Spotted and Syrian, as well as Three-toed and female Lesser Spotted. From juvenile Great Spotted and Syrian it can be told by the gap between its black cheek stripe and black nape, and no black stripe bordering red crown. A restless bird, appearing very barred in flight. Has a repeated 'kik' note, and a 'song' rendered as 'wait, wait' uttered slowly on a rising or falling scale. Drums much less often than Great Spotted. Habitat as Great Spotted, but not in pure conifer forests. 8½ in. (22 cm.).

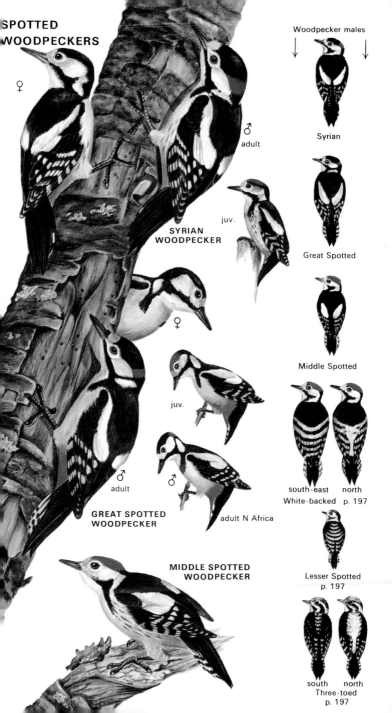

SPOTTED WOODPECKERS

♀

♂
adult

Woodpecker males
↓   ↓

Syrian

juv.

SYRIAN
WOODPECKER

♀

Great Spotted

juv.

Middle Spotted

♂
adult

♂
adult N Africa

GREAT SPOTTED
WOODPECKER

MIDDLE SPOTTED
WOODPECKER

south-east   north
White-backed   p. 197

Lesser Spotted
p. 197

south   north
Three-toed p. 197

WHITE-BACKED WOODPECKER *Dendrocopos leucotos*. The largest black and white woodpecker of the region, differing from all the others, except much smaller Three-toed, in its white or barred rump; from the three on p. 195 in its lack of any white patch on wing, which consequently looks mainly barred, and from Great Spotted and Syrian also by male's red crown and face pattern of both sexes, with black bar on side of neck not joining black nape, as in Middle Spotted. Red of juvenile, both on crown and under tail coverts, is rather pale. Voice not so loud as Great Spotted. Drums with single blows merging into a volley, resembling a creaking branch. Woodland, mainly broad-leaved, less often in areas of scattered trees. 10 in. (25 cm.).

LESSER SPOTTED WOODPECKER or BARRED WOODPECKER *Dendrocopos minor*. The smallest woodpecker of the region, the size of a Hedgesparrow (p. 221); barred appearance is distinctive. Lack of red on under tail coverts distinguishes from all other black and white woodpeckers, except Three-toed. Female is only black and white woodpecker with no red, except Three-toed. Commonest note a rather weak, flat 'pee-pee-pee-pee-pee', not unlike Wryneck but lacking its ringing quality. Less often utters a 'tchik', weaker and more sibilant than Great Spotted's (p. 195). Drums fairly often in spring, not so loud as Great Spotted, but lasting longer, two seconds, with 10–30 blows. Mixed and broad-leaved forests, and areas with scattered timber, such as orchards, parks, large gardens. 5¾ in. (14·5 cm.). ⊙R **Map 149**

THREE-TOED WOODPECKER *Picoides tridactylus*. The most distinctive black and white woodpecker of the region; the only one with mainly black wings, the only one, except White-backed, with a white rump, and the only one, except female Lesser Spotted, with no red at all; male is also the only one with any yellow, on crown. Has various notes resembling Great Spotted but softer. Drums, but rather slowly. Old coniferous forests, also in willow and birch in far north. 8¾ in. (22 cm.).

WRYNECK *Jynx torquilla*. The least woodpecker-like woodpecker of the region, with a longish tail that makes it more like a small brown shrike or a large warbler. From Treecreeper (p. 273) can easily be told by larger size, longer tail, straight bill and brown underparts. Flight less undulating than the true woodpeckers; on ground, where often feeds, hops with tail raised. Call a loud, clear, rather musical 'kew-kew-kew-kew-kew', somewhat like calls of Nuthatch (p. 271), Lesser Spotted Woodpecker or Kestrel (p. 95) and other small birds of prey. Open broad-leaved woodlands, and areas with scattered trees, including parks, orchards and large gardens. Nest normally in tree hole, will use nestbox. 6½ in. (16·5 cm.). ○sM **Map 150**

WOODPECKERS

Woodpecker females

♀

♂

WHITE-BACKED WOODPECKER

Syrian p. 195

♂

♀

Great Spotted p. 195

LESSER SPOTTED WOODPECKER

Middle Spotted p. 195

♀

THREE-TOED WOODPECKER

White-backed

♂

WRYNECK

Lesser Spotted

Three-toed

LARKS: *Alaudidae.* pp. 199–205. The first of the passerine or song-bird families (see p. 10). Small to medium ground-living birds, mostly with sober plumage, sexes alike, and moderately thin bills adapted to both an insect and a seed diet. Song well developed, usually delivered in the air. Larks walk or run but do not hop.

SHORE LARK *Eremophila alpestris.* At a distance appears just like any other lark, though somewhat less streaked than, e.g., Skylark (p. 205), but at close quarters easily told by black and yellow pattern on head, and by male's small black 'horns' in breeding plumage. Has some white in tail which, however, looks mainly black in flight, especially from below. Cf. Temminck's Horned Lark. Song recalls Skylark's, but is briefer, and in its most developed form uttered only from the ground or a stone, also sings frequently, but often only in snatches, in the air. Commonest call is a quite audible-like 'tsip' or 'tseep', similar to Rock Pipit (p. 210) or Yellow Wagtail (p. 212); also a thin, falling 'si-di-wi'. Flight more undulating than Skylark; can run very fast. Breeds in rocky ground in high Arctic or in alpine zones of mountains, but regularly winters on coast, e.g. in Britain, sometimes in company with Snow or Lapland Buntings (p. 281). 6½ in. (16·5 cm.). ○**W   Map 151**

TEMMINCK'S HORNED LARK *Eremophila bilopha.* Smaller, paler and more sandy coloured than Shore Lark, with white instead of yellow on the head, and found only in stony or sandy desert, often quite devoid of vegetation. Voice similar, but call more disyllabic, and song less vigorous, though more often in song flight, with no final plumb drop. 5½ in. (14 cm.)´

BLACK-CROWNED FINCH-LARK *Eremopterix nigriceps.* A small bird much more finch-like than lark-like, male very distinctive with black crown and underparts, but female just like many other small sandy desert passerines; told in flight by black underwing. Twittering song in soaring display flight, followed by butterfly-like descent with wings raised and a final plumb drop. When disturbed may fly round in a circle; on ground does not hop like finches. Unlike most other larks of the desert crouches when stops running. Dry sandy wastes with very sparse vegetation. 4½ in. (11 cm.).

HOOPOE LARK or BIFASCIATED LARK *Alaemon alaudipes.* One of the largest and most distinctive larks, larger than a Skylark (p. 205), with a long slightly curved bill and striking black and white wing-pattern, both features somewhat recalling Hoopoe (p. 191). Prolonged musical whistling and piping song may be uttered on ground or during display flight, when male spirals conspicuously upwards and descends again on outstretched wings, with a final plumb drop. Not very gregarious, and could be mistaken for small courser when running on ground; when it stops does not squat but stands erect. A desert bird. 7½ in. (19 cm.).

LARKS

juv.

winter

N Europe
adult

S E Europe
Asia Minor

SHORE LARK

Morocco

juv.

adult

**TEMMINCK'S
HORNED LARK**

♀

♂

**BLACK-CROWNED
FINCH-LARK**

adult

juv.

HOOPOE LARK

SHORT-TOED LARK *Calandrella cinerea.* Smaller and paler, especially beneath, than Skylark (p. 205), with no crest, shorter bill, unstreaked underparts and a distinctive small dark patch on each side of breast, not always easy to see in the field. Cf. Lesser Short-toed Lark. Song a simple sustained repetition of a few musical notes, often ending with a wistful phrase recalling Willow Warbler (p. 237), usually uttered in aerial display with bird bobbing up and down like a slowly manipulated yo-yo, and with no final plumb drop. Calls include the conversational sparrow-like 'tchi-tchirrp', a short rattling note when flushed, and a 'tee-oo' anxiety note. Has a lark-like flight and on the ground a pipit-like stance. Dry, bare, often sandy ground, steppes, cultivations, semi-deserts, dunes. 5½ in. (14 cm.).
—**A**

LESSER SHORT-TOED LARK *Calandrella rufescens.* Very like Short-toed Lark but greyer and only certainly distinguishable when dark streaks on breast of Lesser Short-toed can be seen. Lacks dark patches on side of breast and slightly capped appearance. Song similar, but usually preceded by a 'prrrit' note and often includes mimicked phrases; uttered in rising spiral or circular flight. Habitat similar, but stonier and less grassy, often at drier margins of marshes. 5½ in. (14 cm.).
—**V**

DESERT LARK *Ammomanes deserti.* Sandy coloured and varying greatly in shade according to the dominant colour of its normal habitat; has some dark but no white feathers in tail. Cf. Bar-tailed Desert Lark and Dupont's Lark; both short-toed larks are partly streaked and have white in tail. Call a plaintive 'tweet'. Deserts, semi-deserts, wadis, rocky and stony ground, sometimes with scattered trees, not normally flocking. 5¾ in. (15 cm.).

BAR-TAILED DESERT LARK *Ammomanes cincturus.* Smaller and less variable than Desert Lark, from which readily distinguished by dark bar at tip of tail. Song weak, fluty, slightly reminiscent of child's trumpet. Fast and sometimes rather jerky flight, running swiftly with frequent sudden stops. More exclusively a desert bird than Desert Lark, usually avoiding bushes and even rocks; frequently seen in small flocks. 5¼ in. (13 cm.).

DUPONT'S LARK *Chersophilus duponti.* Intermediate between Skylark (p. 205) and Short-toed Lark in size, and differing from both in long curved bill, from Skylark in lack of crest and from both short-toed larks in markedly streaked breast. General appearance varies between brown and rufous. Cf. Hoopoe Lark (p. 199). Has a rather nasal song, an even more nasal, greenfinch-like 'dweeje' and a double whistle on a rising scale, 'hoo-hee'. A shy bird, much preferring to run than to fly. Scrub and grassy steppes. 6¼ in. (16 cm.).

LARKS

SHORT-TOED LARK

juv.

LESSER SHORT-TOED LARK

DESERT LARK

BAR-TAILED
DESERT LARK

Morocco to
Central Tunisia

Central Algeria
to N W Egypt

DUPONT'S LARK

Calandra Larks: *Melanocorypha*. Heavily built larks with stout seed-eating bills. Steppes and other any open grassy country.

CALANDRA LARK *Melanocorypha calandra*. A large plump lark, with broad triangular wings and a large black patch on each side of neck. In flight trailing edge of wing is conspicuously white and contrasts with dark underside; cf. Bimaculated Lark. No crest; white outer tail feathers. cf. female Black Lark. Skylark-like song, including both frequent notes mimicked from other birds, and its own jangling corn-bunting-like 'kleetra' call note, uttered either in high wide circular song flight, or lower down with curious slow wing action, or even on ground. Grassy steppes with low scrubby vegetation, cultivations, dry stony ground. 7½ in. (19 cm.).   —V

BIMACULATED LARK *Melanocorypha bimaculata*. Smaller and more rufous than Calandra Lark, with much smaller black neck patches. Most readily distinguished by white eyestripe, no white wing-bar, and white at tip of tail, not on outer feathers. Habits similar. Breeds higher up in mountains, and in winter more often in semi-deserts. 6½ in. (16·5 cm.).   —V

WHITE-WINGED LARK *Melanocorypha leucoptera*. Differs from Calandra Lark most obviously in its much broader white wing-bar, but is also more rufous, especially on male's crown, has narrower wings and lacks the black neck patches. Song like Skylark (p. 205), delivered either in soaring aerial song flight, or flying nearer ground, or on rock or hummock on ground. Dry grassy steppes, stony wastes and semi-deserts. 7 in. (18 cm.).   —V

BLACK LARK *Melanocorypha yeltoniensis*. Male easily distinguished from all other larks by all black summer plumage; in winter black becomes browner. Female and juvenile have no distinctive features, differing from Calandra and White-winged Larks in lack of white in wing. Song like Skylark (p. 205), but in shorter bursts, uttered more often on ground than in low circular owl-like song flights. Flight note also like Skylark, and a piping call note. Grassy, scrubby and in winter also cultivated steppes. 7½ in. (19 cm.)

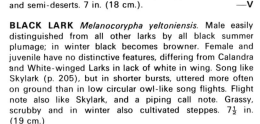

THICK-BILLED LARK *Rhamphocorys clot-bey*. Much the stoutest-billed lark, with breast conspicuously dark-spotted, and black and white patches on each wing and each side of neck. White wing-patches conspicuous in flight. Has very erect carriage, holding head high or even slightly backwards; runs very fast and does not squat but stands upright when stops. Song and song flight distinctive. Calls varied, a low 'coo-ee' and 'sree', and a 'co-ep' flight note. A desert bird, mainly in stony hammada desert, also in grassy wadis. 6¾ in. (17 cm.).

LARKS

CALANDRA
LARK

BIMACULATED LARK

♂

♀

BLACK LARK

WHITE-WINGED LARK

THICK-BILLED
LARK

203

WOODLARK *Lullula arborea*. In flight has noticeably shorter tail than adult Skylark, giving it an almost bat-like outline; young skylarks in late summer and autumn are never quite so short-tailed. Crest not always visible in field. Buff eyestripes meeting on nape, blackish and white mark on leading edge of wing, tail with white tip but no white outer feathers. Mellow fluty song, quite different from Skylark's, often on an interrupted descending scale, usually delivered in circular song flight, sometimes at night. Flight and call note, 'tit-looeet'. All kinds of country with scattered trees, woodland verges, heaths, parkland, alpine meadows, farmland, orchards, olive groves. 6 in. (15 cm.). ⊙R   **Map 152**

SKYLARK *Alauda arvensis*. A rather large plain brown lark, with an often inconspicuous crest, and white outer feathers in fairly long tail. Juvenile has no crest and shorter tail. Best field mark is sustained warbling song, normally delivered in the air, both while ascending and descending almost vertically, and while hovering. Final plummet silent. Flight and call note a liquid 'chirrup'. Crouches rather than runs when disturbed. Flocks on migration and in winter. Open country, farmland, grassland, heaths and moors, alpine meadows, dunes. 7 in. (18 cm.).   ●RmW   **Map 153**

SMALL SKYLARK *Alauda gulgula*. Smaller, but very similar to Skylark, differing chiefly in its thicker bill, and somewhat shorter tail with conspicuous buff edges. Sings more often from a perch. Rare visitor, S Iraq. 6 in. (15 cm.).

CRESTED LARK *Galerida cristata*. Distinguished from Skylark chiefly by longer crest being always erect and conspicuous, and buff instead of white outer feathers in shorter tail; also in flight by orange-buff patch on underwing. Bill slightly curved. Cf. Thekla Lark. Song more plaintive and reedier than Skylark's, and in shorter phases, often mimetic, sometimes delivered in air, but never with soaring display of Skylark. Call a liquid trisyllable 'whe-whee-ooo', rising from first to second and than falling again; also a high-pitched double note. Dry waste, stony and sandy ground, dunes, semi-deserts, wadis, cultivations, oases, also in and around towns and villages, building sites, railway sidings and similar rough places. 6¾ in. (17 cm.).   —V

THEKLA LARK *Galerida theklae*. Not reliably distinguishable from Crested Lark in the field, though tends to have shorter bill and greyer underwing. Best distinction is song, more like Skylark and Short-toed Lark (p. 201), and still more mimetic, delivered either in a fluttering circular display flight, followed by an earthward plummet or, rather more often than Crested Lark, from a bush top or even a tree. Prefers more broken ground, often with scrub, and avoids towns and villages. 6¾ in. (17 cm.).

LARKS

song flights

juv.

adult

WOODLARK

juv.

adult

adult

SKYLARK

juv.

adult

adult

pale form

CRESTED LARK

juv.

adult

adult

adult

pale form

THEKLA LARK

SWALLOWS and MARTINS: *Hirundinidae*. Small slender short-necked aerial birds, with long wings, forked tail and short flattened bill with wide gape; wings relatively shorter than swifts (p. 187). Flight graceful, often fast Gregarious, often feeding over fresh water.

SWALLOW *Hirundo rustica*. The commonest hirundine of the region, easily told by chestnut throat and forehead; adult has long tail streamers, but juvenile has shorter fork. Most frequent call is twittering 'tswit, tswit, tswit'; alarm note a shrill 'tsink, tsink'. Pleasant twittering song, 'feetafeet, feetafeetit'. Usually breeds in buildings. 7½ in. (19 cm.).
●Sm Map 154

CRAG MARTIN *Hirundo rupestris*. Differs from Sand Martin mainly in its brownish underparts, with speckled throat but no marked breast band, also has dark mark on underwing and conspicuous white spots under tail. Juvenile rather more rufous. Cf. also Pale Crag Martin and Plain Sand Martin. Song and call notes both rather feeble and twittering. Breeds on inland and sea cliffs and buildings, sometimes in towns. 5¾ in. (14·5 cm.).

RED-RUMPED SWALLOW *Hirundo daurica*. Readily distinguished by rufous-buff rump and chestnut nape; no white spots in tail streamers. Flight note a long-drawn 'quitsch' or 'guitsch'; alarm note 'keer'. Song less musical and flight slower than Swallow. Usually near cliffs, bridges or buildings, often in towns. 7 in. (18 cm.).   —V

PALE CRAG MARTIN *Hirundo obsoleta*. Smaller, paler and greyer than Crag Martin, and best distinguished by almost white throat and breast; no breast band. 5 in. (12·5 cm.).

PLAIN SAND MARTIN *Riparia paludicola*. Differs from Sand Martin mainly in its brown chin, throat and breast, with no distinct breast band, and from the two Crag Martins in lack of white spots in tail. Habits and habitat as Sand Martin. 4¾ in. (12 cm.).

SAND MARTIN *Riparia riparia*. The smallest hirundine over most of the region, with brown breast band across otherwise white underparts, and no white spots in tail. Calls reedier and much less musical than Swallow or House Martin, twittering song being little more than a repetition of call note. Usually in open country fairly near fresh water, but not far up in hills or in towns; nests colonially in holes excavated in sand and gravel banks. 4¾ in. (12 cm.).
●Sm Map 155

HOUSE MARTIN *Delichon urbica*. Prominent white rump is best field mark, together with pure white underparts; but cf. the two white-rumped swifts (p. 187) and Red-rumped Swallow. Juvenile's upperparts tinged brown. Usual call a spluttering 'chirrp' or 'chichirrrrp'; alarm note 'tseeep', gentle, twittering song, delivered on wing or from perch. Breeds in or near human settlements, also on cliffs, quarries and bridges. 5 in. (12·5 cm.).   ●Sm Map 156

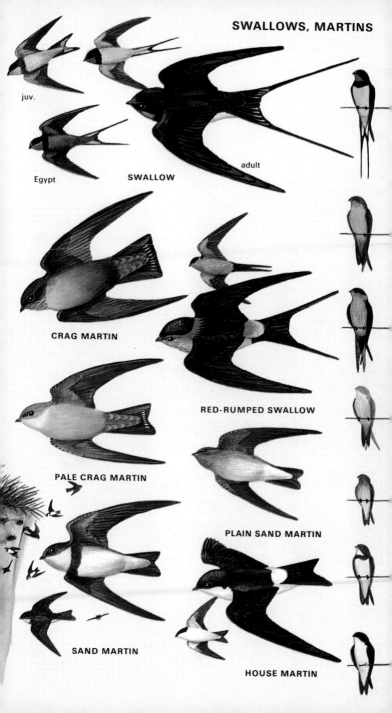

SWALLOWS, MARTINS

juv.

Egypt

SWALLOW

adult

CRAG MARTIN

RED-RUMPED SWALLOW

PALE CRAG MARTIN

PLAIN SAND MARTIN

SAND MARTIN

HOUSE MARTIN

Small, rather slim, long-tailed insectivorous land birds, with sexes alike, divided in our region into pipits *Anthus* and wagtails *Motacilla* (p. 212). Pipits are brown, with paler underparts, usually with darker streaks on breast; tail shorter than wagtails, usually with white outer feathers. Appearance and habits often lark-like, e.g. undulating flight, aerial song flights, walking and running gait, tendency to avoid perching in trees. Call note often the decisive clue in identification.

TREE PIPIT *Anthus trivialis*. Very like Meadow Pipit. Requires presence of trees in breeding season, when frequents open woodland, heaths, and other areas with scattered timber, though not usually in or very close to human settlements. 6 in. (15 cm.).　　●**Sm　Map 157**

MEADOW PIPIT *Anthus pratensis*. Can most easily be distinguished from Tree Pipit by voice; legs of adult generally dark flesh-pink, those of immature and of Tree Pipit flesh-pink. Juvenile tinged yellow-buff. Usual call a single or more often triple 'pheet', closely resembling Rock Pipit (p. 211) and quite distinct from Tree Pipit's rather loud harsh 'teez', which is more like Yellow Wagtail (p. 213). Both have undistinguished trilling song, but Tree Pipit's normally ends with distinctive far carrying 'see-er, see-er, see-er'. Song of both uttered in aerial display, normally flying up either from ground (Meadow) or tree or bush (Tree). Breeds in all kinds of open uncultivated country, moors, bogs, grassy hills, alpine meadows, tundra, heaths, dunes. In winter resorts to damp grassland, fresh-water margins, marshes and estuaries, often in flocks. Present in region throughout year. 5¾ in. (14·5 cm.).　　●**SrMW　Map 158**

RED-THROATED PIPIT *Anthus cervinus*. Darker than Meadow Pipit, and always distinguishable both by strongly streaked rump and underparts and by distinctive call. In breeding plumage has reddish throat and sometimes also breast. Song not unlike Meadow Pipit, but more prolonged and musical and often delivered at greater height. Calls a loud sharp 'chup' and a tree-pipit-like 'skee-eaz'. Open or shrub tundra and its coasts. 5¾ in. (14·5 cm.).　　—**A**

OLIVE-BACKED PIPIT *Anthus hodgsoni*. Strikingly olive-green above, with a marked eyestripe (orange-buff in front and white behind eye) and white underparts, breast boldly spotted, with a larger blackish smudge on side of neck. Call a loud 'tsee' or 'tseet', like Red-throated Pipit. Coniferous forest. 5¾ in. (14·5 cm.).　　—**V**

PECHORA PIPIT *Anthus gustavi*. Best distinguished by its call, a loud 'pwit', softer and lower-pitched than Meadow Pipit and usually repeated 2–3 times. Has two pale streaks down back, buffish outer tail feathers, and rump and underparts boldly streaked. Song has a wood-warbler-like trill, followed by a low throaty warble; delivered in aerial song flight. Wooded and shrub tundra, and fringes of coniferous forests. 5¾ in. (14·5 cm.).　　—**V**

PIPITS

song flight

TREE PIPIT

song flight

MEADOW PIPIT

summer

summer

winter

very variable
in summer

RED-THROATED PIPIT

OLIVE-BACKED PIPIT

PECHORA PIPIT

209

↑ Water Pipit   Rock Pipit ↓

WATER and ROCK PIPITS *Anthus spinoletta*. A dark-legged pipit with well marked races occupying two distinct breeding habitats, mountain (Water Pipit) and coastal (Rock Pipit), all appreciably larger and greyer than Meadow or Tree Pipits (p. 209). Water Pipit greyer, paler than Rock Pipit with white, not greyish outer tail feathers. Voice of all races similar: a meadow-pipit-like song, delivered in aerial song flight, rising from and returning to either ground or a rock; and a sharp 'phist', less high-pitched than Meadow Pipit's and rarely uttered in triplicate. Rocky coasts, mountain tops, alpine meadows and scrub; other sea-coasts and lowland marshes in winter. 6½ in. (16·5 cm.). ● Rw **Map 159**

TAWNY PIPIT *Anthus campestris*. The palest and most wagtail-like of the pipits, with its almost uniform sandy-brown plumage (scarcely streaked above, unstreaked below), long tail, and wagtail-like stance. Buff eyestripe noticeable. Paler, less streaked and shorter-legged than slightly larger Richard's Pipit. Juvenile has streaked breast, like juvenile Richard's. Song a simple metallic 'chivee-chivee-chivee', uttered in high display flight, from which plummets to ground. Calls varied, a yellow-wagtail-like 'tseep', also 'tsip', 'tsup', 'tseuc' and 'tsi-uc', and a sparrow-like chirrup, like Richard's Pipit. Dry, usually rather open, often sandy country, heaths, dunes, hillsides, savannas, cultivations, vineyards. 6½ in. (16·5 cm.).   **—A**

LONG-BILLED PIPIT *Anthus similis*. Like a large pale Tawny Pipit, almost uniformly brown above and paler beneath, though faintly streaked on each, but outer tail feathers buff not white. Fairly musical song, uttered either on ground or in air. Barren or grassy ground, with scattered rocks and sometimes bushes. 7½ in. (19 cm.).

BERTHELOT'S PIPIT *Anthus berthelotii*. Like Meadow Pipit (p. 209), but greyer; habits like Tawny Pipit. Song a repeated 'tsiree', sometimes delivered in air; call a low 'tsik', also 'chi-ree', like song. Inhabits all natural habitats in Canaries, but only upland ones in Madeira. 5½ in. (14 cm.).

RICHARD'S PIPIT *Anthus novaeseelandiae*. One of the largest and longest-legged pipits of the region, with eyestripe rather conspicuous, boldly patterned underparts; Tawny Pipit adult has equally long tail but is much less streaked. Most likely to be confused with immature Tawny Pipit, which has streaked breast. Pale legs distinguished from Water Pipit. Has a most distinctive harsh call, 'r-r-ruup', and a rather upright stance. A wanderer from Siberia, occurring annually in western Europe in some numbers, mainly in autumn. 7 in. (18 cm.).   **—A**

PIPITS

summer

Rock pipit

Fenno-Scandia

Faeroes,
British Isles,
N W France

winter

WATER PIPIT

juv. before
moulting

adult

TAWNY PIPIT

LONG-BILLED PIPIT

BERTHELOT'S PIPIT

RICHARD'S PIPIT

211

Wagtails: *Motacilla*. Wagtails are longer-tailed than pipits (p. 209), with plumage in combinations of black, grey, white and yellow, and white outer tail feathers. They repeatedly wag their tail up and down. Flight notably bounding, gait a quick, often rather jerky, run. Gregarious after breeding season.

WHITE and PIED WAGTAILS *Motacilla alba*. The only small black and white bird of its size with such a long tail. Colour of rump, grey in White Wagtail, subspecies *alba*, and black in British Pied Wagtail *yarrellii* (p. 215), is only absolutely reliable field character for these two races at all times. Flight note a distinctive high-pitched 'tschizzick'; also a monosyllabic 'tchik'. Twittering song, based on calls, may be delivered in air, on ground or from a perch. Open country from tundra to farmland and semi-desert, often in or near human settlements and near fresh water. In winter more often on farmland. 7 in. (18 cm.).　●RSM　Map 160

GREY WAGTAIL *Motacilla cinerea*. In outline and behaviour more like White than Yellow Wagtail, but with appreciably longer tail; cf. also Citrine Wagtail and p. 215. Is always blue-grey above, with yellow-green rump, and yellow beneath, though breeding male is brighter yellow and has a distinctive black throat. Juvenile has a slightly speckled breast, and is really yellow only on the under tail coverts. Call-note like White Wagtail's but more staccato and metallic and often reduced to a single sharp 'tit'. Song, rather infrequent, is a shrill treble or quadruple 'tsee-tee-tee', rather like a Spotted Flycatcher (p. 241), uttered either from a perch or, in a more trilling version, in flight. Breeds by fast flowing streams in hill districts, also in lowlands at weirs. In winter more widely at freshwater margins; on migration even at quite small pools in towns. 7 in. (18 cm.).
　　　　　　　　　　　　　　　　　　　●Rs　Map 161

BLUE-HEADED and YELLOW WAGTAILS *Motacilla flava*. Smaller and shorter-tailed than other White and Grey Wagtails, and only confusable with Grey and Citrine Wagtails. Has many races, as shown on p. 214, whose breeding males have distinctive head patterns greenish-brown above and yellow beneath, juveniles with a blackish band on the breast. Females are much harder to distinguish, and juveniles generally impossible. Flight note 'tsweep' is quite distinct from Grey and White Wagtails; brief trilling song, not often heard, somewhat robin-like, may be delivered in bounding song flight or from perch. Grasslands, generally damp but sometimes dry and healthy, also saltmarshes, cultivations, and on passage at freshwater margins, often associated with cattle. 6½ in. (16·5 cm.).　　　　●Sm　Map 162

CITRINE WAGTAIL *Motacilla citreola*. Breeding male unmistakable with yellow head and underparts, grey upperparts and black collar on nape. Female and winter male have grey upperparts, and underparts, forehead and superciliary stripe yellow. Juvenile hardly separable from some races of Yellow Wagtail. Stance and behaviour more like Grey Wagtail, including more vigorous wagging of tail, and call note, a sharp double 'tit, tit'. Tundras, marshes, wet moors; in winter in open country, by fresh water. 6½ in. (16·5 cm.).
　　　　　　　　　　　　　　　　　　　　　　—V

WAGTAILS

juv.

winter

adult summer

WHITE WAGTAIL

juv.

♂

♀

GREY WAGTAIL

white phase

juv.

winter

♂

♀

BLUE-HEADED WAGTAIL

juv.

♂

♀

CITRINE WAGTAIL

213

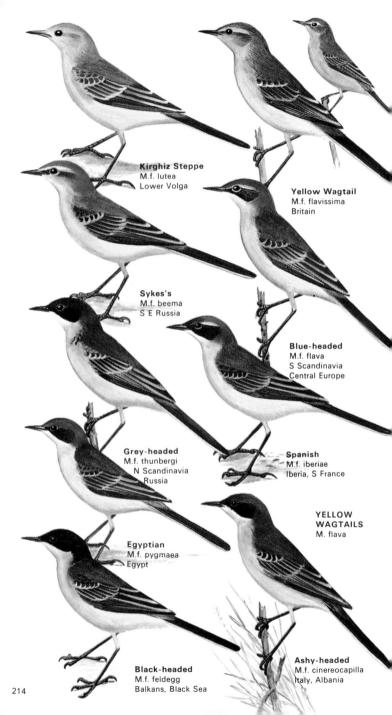

Kirghiz Steppe
M.f. lutea
Lower Volga

Yellow Wagtail
M.f. flavissima
Britain

Sykes's
M.f. beema
S E Russia

Blue-headed
M.f. flava
S Scandinavia
Central Europe

Grey-headed
M.f. thunbergi
N Scandinavia
Russia

Spanish
M.f. iberiae
Iberia, S France

Egyptian
M.f. pygmaea
Egypt

**YELLOW
WAGTAILS**
M. flava

Black-headed
M.f. feldegg
Balkans, Black Sea

Ashy-headed
M.f. cinereocapilla
Italy, Albania

214

RACES OF WAGTAILS

all in summer plumage
males

Canary Is.

M.c. canariensis

Europe
Africa
Asia Minor

M.c. cinerea

GREY WAGTAIL
M. cinerea

RACES OF WAGTAILS. The Blue-headed
or Yellow Wagtail is an exceptionally variable
species. In Africa and on migration in Southern
Europe several races may be seen together.
Intermediates occur, and especially confusing
birds may be seen in the zones where two
races overlap. Females and juveniles of both
blue-headed and white wagtails are frequently
impossible to assign to any particular race.

Europe
Asia Minor

M.a. alba

♀

British Isles

M.a. yarrellii
Pied Wagtail

S W Morocco

M.a. subpersonata

WHITE WAGTAIL

M. alba

Upper Egypt

M. aguimp vidua

215

GREY HYPOCOLIUS *Hypocolius ampelinus.* (Bomby-cillidae). Somewhat like a long-tailed grey shrike (p. 219), but bill not hooked, and plumage mainly pinkish grey, with bold black markings on cheek, wing tips and tip of tail; female browner with no black on head. Flight direct, not undulating like a shrike, and alighting in middle rather than on top of tree. Can be very tame. Rather silent, but has a scolding chirp, and a low churring alarm note. Bushes and scrub, in semi-deserts and cultivations, also in gardens and palm groves. 9 in. (23 cm.).

WAXWING *Bombycilla garrulus.* The only crested brown bird of the region that has yellow and red markings on wings and tail, tipped yellow. Flies rather like Starling (p. 303), but less strongly, and can always be distinguished by grey rump. Song also used as call note, a rather high-pitched weak trilling 'sirrrrr'; various chattering, piping and wheezing notes described but evidently not common. Breeds in fairly open coniferous and birch forests, especially in the taiga, but during periodic westward eruptions nearly always seen at berried shrubs, in parks and gardens or in hawthorn scrub. 7 in. (18 cm.). ○mW **Map 163**

● **BULBULS:** *Pycnonotidae.* Medium, often gregarious, usually soberly coloured land birds, with fairly slender bill and rather long tail. Not strong fliers. In our region regularly in human settlements.

COMMON BULBUL *Pycnonotus barbatus.* North African races *barbatus* and *arsinoe* very soberly dressed, like an immature male blackbird but with head and tail darker, whitish vent and no yellow bill. S W Asiatic race *xanthopygos* has strikingly yellow under tail coverts, with whitish ring round eye. Song rich and fluty, but staccato. Noisy and gregarious, especially at roosts. Common in gardens and orchards in towns and villages, also in palm groves and among bushes in remote wadis. An inquisitive bird. 7½ in. (19 cm.).

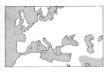

WHITE-EARED BULBUL *Pycnonotus leucogenys.* Shares yellow vent with Asiatic form of Common Bulbul, but easily distinguished by large white patch on each cheek, also by white spots at tip of tail. Head of immature brown, not black. Noisy chattering birds. A common town and village bird, in gardens, orchards and palm groves, and in open bushy country. 7 in. (18 cm.).

BLACK-HEADED BUSH SHRIKE *Tchagra senegala* (Laniidae, see p. 218). Strikingly plumaged; rufous wings, grey rump and white-tipped black tail are most conspicuous as this rather skulking bird dives for the nearest cover; also has black crown with black and white eyestripes. Has a pigeon-like display flight, rising high into the air—sometimes up to 200 feet—with sharply flapping wings, and gliding or spiralling down to a bush. Song a succession of vigorous, but plaintive, piping notes, rapid at first but later clear and bell-like, uttered either from perch or in flight. Alarm note churring. Habitat among bushes or scrub. 8½ in. (22 cm.).

GREY
HYPOCOLIUS

♀

♂

juv.

WAXWING

Middle East

Blackbird
N Africa

♀

COMMON
BULBUL

N E Africa

WHITE-EARED
BULBUL

BLACK-HEADED
BUSH SHRIKE

● **SHRIKES**: *Laniidae*. pp. 217–19. Small-medium to medium-sized land birds, with sexes generally alike, juveniles usually lightly barred, longish rounded or graduated tail, and bill slightly hooked. Aggressive birds, often perching on prominent lookouts before swooping on large invertebrate or small vertebrate prey, which is often impaled on thorns or other spikes as 'larder'. Flight usually dipping; often hovers to catch prey. All *Lanius* shrikes have harsh chattering cry and alarm note, similar to 'shek, shek' or 'chack, chack', rather subdued song mixing pleasing and harsh notes with calls mimicked from other birds. Woodland edges, heaths, hedgerows, orchards, olive groves, and other areas with scattered tall bushes.

GREAT GREY SHRIKE *Lanius excubitor*. The largest shrike of the region, with plumage all black, white and grey, with forehead grey, usually a white stripe above eye, and either one or two white wing-bars; cf. Lesser Grey Shrike. In N Europe the only medium-sized black, white and grey bird that perches on prominent lookouts. In S variable, with several distinct races. Hen and immature both have faint grey bars on breast; juvenile brownish. 9½ in. (24 cm.).

⊙mW **Map 164**

LESSER GREY SHRIKE *Lanius minor*. Differs from Great Grey Shrike especially in broad black band across forehead, lack of white eyestripe, underparts tinged pink, and relatively longer wings, shorter tail and stouter bill. White wing-bar conspicuous in flight. Juvenile tinged pale yellowish-brown. Flight much less undulating than Great Grey, hovering more, and erecter when perched. 8 in. (20 cm.).

—**A**

MASKED SHRIKE *Lanius nubicus*. Has black and white flight pattern similar to Woodchat, but in other ways is its obverse, with black crown, nape and rump, white forehead and rufous flanks. Female browner, juvenile browner still. Perches less conspicuously than other shrikes. Most frequent call a harsh but shrill 'keer, keer, keer'. Song resembles Icterine and Olive-tree Warblers (p. 229) 6¾ in. (17 cm.).

WOODCHAT SHRIKE *Lanius senator*. The only shrike in the region with a rich chestnut crown and nape, also showing conspicuous white wing-bars, shoulder patches and rump in flight. Corsican race *badius* lacks wing-bar. Female duller than male. Juvenile very like a pale juvenile Red-backed Shrike, but with pale marks on wings, shoulders and rump where adult Woodchat has white. Song more musical than most shrikes. 6¾ in. (17 cm.).   —**A**

RED-BACKED SHRIKE *Lanius collurio*. Male's combination of blue-grey head and rump with chestnut back unique among shrikes of region; dark cheeks with white stripe above and below. Female and juvenile mainly brown with crescentic marks on underparts. Juvenile has crescentic bands on upperparts too; cf. Woodchat Shrike. No white on wing, but shows white on either side of base of tail in flight. Eastern races have reddish tails. Song slightly reminiscent of Garden Warbler (p. 231). 6¾ in. (17 cm.).

⊙SM **Map 165**

SHRIKES

adult

GREAT GREY SHRIKE

1 S France, Spain
2 S Morocco to Sinai
3 N Morocco to Cyrenaica

1

2

3

adult

LESSER GREY SHRIKE

♂

♀

MASKED SHRIKE

juv.

adult

**WOODCHAT
SHRIKE**

juv.

♀

♂

1

♂

2

♂

Eastern races
1 *L.c. phoenicuroides*
2 *L.c. isabellinus*

RED-BACKED SHRIKE

219

ACCENTORS: *Prunellidae.* Mainly montane, generally solitary sparrow-like birds, distinguished from sparrows by their thin insect-eating bills. Sexes alike; flanks with dark streaks.

HEDGESPARROW or DUNNOCK *Prunella modularis.* At first glance not unlike a female House Sparrow (p. 299), but easily distinguished by grey head and underparts, well streaked flanks and thin bill. Chief call-note, a high-pitched 'tseep', often first betrays presence of this inconspicuous rather than actually skulking bird. Song, a rather flat little warble, has neither the vehemence of the Wren (p. 273) nor the sweetness of the Robin (p. 253). Inhabits bushy places of all kinds, scrub, heaths, parks, gardens (one of the commonest suburban birds in the West), also both broad-leaved and coniferous woodland, going quite high on mountains. 5¾ in. (14·5 cm.).   ●Rm   Map 166

BLACK-THROATED ACCENTOR *Prunella atrogularis.* A rather secretive bird of tangles of undergrowth confined in our region to the northern end of Urals. Black head with cinnamon-brown eyestripe and moustachial stripe recall male Whinchat (p. 243), but rest of plumage much paler, with underparts cinnamon-yellow. After breeding black becomes less intense. 5½ in. (14 cm.).

SIBERIAN ACCENTOR *Prunella montanella.* A wanderer to Central and Southern Europe that differs from Black-throated Accentor especially in lack of black on throat, also by amount of reddish-cinnamon on back and by yellow underparts with flanks streaked rufous; rump and tail grey. Song loud; rather shy, general behaviour like Hedgesparrow. Spruce/fir taiga with some birches and rowans in Siberian Urals. 6¼ in. (16 cm.).

RADDE'S ACCENTOR *Prunella ocularis.* Differs from Black-throated Accentor in lack of black throat, but also has brownish-black head, paler greyish back with dark markings, paler buff underparts and warm buff wash on breast. Another secretive bird, most easily located by call, a brief tri- or quadri-syllabic warble. Scrub, especially juniper, on high mountain slopes. 6 in. (15 cm.).

ALPINE ACCENTOR *Prunella collaris.* The largest accentor of the region, very rarely seen away from mountains. Like a large and rather brightly coloured Hedgesparrow, with chin and throat spotted black and white, and flanks still more strongly streaked chestnut, showing as rufous blaze at a distance. In flight shows pale double wing-bar enclosing a blackish patch and pale tip to tail; often jerks tail like chats. Song an almost skylark-like warble, much more musical than Hedgesparrow; rippling call-note also reminiscent of Skylark (p. 205), with sometimes a more metallic 'churrp'. High mountain slopes, stony or rocky, with or without sparse vegetation. 7 in. (18 cm.).

—V

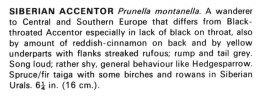

ACCENTORS

adult

juv.

HEDGESPARROW

♀

House Sparrow p. 299

BLACK-THROATED
ACCENTOR

SIBERIAN
ACCENTOR

ALPINE
ACCENTOR

RADDE'S ACCENTOR

221

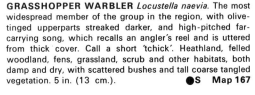

● **WARBLERS:** *Sylviidae.* pp. 223–39. Small or very small migratory land birds, with thin insect-eating bill. Voice is often one of the key field marks of the group. Sexes generally alike and juvenile usually similar to adult. Flight flitting. Habitat requiring some cover, from trees to low bushes or reeds; nest usually in bush or on ground. *Locustella:* A group of extremely shy brown warblers, with an obscure white eyestripe, distinguished especially by their rounded, almost graduated tail, which appears heavy when they do (rarely) take flight, and by their reeling songs. These recall certain types of grasshopper, and appear louder or softer as the bird turns its head. Inhabit dense scrub and other vegetation, often in marshes, skulking in thick cover, through which they can run rapidly like a mouse, though some species sing from prominent perch.

GRASSHOPPER WARBLER *Locustella naevia.* The most widespread member of the group in the region, with olive-tinged upperparts streaked darker, and high-pitched far-carrying song, which recalls an angler's reel and is uttered from thick cover. Call a short 'tchick'. Heathland, felled woodland, fens, grassland, scrub and other habitats, both damp and dry, with scattered bushes and tall coarse tangled vegetation. 5 in. (13 cm.). ●S **Map 167**

SAVI'S WARBLER *Locustella luscinioides.* Rather larger and less skulking than Grasshopper Warbler, with more rufous and unstreaked upper-parts, conspicuously white chin, and a louder, slower, lower-pitched song, uttered in shorter bursts. Calls a liquid 'puitt', a scolding 'tzwick' and a harsh chatter. Breeds in marshes, swamps and fens among reeds, sedge and reed-mace. 5½ in. (14 cm.). ○S **Map 168**

RIVER WARBLER *Locustella fluviatilis.* Differs from Grasshopper Warbler in unstreaked upperparts, and from both Grasshopper and Savi's in earth-brown upperparts and obscurely streaked breast, as well as in distinctive song, slower than Grasshopper and more rhythmic than either, pairs of fast and slow notes alternating: 'derr-derr, derr derr, derr-derr', uttered from top of bush. Call note rather harsh. Bushy and well vegetated swamps and freshwater margins, often in forests, sometimes in open steppes and even in town parks. 5 in. (13 cm.). —V

PALLAS'S GRASSHOPPER WARBLER *Locustella certhiola.* A vagrant from Siberia, with rufous rump and tail coverts, and grey-brown tail with dark tip, most feathers tipped grey. Juvenile has yellowish underparts with band of dark spots across breast. Call 'chir-chirr'. 5¼ in. (13·5 cm.). —V

LANCEOLATED WARBLER *Locustella lanceolata.* The smallest *Locustella* of the region, greyer and more heavily streaked above than Grasshopper Warbler, and with distinctive dark streaks in a band across breast and down flanks. Song a trill recalling Grasshopper Warbler, but more modulated and including various rattling and whistling notes, uttered from top of bush. Call 'chir-chir'. Thick vegetation by fresh water, tall grass and other plants in open forests and taiga. 4½ in. (11·5 cm.). —V

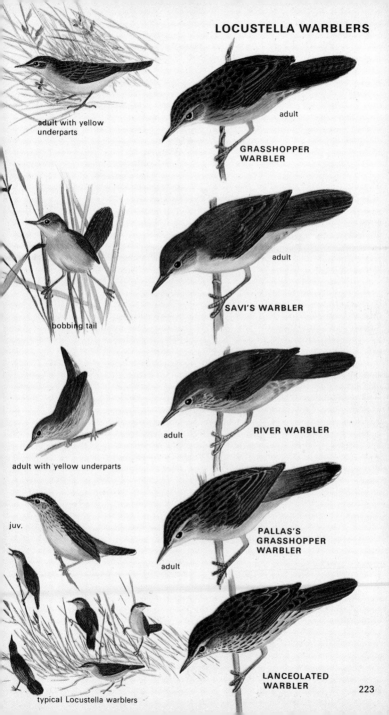

LOCUSTELLA WARBLERS

adult with yellow underparts

adult

GRASSHOPPER WARBLER

bobbing tail

adult

SAVI'S WARBLER

adult with yellow underparts

adult

RIVER WARBLER

juv.

adult

PALLAS'S GRASSHOPPER WARBLER

typical Locustella warblers

LANCEOLATED WARBLER

223

Reed Warblers: *Acrocephalus.* pp. 225–7. A difficult group, with very similar plumage, brown above and paler below, with whitish throat; tail rounded. Most easily distinguished by their often rather repetitive and mimetic songs; churring and scolding call notes rather similar. Generally in marshy or swampy habitats; skulking in habit, but may sing from prominent perch. In hand, best distinctions are wing formulae.

REED WARBLER *Acrocephalus scirpaceus.* Undistinguished except for rather rufous tinge of upperparts, especially on rump and in juveniles. Only safe distinction from Marsh and Blyth's Reed Warblers is song, rather monotonous, with general pattern 'churr-churr-churr . . . chirruc-chirruc-chirruc', like two pebbles rubbed together, mimetic, but normally with no harsh interjections. Rarely breeds away from reed beds. 5 in. (12·5 cm.).
●**Sm   Map 169**

MARSH WARBLER *Acrocephalus palustris.* Virtually impossible to distinguish from Reed and Blyth's Reed Warblers in field except by song, though adults rather more olive-brown with whiter throat and pinker legs. Typical song often consists mainly of mimicry, and much louder and jerkier, more musical and less uniform than Reed or Sedge Warbler (p. 227). Sings from prominent perch fairly often, and more continuously at night. Bushy places, with tall dense vegetation, often near fresh water, also in cornfields or gardens. 5 in. (12·5 cm.).
○**Sm   Map 170**

PADDYFIELD WARBLER *Acrocephalus agricola.* Confusingly similar to Reed, Marsh and Blyth's Reed Warblers, but more rufous and with more distinct pale eyestripe. Song very like Marsh, but with no harsh chirps. Among bushes and thick vegetation near fresh water or in swamps. 5 in. (12·5 cm.).
—V

BLYTH'S REED WARBLER *Acrocephalus dumetorum.* Best distinguished by steeper forehead, longer, thin bill, longer tail, and shorter, more rounded wings, resulting in whirring, wren-like flight, as well as by loud musical mimetic song. By day song comes in bursts, but at night it is more or less continuous. Call a distinctive 'chek', often repeated two or three times. Wide range of habitats with bushes and tangled vegetation. 5 in. (12·5 cm.).
—V

GREAT REED WARBLER *Acrocephalus arundinaceus.* Much the largest warbler of the region, almost song-thrush-sized; otherwise like a giant Reed Warbler but with more conspicuous pale eyestripe, stouter bill and distinctive loud croaking and grating voice. Song loud and far-carrying, frog-like, with croaking notes, e.g. 'karra-karra-karra', krik, krik' and 'gurk, gurk, gurk'. Less mimetic. Mainly reed-beds, but often at other freshwater margins. 7½ in. (19 cm.).
—A

CLAMOROUS REED WARBLER *Acrocephalus stentoreus.* Slightly smaller than Great Reed Warbler, but scarcely distinguishable in field, though has longer, thinner bill, paler lores and plumage a different shade of brown; largely separated geographically. Voice and behaviour very similar, but has strangled churring note interspersed with 'squark' and 'squeerk', and prefers papyrus beds to reeds. 7¼ in. (18 cm.).

REED WARBLERS

REED WARBLER

MARSH WARBLER

PADDYFIELD WARBLER

BLYTH'S REED WARBLER

GREAT REED WARBLER

CLAMOROUS REED WARBLER

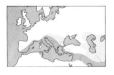

MOUSTACHED WARBLER *Acrocephalus melanopogon*. Differs from Sedge Warbler by much darker crown, more rufous upperparts, whiter square-ended eyestripe, darker cheeks, and whiter throat, and habit of cocking up and spreading graduated tail. Song more musical and some nightingale-like 'tu-tu-tu-tu' notes. Calls a soft 't-trrt' and a louder 'tchuck', repeated as a churring alarm. Resident in freshwater margins, mainly with reeds. 5 in. (13 cm). —**V(b)**

AQUATIC WARBLER *Acrocephalus paludicola*. Looks distinctly yellowish, with head more strikingly marked than Sedge and Moustached Warblers, a buff stripe over each eye and conspicuous pale buff stripe on crown; rump as well as mantle streaked. Voice very like Sedge, but song has more regular pattern in short distinct phrases. Freshwater margins, mainly with reeds, reed-mace or sedge. 5 in. (13 cm). —**A**

SEDGE WARBLER *Acrocephalus schoenobaenus*. Distinguished by broad whitish eyestripe and dark streaks on upperparts; rump rufous, unstreaked. Cf. Aquatic and Moustached Warblers. Juvenile has buffish eyestripe. Song a jumble of many contrasting sweet and harsh notes, all mingled with mimicry; also a harsh churr and a scolding 'tucc'. Breeds among coarse vegetation, bushes and hedgerows fairly near water. 5 in. (13 cm). ●**Sm   Map 171**

CETTI'S WARBLER *Cettia cetti*. Much more easily identified by distinctive song than during the brief glimpses its skulking habits usually permit; upperparts dark rufous brown tail rounded, and often cocked up. Song, uttered in loud staccato bursts, 'chewee, chewee, cheweeweeweewee' or 'pit, pit, pitipit, pitipit'. Calls include 'chee', 'twic', 'huit' and a churring note. Dense bushy vegetation and thickets by fresh water and in marshes. 5½ in (14 cm). —**V**

FAN-TAILED WARBLER *Cisticola juncidis*. Diminutive and most easily detected during its jerky high aerial song flight, when utters an insistent 'chip, chip, chip'; call 'tew'. Rather restless but skulking on ground. Tail short, graduated, with black and white tip. Freshwater margins with vegetation, also marshes, dry grassland, farmland and road verges. 4 in. (10 cm). —**V**

GRACEFUL WARBLER *Prinia gracilis*. A very small warbler, with streaked greyish upperparts, and a long graduated tail, tipped black and white, often cocked up and fanned out, and sometimes loosely twitched from side to side. Song, a repeated high-pitched, slightly tinkling 'zerwit'; calls include breeping, ticking and jitting notes; triple wing-snapping 'brrrp' note in display, in flight or at rest. Bushes and low vegetation in semi-deserts, cultivations, gardens, palm groves. 4 in. (10 cm).

SCRUB WARBLER *Scotocerca inquieta*. Restless, excitable, rather pale, with a long graduated tail, which it cocks up like Graceful Warbler, from which it differs especially in its uniform scarcely streaked upperparts and tail; dark streaks on head. Often skulks in bush, can also get very agitated at approach of observer. Desert or semi-desert, with sparse bushes, wadi beds. 4 in. (10 cm).

REED WARBLERS

MOUSTACHED
WARBLER

AQUATIC WARBLER

SEDGE WARBLER

CETTI'S WARBLER

FAN-TAILED
WARBLER

GRACEFUL
WARBLER

SCRUB WARBLER

227

Hippolais Warblers: Uniformly coloured, differing from the unstreaked reed warblers (p. 225) chiefly in their square tail, pale lores and broader, flatter bill. High forehead separates from leaf warblers (p. 237). Young like adults. Best identified by songs, all distinctive, sustained, varied and babbling, usually delivered from prominent perch. Have habit of raising crown feathers when excited.

ICTERINE WARBLER *Hippolais icterina*. Resembles an outsize leaf warbler (p. 237) with yellow underparts; immatures greyer. Legs pale or dark bluish-grey; bill pink. Very hard to tell from Melodious Warbler except by voice and distribution, but slightly larger, tends to be more brightly coloured, and has a peaked crown, and longer, more pointed wings, each with a pale patch. Cf. Wood Warbler (p. 237). Song reminiscent of Marsh Warbler (p. 225), a vehement repetitive medley of harsh, discordant and musical notes, the discordant ones often predominating. Calls include a distinctive liquid 'dideroid', a hard blackcap-like 'tek, tek' and a softer chiffchaff-like 'hooeet'. Forest edges, parks, gardens, orchards and riversides. 5¼ in. (13·5 cm.)
○**M**

MELODIOUS WARBLER *Hippolais polyglotta*. The southern counterpart of the Icterine, most easily distinguished by voice; wings shorter, more rounded; legs vary from blue-grey to brownish-flesh. Song more liquid, musical, mimetic and hurried, often including its own characteristic sparrow-like chirping call-note; has similar 'hooeet', but distinctive 'tit, tit'. 5 in. (13 cm.). —**A**

BOOTED WARBLER *Hippolais caligata*. The smallest *Hippolais* of the region, differing from Olivaceous in its shorter slenderer bill and underparts being buffer in summer, more silvery in winter, whitish outer tail feathers distinctive. A skulking bird, best identified by song, babbling variations on its 'chrek-chrek' and chirping call notes. Bushy places, forest edges, semi-deserts, gardens, cultivations. 4½ in. (11·5 cm.). —**V**

OLIVACEOUS WARBLER *Hippolais pallida*. Plain grey-brown or olive-grey, with whitish eye-rings, not unlike Garden Warbler, but differs in its longer broader bill, more distinct pale eyestripe, flatter forehead and whitish tips to tail feathers, and much more varied song. Call a hard 'trrk' or 'tak, tak', also a 'tic, tic' alarm note. Bushy places from semi-deserts to parks, orchards, cultivations and gardens, even in cities. 5¼ in. (13·5 cm.). —**V**

UPCHER'S WARBLER *Hippolais languida*. Rather larger than Olivaceous Warbler, but hardly identifiable in field, except by distinctive call-note. Scrub, gardens, vineyards, in the hills at greater altitudes. 5½ in. (14 cm.).

OLIVE-TREE WARBLER *Hippolais olivetorum*. The largest *Hippolais* of the region, grey-brown with a markedly long deep bill, blue-grey legs, slightly peaked crown, rather conspicuous eyestripe and pale panel on wing. Cf. immature Barred Warbler (p. 231). Song louder and deeper than other *Hippolais* warblers, call 'tuc' or 'tr-trck'. A skulking bird, in areas of scattered trees, open woodland, orchards, scrub. 6 in. (15 cm.).

HIPPOLAIS WARBLERS

ICTERINE WARBLER

MELODIOUS WARBLER

OLIVACEOUS WARBLER

BOOTED WARBLER

UPCHER'S WARBLER

OLIVE-TREE WARBLER

229

Sylvia Warblers: *Sylvia.* pp. 231–5. Tail graduated, rounded at tip. Most have two characteristic notes, a harsh churr and a hard 'tacc' note. Bushes, scrub, tall vegetation. Males usually brighter than females.

WHITETHROAT *Sylvia communis.* Male differs from all other warblers of region by combination of grey head, conspicuous white throat and rufous wings; female also has rufous wings and both have white feathers in tail. Juvenile's throat less markedly white. Brief staccato song, 'wheet' or 'whit'. Tangled vegetation, scrub, hedgerows, sometimes in gardens after breeding. 5½ in. (14 cm.).
●Sm   Map 172

*DESERT LESSER WHITETHROAT *Sylvia minula.* Rather smaller than Lesser Whitethroat, pale brown, with no dark patch and a weaker bill. Bushes and open scrub in deserts and semi-deserts, oases. 5¼ in. (13·5 cm.).

LESSER WHITETHROAT *Sylvia curruca.* Greyer than Whitethroat, with no rufous on wings and a more distinct dark patch on ear coverts than any other white-throated warbler of the region. More skulking than Whitethroat, with no song flight, the simple song, a tuneless rattle recalling Cirl Bunting (p. 277), being uttered from a well hidden perch; also a pleasant warbling subsong, more reminiscent of Whitethroat. Scrub, tall bushes and low trees, more often in open woodland, parks and gardens. 5¼ in. (13·5 cm.).
●Sm   Map 173

*HUME'S LESSER WHITETHROAT *Sylvia althaea.* Darker than Lesser Whitethroat, with a much larger stouter bill. Breeds in broad-leaved and juniper woods and scrub in mountains, wintering in plains. 5¼ in. (13·5 cm.).

GARDEN WARBLER *Sylvia borin.* Uniform plumage lacking any distinctive feature, even a white throat or a pale eyestripe, is most important visual field character; roundish head and rather short bill are useful pointers; legs grey-brown. Best identified by song, usually delivered from well hidden perch, normally a very even musical warble, mellower, lower-pitched and more sustained than Blackcap (p. 233), but occasionally in snatches; Blackcap may mimic Garden Warbler. Woodland with shrub understory, scrub, parks, large gardens. 5½ in (14 cm.).   ●Sm   Map 174

BARRED WARBLER *Sylvia nisoria.* One of the two largest *Sylvias* of the region, stout, long-tailed and greyish, adult with barred underparts, two white wing-bars and a yellow eye. Female is browner with less distinct bars. Juvenile unbarred, like a rather large, long-tailed Garden Warbler with noticeably pale tips to outer flight feathers and a steeper forehead; cf. Olive-tree Warbler (p. 229) and immature Orphean Warbler (p. 233). Song similar to Garden Warbler, but in shorter bursts, and interspersed with loud harsh chattering 'charr-charr-charr', also used as call note; delivered from perch or in dancing display flight. Scrub, woodland edges, hedgerows. 6 in. (15 cm.).
—A   Map 175

*Now often regarded as races of the Lesser Whitethroat.

display flight

♂

♀

WHITETHROAT

DESERT LESSER
WHITETHROAT

♂

♂

LESSER
WHITETHROAT

HUME'S LESSER
WHITETHROAT

♂

GARDEN WARBLER

adult

juv.

BARRED WARBLER

231

BLACKCAP *Sylvia atricapilla.* Easy to identify by colour of crown, not extending to cheeks, black in adult male, blackish-brown in immature male, brown in female and juvenile. Song is higher-pitched, less sustained and more mimetic than Garden Warbler (p. 231), but a variant, possibly mimicking Garden Warbler, is sometimes hard to tell. Forests, open woodland, scrub with scattered trees, parks, large gardens. 5½ in. (14 cm.). ●**Smw   Map 176**

ORPHEAN WARBLER *Sylvia hortensis.* Appreciably larger and stouter than Blackcap, with its staring white eye and jet-black cheeks as well as crown, contrasting with white throat; also has white outer tail feathers. Female's head duller black. Larger and longer-billed than Sardinian Warbler. Immature has shorter tail than immature Barred Warbler (p. 231), with no pale spots at base of tail. Song a pleasant thrush-like warble, repetitive but with no discordant notes, more repetitive in the W, more thrush-like in the E. Has a loud rattling 'trrr' alarm note. Open woods, scrub, parkland. 6 in. (15 cm.).   —**V**

MÉNÉTRIES' WARBLER *Sylvia mystacea.* Very like Sardinian Warbler, but underparts pink and eye-ring pale yellow; white line separates black cheeks from pink throat. Restless and skulking with voice and general habits like Sardinian, but song of poor quality, rattling and hissing. Thickets, especially of tamarisk, and along rivers, gardens and orchards. 5¼ in. (13·5 cm.).

SARDINIAN WARBLER *Sylvia melanocephala.* Male like a male Blackcap with whole head jet black, except for white chin and front of neck, and with conspicuously red eye and eye-ring and white outer tail feathers; female browner with scarcely contrasting cap. Cf. Orphean, Rüppell's and Ménétries' Warblers. Song, uttered from perch or in dancing display flight, rather whitethroat-like, but more musical and including snatches of alarm note, a wren-like chittering scold. Scrub, open woodland, parks, gardens, very locally in towns. 5¼ in. (13·5 cm.).   —**V**

RÜPPELL'S WARBLER *Sylvia rüppelli.* Male is only warbler of region with whole head and throat black, and a white moustachial stripe, sharing a red eye with male Sardinian Warbler from which black throat and white moustache separate it; female greyer and browner, scarcely black on head, but moustache still visible. Both sexes have distinctive red legs. Song like Sardinian, but interspersed note is a harder more staccato rattle. Scrub, low bushes, gardens. 5½ in. (14 cm.).

CYPRUS WARBLER *Sylvia melanothorax.* Very similar to Sardinian Warbler, but has underparts strongly marked with black, reddish legs and no red eye-ring. 5¼ in. (13·5 cm.). Restricted to Cyprus.

SYLVIA WARBLERS

Marsh Tit p. 269

Canary Is.
Madeira
melanistic

♂

BLACKCAP

♀

ORPHEAN WARBLER

♀

♂

♀

♂

MÉNÉTRIES'
WARBLER

SARDINIAN
WARBLER

♂

♀

♀

♂

RÜPPELL'S WARBLER

CYPRUS WARBLER

233

TRISTRAM'S WARBLER *Sylvia deserticola*. Like a small paler Dartford Warbler with rufous wings. Differs from Spectacled Warbler in its dark throat, from Subalpine Warbler in lack of white moustache; female paler. Song like Dartford, but call distinctive, a sharp 'chit' or 'chit-it'. Breeds in open woodland and scrub in hills, in winter also in desert. 4¾ in. (12 cm.).

DESERT WARBLER *Sylvia nana*. Smallest and palest scrub warbler, not unlike a small pale uniformly sand coloured Whitethroat (p. 231), but with rufous at base of and in centre of otherwise white-edged darker tail. Sexes alike. Song delivered in bush or in aerial display flight, simple and harmonious, like jingling of small silver bell; also has rattle like Scrub Warbler (p. 227). Scattered bushes in deserts and semi-deserts. 4½ in. (11·5 cm.).   **—V**

SUBALPINE WARBLER *Sylvia cantillans*. Like a small pale Dartford Warbler with a conspicuous white moustachial stripe, recalling Rüppell's Warbler (p. 233). throat never spotted, and whiter edging to shorter tail. Differs from Ménétries' Warbler (p. 233) in red eye-ring and much paler head. Song like Sardinian Warbler (p. 233) but more musical and with no harsh notes; delivered in dancing display flight. Distinctive call a soft 'tec, tec', also a chattering alarm note. Scrub and maquis. 4¾ in. (12 cm.).   **—A**

SPECTACLED WARBLER *Sylvia conspicillata*. Resembles a dark Whitethroat (p. 231) or a pale Subalpine Warbler, differing from the first in its darker head, whiter throat and pinkish breast, from the second in its rufous wings, white throat and paler breast, and from both in its yellow legs; pale eye-rings not conspicuous. Female and juvenile have striking chestnut wing patch. Song a pleasant little musical whitethroat-like ditty, uttered from perch or in display flight; alarm note 'tac, tac' and a rattling 'kirrrrrr'. Dry open country with low bushes but no tall shrubs or trees. 5 in. (12·5 cm.).   **—V**

MARMORA'S WARBLER *Sylvia sarda*. A small all-dark warbler with red eye and eye-ring, differing from Dartford Warbler in its grey underparts. Habits and song like Dartford, but usual call a distinctive 'tsig', uttered either singly or as a rattle, and inhabits rather more open scrub and maquis. 4¾ in. (12 cm.).

DARTFORD WARBLER *Sylvia undata*. Combination of dark grey-brown upperparts and dark pinkish- or purplish-brown underparts, together with long, frequently cocked-up, graduated, white-edged tail, is unique among warblers of N W Europe but usually one only sees a small dark long-tailed bird dive into a bush. Throat spotted white; eye and eye-ring red; legs yellow. Whitethroat-like song delivered in dancing display flight; alarm a scolding 'jer-jit'. Dense scrub, in England especially gorse and long heather. 5 in. (12·5 cm.).
    ⊙**R**   **Map 177**

SYLVIA WARBLERS

Russia

N Africa

DESERT WARBLER

TRISTRAM'S
WARBLER

♂

♀

♂

SPECTACLED
WARBLER

♂

♀

SUBALPINE WARBLER

♀

♂

♀

MARMORA'S
WARBLER

♀

DARTFORD
WARBLER

♂

♀

235

Leaf Warblers: *Phylloscopus.* pp. 237–9. Small greenish or yellowish warblers most easily identified by their songs. Low forehead separates from *Hippolais* (p. 228). Typical habit of flicking wings and tail, which appears slightly forked.

WILLOW WARBLER *Phylloscopus trochilus.* The commonest warbler over much of N Europe, with underparts tinged yellow, especially in juvenile; legs dark brown to flesh-coloured. Some eastern birds browner above and white beneath. From Chiffchaff only safely distinguishable by song, a fluent series of similar wistful descending notes, and call-note, a gentle disyllabic 'hooeet'. Woodland, areas with scattered trees and bushes, gardens. 4¼ in. (11 cm.).
●Sm   Map 178

CHIFFCHAFF *Phylloscopus collybita.* Best distinction from Willow Warbler is song, a repeated monotonous 'chiff-chaff' or 'zip-zap', sometimes interspersed with a guttural 'chirr-chirr'; call-note monosyllabic, 'hweet'. Less tinged green and yellow; legs always dark. N European race *abietinus* is greyer above and whiter below; Siberian race *tristis*, rare autumn visitor to W, is greyer still, and has distinctive 'sad' single note, which forms basis of quite distinct song. S W Asian race *lorenzii* is darker grey and even less green than *tristis*, with tawny buff breast and flanks; call as *abietinus*. Habitat similar to Willow Warbler, but needs taller trees and fewer bushes. 4¼ in. (11 cm.).
●Smw   Map 179

WOOD WARBLER *Phylloscopus sibilatrix.* The largest breeding leaf warbler of the region, with noticeably yellow breast and white underparts and a distinct yellow eyestripe, distinguished from Icterine and Melodious Warblers (p. 229) by white belly, shorter bill, less angled head and yellow legs. Has two quite different songs, a long quivering trill and a plangent repetition of its anxiety note, a mellow plaintive bullfinch-like 'dee-ur' or 'püü'. Forests and woods, especially beech. 5 in. (12·5 cm.).
●Sm   Map 180

BONELLI'S WARBLER *Phylloscopus bonelli.* Greyer than Willow Warbler, especially on head, and with whiter underparts, yellowish patches on wing and rump. Song a short wood-warbler-like trill, based on its 'hoo-eet' call note, more distinctly disyllabic than Willow Warbler. Woods and forests in the hills. 4½ in. (11·5 cm.).
—A

RADDE'S WARBLER *Phylloscopus schwarzi.* Large, rather grey-brown and thick-billed, with longish tail, conspicuous creamy eyestripe, creamy white underparts and yellowish legs. Call a delicate whistling 'twit, twit'. Vagrant from Asia; skulks in low cover. 5 in. (12·5 cm.)
—V

DUSKY WARBLER *Phylloscopus fuscatus.* Another Siberian vagrant, much smaller and thinner-billed than Radde's Warbler and the darkest leaf warbler of the region, distinguished by general brown appearance, lack of any green or yellow tinge, and buff eyestripe. Call a distinctive, rather *Sylvia*-like 'tak, tak'. Feeds much on ground. 4¼ in. (11 cm.).
—V

LEAF WARBLERS

juv.

adult

WILLOW WARBLER

juv.

Canary Is.

adult

Caucasus

CHIFFCHAFF

BONELLI'S WARBLER

WOOD WARBLER

DUSKY WARBLER

RADDE'S WARBLER

237

ARCTIC WARBLER *Phylloscopus borealis.* Intermediate between Willow and Wood Warblers (p. 237) in size, and distinguished from both by whitish throat, dark stripe through eye and two whitish wing-bars, one often obscured, from Willow also by whitish underparts and more marked pale stripe above eye; bill dark. Legs pale. Cf. Greenish Warbler. Song a short rather tuneless, buzzing trill, usually preceded by a hard 'tzick'; calls 'tzick', 'tswee-ep' and a short rattle or chatter. Arctic and sub-arctic forests and scrub. 4¾ in. (12 cm.).
—A

GREENISH WARBLER *Phylloscopus trochiloides.* Varies from greenish to greyish-brown, differing from Willow Warbler (p. 237) in its narrow pale wing-bar, more marked eyestripe and whiter underparts; legs dark. Smaller and greyer than Arctic Warbler. Song a rapid and high-pitched warbling wren-like trill, often preceded by repetition of disyllabic call, 'tiss-yipp'. Open woodland, forest edges. 4¼ in. (11 cm.). —A

YELLOW-BROWED WARBLER *Phylloscopus inornatus.* Smaller, greener above and with more marked pale eyestripe than Willow Warbler (p. 237), and readily distinguished by double pale wing bar. Cf. Goldcrest and Firecrest. Song a rapid monosyllabic trill; call not unlike Chiffchaff but louder. Forests and woodlands. Vagrant from Asia. 4 in. (10 cm.). —A

GREEN WARBLER *Phylloscopus nitidus.* Identified by combination of bright green upperparts and bright yellow underparts, like a small Wood Warbler (p. 237), with a yellow wing-bar. Song repetitive, 'ts-tri-tsi', in Willow Warbler pattern; call a cheerful 'chi-wee'. Breeds in mountain woods. 4¼ in. (11 cm.).

PALLAS'S WARBLER *Phylloscopus proregulus.* Smallest leaf warbler of region, greener than Yellow-browed, with yellow crown-stripe and eyestripes, double yellow wing bar and yellow rump, most obvious when hovering. Cf. Goldcrest, Firecrest. Call soft, disyllabic. Vagrant from Asia. 3½ in. (9 cm.).
—V

GOLDCREST *Regulus regulus.* With Firecrest the smallest breeding bird of the region, differing from all leaf warblers in its tiny bill, black-bordered crest, orange in cock, yellow in hen, and dark mark alongside double wing-bar. Cf. Firecrest. Very high-pitched song, 'cedar-cedar-cedar-cedar-sissu-pee'. Call note a thin 'zi' or 'zi-zi-zi', confusable with similar cries of Treecreeper (p. 273) and Coal and other tits (p. 267), except when uttered in intensified form, 'zi-zi-zi-zeee-zeee-zeee-zi-zi'. Woods, scattered trees, large gardens; especially near conifers. In winter also in bushy places away from conifers. 3½ in. (9 cm.). ●RMW Map 181

FIRECREST *Regulus ignicapillus.* Black and white eyestripes separate from Goldcrest; bronze patch on side of neck. Voice less high-pitched and intense; 'peep' rather than 'zi'. Habitat as Goldcrest but no preference for conifers. 3½ in. (9 cm.). ☉sMw Map 182

LEAF WARBLERS, GOLDCRESTS

ARCTIC WARBLER

GREENISH WARBLER

YELLOW-BROWED WARBLER

GREEN WARBLER

PALLAS'S WARBLER

juv.

♀

♂

GOLDCREST

♂

♀

FIRECREST

juv.   Canary Is.   Madeira   239

FLYCATCHERS: *Muscicapidae.* Small birds, with rather broad flattened bill for feeding on flying insects, caught by persistent sallies from perch, to which bird usually returns. Chat-like alarm-note 'whee-tucc-tucc'. Rarely on ground except to fly down and pick up an insect. Nest in hole or on ledge.

SPOTTED FLYCATCHER *Muscicapa striata.* Grey-brown with dark streaks on head and breast; sexes alike, juvenile spotted paler. Song, some half a dozen shrill, rather grating and squeaky notes, sounding at first as if made by more than one bird; call a shrill robin-like 'tzee'. Forest edges, parks, orchards, gardens and other places with scattered trees; frequent in suburbs. 5½ in. (14 cm.).
●Sm   Map 183

BROWN FLYCATCHER *Muscicapa latirostris.* Vagrant from Siberia, appreciably smaller than Spotted and unstreaked, more closely resembling female Red-breasted but with no white at base of tail, or female Pied or Collared but with no white mark on wing. White eye-ring diagnostic at close range. Sexes alike. Juvenile conspicuously mottled paler. Voice similar to Spotted. 4¾ in. (12 cm.).

PIED FLYCATCHER *Ficedula hypoleuca.* Breeding males strikingly black and white, and with Collared are only small black and white birds with fly-catching habit. Female, winter male and juvenile all greyish-brown above, male distinguished by white forehead, juvenile by pale spots. In some districts males breed in brown plumage. Distinguished from other flycatchers, except Collared, by white wing bar. Cf. Collared Flycatcher. Song, usually delivered from a perch, is rather varied, not unlike Redstart in one phase, and has been aptly rendered 'tree, tree, tree, once more I come to thee'; call a swallow-like "whit'. Woods and forests, parks, orchards, large gardens. 5 in. (13 cm.).   ●SM   Map 184

COLLARED FLYCATCHER *Ficedula albicollis.* Breeding male differs from Pied by conspicuous white collar, white rump and more white on forehead and wings, these markings still visible but fainter in brownish winter plumage. Eastern race *semitorquata* lacks white collar and has grey rump. Female and juvenile doubtfully distinguishable from Pied but generally greyer; female may have faint whitish collar and rump, and usually appears white on wing. Voice and habitat similar to Pied but song softer and more uniform. 5 in. (12·5 cm.).   —V

RED-BREASTED FLYCATCHER *Ficedula parva.* The smallest flycatcher of the region, rather variable, the male distinctive, with red throat and breast. Tail frequently flicked up, revealing striking white marks at base of tail in both sexes; no white wing-bar. Song variable, including some clear bell-like notes and others reminiscent of Wood Warbler (p. 237). Calls a sharp 'chik' and a wren-like chatter. Broad-leaved forests and woodlands. 4½ in. (11·5 cm.).
—A   Map 185

FLYCATCHERS

adult

juv.

SPOTTED FLYCATCHER

BROWN FLYCATCHER

♀

♂ winter

PIED FLYCATCHER

♂

♀

COLLARED FLYCATCHER

♂

♀

♂

Asia Minor

RED-BREASTED FLYCATCHER

241

● **THRUSHES, CHATS and ALLIES:** *Turdidae.* pp. 243–61. A large subfamily containing some of the finest songsters. CHATS: *Saxicola.* Small robin-like thrushes, with habit of perching upright on prominent lookout, often flicking tail jerkily and uttering harsh chacking note. Juveniles like females but speckled.

CANARY ISLANDS CHAT *Saxicola dacotiae.* Intermediate between Stonechat and Whinchat, male having general pattern, black head and no white in tail of male Stonechat, but paler appearance, white throat and eyestripe of Whinchat; less chestnut on breast than either. Female duller. Alarm-note louder and sharper than Stonechat; ·song resembles Spectacled Warbler (p. 235). Scrub and farmland on Fuerteventura and two islets in Canaries. 5 in. (12·5 cm.).

STONECHAT *Saxicola torquata.* Male distinctively black and chestnut, and white on neck, wings and rump; black becomes brownish in winter. Female and juvenile brown, streaked darker. All show white wing-bars in flight. Song a brief squeaky warble, sometimes in dancing song flight; chief call a grating 'tsak, tsak' or 'hwee-tsak-tsak'. Moors, heaths, gorsy sea-cliffs, alpine meadows, farmland, low scrub. 5 in. (12·5 cm.). ●Rs **Map 186**

WHINCHAT *Saxicola rubetra.* Summer visitor, male readily told from Stonechat by white or buffish eyestripe and white sides to base of tail; female similar but duller; both have white wing-patch, especially conspicuous in flight. Song like Stonechat, but call a less grating 'tic-tic' or 'u-tic'. Habitat also as Stonechat, but more often in riverside meadows, waste ground and railway embankments. 5 in. (12·5 cm.). ●Sm **Map 187**

PIED STONECHAT *Saxicola. caprata.* Male black, with white wing-patch, rump and lower belly; female, immature brown with pale belly and rufous rump and upper tail. Song louder, more resonant than Whinchat. 6½ in. (16·5 cm.).

BLUE ROCK THRUSH *Monticola solitarius.* Male most distinctively all blue with dark wings and tail; female differs from paler female Rock Thrush in having no rufous in tail. Song fluty and repetitive warbling, blackbird-like in tone; calls a chat-like 'chuck', a nuthatch-like 'uit-uit' and a high-pitched 'tseee'. Rocky places, from mountain tops to sea level; replaces Blackbird (p. 257) in towns in S Europe. 8 in. (20 cm.).

ROCK THRUSH *Monticola saxatilis.* Male is one of the most striking mountain birds, with strongly contrasted blue and rufous chestnut plumage, and white back and rump. Female and young mottled brown with chestnut tail; cf. Blue Rock Thrush. A shy bird as often heard as seen, with its chat-like 'chack, chack', and its clear piping song, like a Wheatear's sung by a Blackbird. Open rocky ground and ruins; in the W only in mountains. Summer visitor. 7½ in. (19 cm.). —V

♂

♀

CANARY ISLANDS CHAT

♂

♀

STONECHAT

♂

♂

♀

PIED STONECHAT

WHINCHAT

♀

♂

♂

♀

BLUE ROCK THRUSH

ROCK THRUSH

243

Wheatears or Chats: *Oenanthe*. pp. 245–9. Small thrush-like land birds, with rump usually conspicuously white, and tail usually with white sides and black centre and tip. Males (see Key on p. 248) distinctive but females hard to tell apart; juveniles usually speckled paler. Song usually a brief staccato warble, uttered from a low eminence or in aerial display. Mostly on ground, frequently bobbing and chasing after flies; flight flitting, sometimes hawking for flies.

WHEATEAR *Oenanthe oenanthe*. Breeding male distinguished from all other wheatears by head pattern (grey crown, white eyestripe, black cheeks); winter male, female and juvenile browner. Many individuals of Greenland race *leucorrhoa* migrating through W Europe in spring are larger and brighter, but others not distinguishable in field. Male of North African race *seebohmi* has throat black. Song a squeaky little warble; call a grating 'chack, chack' or 'weet-chack, chack'. Tundra, moors, grassy downs, deserts and other open country. 5¾–6 in. (14·5–15 cm.).
●**SM   Map 188**

DESERT WHEATEAR *Oenanthe deserti*. Differs from all other wheatears of region in almost completely black tail, male otherwise rather like black-throated form of Black-eared Wheatear, but with more white on the wings and with black of wings joining black of throat. Song rather plaintive, 'see-dool-a-dol' or 'trütrütitü', call a plaintive whistle. Dry desert and semi-desert areas, in winter also in cultivations. 5¾ in. (14·5 cm.).   —**V**

ISABELLINE WHEATEAR *Oenanthe isabellina*. A large pale sandy, rather upright and long-legged wheatear, sexes alike, hardly distinguishable from large pale female Greenland Wheatear, though underwing whiter. Loud mimetic song, sometimes uttered in striking fluttering display flight. Calls unchatlike, chirping and whistling. Steppes, deserts, stony plains and hillsides. 6½ in. (16·5 cm.).   —**V**

RED-TAILED WHEATEAR *Oenanthe xanthoprymna*. Differs from all other wheatears of region, except Red-rumped Wheatear (p. 247) in rufous base of tail; from Red-rumped male differs in pale brown, not black, mantle, no white on wings and more deeply rufous rump, female differs in grey-brown not rufous head. Western males differ from eastern in black, not brown, throat and sides of face and neck, and white not rufous outer tail feathers; intermediates exist. Song strongly mimetic. Breeds on rocky hillsides, in winter in semi-desert. 5½ in. (14 cm.).

BLACK-EARED WHEATEAR *Oenanthe hispanica*. Breeding male very striking, creamy buff, sometimes almost white, except for black wings, cheeks, tip and centre of tail, sometimes also throat; eastern birds have more black on cheeks and throat. Winter male has darker head. Female like Wheatear, but wings and cheeks darker; cf. Desert Wheatear, Pied Wheatear (p. 247). Song like Wheatear, preceded by soft 'plit' note; call rather rasping. Dry open country with scattered bushes. 5¾ in. (14·5 cm.).   —**V**

WHEATEARS

'Seebohm's Wheatear'
N Africa

♂

♀

♂

WHEATEAR

♀

♂

DESERT
WHEATEAR

ISABELLINE WHEATEAR

♀

♂

RED-TAILED
WHEATEAR

pale form

♂

♀

black-throated form

♂

♀

BLACK-EARED
WHEATEAR

245

MOURNING WHEATEAR or MOURNING CHAT
Oenanthe lugens. Male differs from black-throated form of
Black-eared Wheatear (p. 245) in black mantle and black
of wings being joined to black throat; from Red-rumped
Wheatear in white rump and all-black wings; from Pied
Wheatear in white breast, less black on mantle and rufous-
tinged under tail coverts; and from all in very narrow white tip
to tail. Female in Asian races similar to male, in N African race
halophila has whole crown, nape and mantle grey. Song
variable, short and repetitive or longer and warbling. Call
'tchut, tchut'. Wadis and other wild rocky desert country.
5¼ in. (13·5 cm.).

PIED WHEATEAR *Oenanthe pleschanka*. Male differs from
Mourning Wheatear especially in its buff-tinged underparts, white under tail coverts and black-tipped tail; from
black-throated form of Black-eared Wheatear (p. 245) in
black-mantle and buff-tinged underparts; cf. also Finsch's
Wheatear. Female (except in Cyprus) indistinguishable from
female Black-eared Wheatear, and very similar also to female
Wheatear (p. 245) and Isabelline Wheatear (p. 245). Song
like Black-eared Wheatear, call 'zack'. Wide range of open
stony country, low cliffs, hillsides, with some bushes, also
in cultivations and even gardens. 5¾ in. (14·5 cm.).　　**—V**

FINSCH'S WHEATEAR or FINSCH'S CHAT *Oenanthe
finschii*. Male whiter on upperparts than any other wheatear,
in fact like black-throated form of Black-eared Wheatear
(p. 245) with white continuous from crown to tip of tail, and
black continuous from throat on to wings. Female duller and
may have throat either pale or black, but very similar to other
female wheatears. A shy uncommon bird of deserts and
neighbouring cultivations. 5¼ in. (13·5 cm.).

RED-RUMPED WHEATEAR *Oenanthe moesta*. One of
the largest wheatears of the region, different in many ways
from the Red-tailed Wheatear (p. 245), the only other wheatear with a rufous rump, being in fact rufous only on the sides
of the rump and tail. Apart from this, more closely resembles
Mourning Wheatear, but much whiter on wings and tail
black. Female easily told by rufous head. Remarkable
whirring song, on an ascending scale, uttered by both sexes
throughout year. Desert edges with sparse bushes. 6½ in.
(16·5 cm.).

HOODED WHEATEAR *Oenanthe monacha*. A mainly
black wheatear, but with white crown and belly, differing
from all other wheatears except White-crowned Black
Wheatear in having outer tail feathers white to the tip; black
breast further distinguishes from Mourning Wheatear
(p. 247), which also has shorter bill and longer legs. Flight
buoyant, butterfly-like. Song a sweet subdued warble.
Wild unvegetated wadis and ravines in the desert, uncommon. 6¾ in. (17 cm.).

WHEATEARS

MOURNING WHEATEAR ♂ ♀

PIED WHEATEAR ♂ ♀

FINSCH'S WHEATEAR ♂ ♀

RED-RUMPED WHEATEAR ♂ ♀

HOODED WHEATEAR ♂ ♀

WHITE-CROWNED BLACK WHEATEAR *Oenanthe leucopyga*. White-capped male resembles Hooded Wheatear (p. 247), but with a dark belly; female, immature male and occasional adult male breeding in immature plumage are distinguishable from Black Wheatear only by outer tail feathers being white to tip. Song short and subdued. Wild desert country, also in towns and villages. 6¾ in. (17 cm.).

HUME'S WHEATEAR or HUME'S CHAT *Oenanthe alboniger*. A highly contrasted black and white wheatear, the only one of the region which has whole head and upperparts black and whole breast white. Wild rocky gorges, ravines and mountain valleys. 6½ in. (16·5 cm.).

BLACK WHEATEAR *Oenanthe leucura*. A large wheatear, the male all black except for white rump, under tail coverts and outer tail feathers, though wings appear paler; female browner. Cf. female and immature White-crowned Black Wheatear. Song a typical staccato chat performance, with some musical warbling notes. Call 'pee-pee-pee'. Cliffs, ravines and other rocky places. 7 in. (18 cm.).   **—V**

BLACKSTART *Cercomela melanura*. Male is a small grey bird with an all-black tail, which it flicks constantly; cf. immature Black Redstart (p. 251) which has red tail. Female browner, but still with black tail. Song a pleasant but rather monotonous subdued warble; call chirping. Desolate and rocky desert country. 5½ in. (14 cm.).

KEY TO MALE WHEATEARS
Head black: Hume's, Black.
Crown grey: Wheatear, Red-tailed; Black-eared (pale form), Mourning Finsch's, Red-rumped; **buff:** Isabelline. Black-eared, Desert, Red-tailed; **white:** Pied, White-crowned Black, Hooded.
Cheeks contrastingly black: Wheatear, Black-eared.
White eyestripe: Wheatear.
Rump rufous: Red-tailed, Red-rumped (sides only).
Tail white at extreme tip: Mourning; **with outer feathers white to tip:** White-crowned Black, Hooded; **almost completely black:** Desert.
Whole underparts black: Black, White-crowned black; **white:** Hume's; **buff:** Wheatear, Isabelline.
Throat and breast black: Pied (upper breast), Hooded; **and cheeks black:** Wheatear (North African race), Black-eared, Desert, Red-tailed, Mourning, Finsch's, Red-rumped.

Wheatears with black throats. All males.

| Seebohm's | Black-eared | Desert | Red-tailed | Red-rumped |

WHEATEARS

imm.

WHITE-CROWNED BLACK WHEATEAR

HUME'S WHEATEAR

♀

♂

BLACKSTART

♂

♀

BLACK WHEATEAR

| Finsch's | Mourning | Pied | Hooded | Hume's |

249

Redstarts: *Phoenicurus.* Robin-like birds characterised especially by rufous tail of both sexes at all ages, and by generally chat-like voice and behaviour. Juvenile like female but speckled. Habits include flycatching sallies and curious tail-shivering display. Hole-nesters.

BLACK REDSTART *Phoenicurus ochruros.* Breeding male distinctively all black except for white wing patch and rufous tail; winter male greyer. Female and juvenile greyer than Common Redstart, especially on underparts. Song a staccato redstart-like warble, interspersed with a remarkable sound like the grinding together of little metal balls. Most frequent calls 'tsip', 'tic' and redstart-like 'tucc-tucc'. Rocky hill and mountain slopes, cliffs, villages and towns; in Germany the Black Redstart is the 'house redstart' and the Redstart the 'garden redstart'. 5½ in. (14 cm.).
⊙SMw   **Map 189**

REDSTART *Phoenicurus phoenicurus.* Breeding male handsome, with white forehead, black throat and grey mantle offsetting fiery chestnut tail and underparts. In S. W. Asia and Greece males of *samamisicus* race have white patch on wing. Female and winter male browner and duller; Cf. Black Redstart. Song a rather squeaky warble, but very varied and often mimetic, recalling at times chats (p. 243), Chaffinch (p. 285) and Pied Flycatcher (p. 241). Chief calls a chat-like 'hwee-tucc-tucc' and a loud willow-warbler-like 'hooeet'. Broad-leaved and pine woodland, orchards, gardens, areas with scattered old trees, such as parks and river banks, and hill districts with stone walls and old quarries. 5½ in. (14 cm.).   ●Sm   **Map 190**

GÜLDENSTÄDT'S REDSTART *Phoenicurus erythrogaster.* The largest redstart, males being easily told by their white crown and nape and large white wing-patch, black cheeks, back and breast, and rufous tail and underparts. The wing-patches are especially conspicuous during the aerial song flight. Female like large female Redstart. High rocky mountain slopes, descending to tree level in winter. 7 in. (18 cm.).

MOUSSIER'S REDSTART *Phoenicurus moussieri.* A small endemic redstart of North Africa, where it is much more widespread than the Redstart, from which male differs in its strongly contrasting black and white upper-parts, black on crown, cheeks, back, wings and in centre of rufous tail, and white in a broad eyestripe back on to neck and a large wing patch. Female similar to a small female Redstart. Call 'wheet' followed by a rasping note. Forests and hill or mountain sides, with or without vegetation. 4¾ in. (12 cm.).

EVERSMANN'S REDSTART *Phoenicurus erythronotus.* A rare passage migrant and winter visitor to Transcaspia and S Iraq, best told by its large size and dark rufous back, and the small white patches on forehead and wings of male. 6¼ in. (16 cm.).

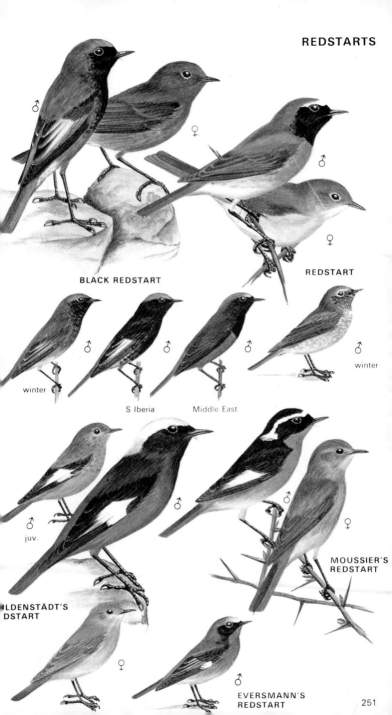

REDSTARTS

♂
♀
♂
♀

BLACK REDSTART

REDSTART

winter

♂ winter

♂
S Iberia

♂
Middle East

♂ winter

♂
juv.

♂

♂

♀

MOUSSIER'S REDSTART

GÜLDENSTÄDT'S REDSTART

♀

♂

EVERSMANN'S REDSTART

RED-FLANKED BLUETAIL *Tarsiger cyanurus*. Male like a bright blue Redstart, with tail and whole upperparts blue and bright rufous flanks; female olive-brown with rufous flanks but blue on tail only; juvenile with only upper tail blue, otherwise like Robin. Behaviour reminiscent of flycatchers, tits (creeping about trees) and redstarts (tail jerking). Song, not loud, includes repetitive song-thrush-like notes, usually delivered from tree; call 'tic, tic', like Robin. Coniferous forest, with shrub understory, usually on damp soil. 5½ in. (14 cm.). —V

ROBIN *Erithacus rubecula*. Much smaller than American Robin (p. 260). Britain's National Bird is one of the easiest European birds to identify; its red face distinguishes it from all other red-breasted birds. Shows pale under tail coverts as it flies away. In Britain, speckled juvenile much tamer and easier to approach than similarly speckled juvenile nightingales (p. 255) and chats (p. 243), but elsewhere often shy. Pleasant, rather thin warbling song almost throughout year, commonest call 'tic, tic', also a thin 'tsit' and a high-pitched 'tswee', recalling Spotted Flycatcher (p. 241), especially from juveniles. Forests, scrub, gardens, hedgerows, town parks; a common suburban bird in the W. 5½ in. (14 cm.). ●Rsmw   Map 191

SIBERIAN RUBYTHROAT *Luscinia calliope*. Larger than Bluethroat, and with whole throat of male bright red, differing from Robin in its two eyestripes and red not extending on to breast or forehead. Female has throat whitish, and both sexes have whitish stripe both above and below eye. Song loud, nightingale-like but less sustained, often beginning mimetically. Calls a loud whistling 'tiuit, tiuit' and a rattling alarm note. Thickets in the taiga, often in damp valley bottoms. 6¼ in. (16 cm.).

BLUETHROAT *Luscinia svecica*. A shy robin-like bird, distinguishable in all plumages by rufous base of tail, distinct pale eyestripe and black band on breast. Blue-throated breeding males very distinctive, in two or three forms: Red-spotted Bluethroats *svecica* Scandinavia and N Russia and *pallidogularis* from E Europe, both with a conspicuous red spot in the middle of the blue; White-spotted Bluethroats *cyanecula* from C and S Europe with the spot white instead of red, and *magna* from Turkey, E Iraq and W Iran with either no spot or a small white one. Immature and winter adult males also have unspotted blue throat. Song loud, rich, varied and mimetic, incorporating a distinctive metallic 'ting-ting-ting' and some nightingale-like notes. Chief calls are nightingale-like 'hweet' and 'tacc, tacc'. Swampy and marshy thickets by fresh water and on tundra. 5½ in. (14 cm.). ○M(b)   Map 192

summer   summer   winter   winter

↑ Asia Minor   Red-spotted race →

ROBIN, BLUETHROAT

RED-FLANKED BLUETAIL

♀

♂

Grand Canary, Tenerife

adult

juv.

ROBIN

♂

♀

juv.

SIBERIAN RUBYTHROAT

white-spotted race
summer

juv.

♂

♀

♂
winter

BLUETHROAT

253

THRUSH-NIGHTINGALE or **SPROSSER** *Luscinia luscinia.* Only distinguishable from Nightingale at close quarters when darker brown plumage, less rufous tail and lightly speckled breast can be clearly seen. Song also extremely similar, according to some hearers richer and more beautiful, but equally variable and sometimes consisting almost entirely of harsh notes; lacks Nightingale's crescendo. Calls rather higher-pitched. More exclusively confined to damp thickets. 6½ in. (16·5 cm.). —**V**

NIGHTINGALE *Luscinia megarhynchos.* Like a large, all-brown Robin (p. 253), with a conspicuously rufous tail which is often all that can be seen of this usually rather skulking bird as it dives for the nearest cover. Cf. extremely similar Thrush-Nightingale. Juvenile also like outsize juvenile Robin, but with rufous tail (less rufous than juvenile Redstart p. 251), and paler underparts. Song outstandingly rich in volume and range of notes, including several, such as 'jug, jug' or 'chooc, chooc' and a crescendo based on 'pioo' that only Thrush-Nightingale can approach, but also with many harsh guttural and almost frog-like notes, recalling Great Reed Warbler (p. 225) and other acrocephalines. In some parts of range, e.g. British Isles, song invariably delivered from thick cover, but elsewhere, e.g. Mediterranean Europe, often also from open perches; as often by day as by night. Calls include a soft leaf-warbler-like 'hweet', a hard chat-like 'tacc, tacc', a scolding 'krrr' and a grating 'tchaaa'. Broad-leaved forests, woodland, thickets of all kinds, overgrown hedgerows, shrubberies, large gardens. 6½ in. (16·5 cm.). ●**S Map 193**

Nightingale, juv.

WHITE-THROATED ROBIN *Irania gutturalis.* Male easily identified by its striking head pattern, with white throat and eyestripe and black cheeks, together with rufous underparts and black tail. Female much browner grey, with cheeks grey and no white eyestripe. Juvenile spotted. Song loud and bell-like. Tail may be fanned out in descending flight. Scrub, especially on stony ground and in mountain ravines, usually skulking nightingale-like in the bushes, but sometimes perching boldly out on stones, often with tail cocked up. 6½ in. (16·5 cm.).

RUFOUS BUSHCHAT *Cercotrichas galactotes.* Intermediate between thrushes and warblers in appearance, and characterised by long graduated rufous tail, conspicuously tipped black and white and frequently fanned and jerked. Western birds *galactotes* have whole upperparts largely rufous, but eastern birds *syriacus* are rufous only on rump and tail, otherwise greyish brown. Song musical, varied, rather lark-like, but often somewhat disjointed; delivered from conspicuous perch or in butterfly-like descending display flight; call a hard 'teck, teck'. Scrub, either near human settlements, in gardens, orchards, vineyards, olive groves and among palms and cacti, or in oases, wadi-beds and other semi-desert environments. 6 in. (15 cm.). —**V**

NIGHTINGALES

THRUSH-
NIGHTINGALE

NIGHTINGALE

♂

WHITE-THROATED
ROBIN

♀

juv.

song in flight

western race

eastern race

RUFOUS
BUSHCHAT

255

Thrushes: *Turdus.*   pp. 257–61. Medium-sized song birds with square tail and fairly thin bill adapted to diet of earthworms, molluscs and other invertebrates. Most also eat berries. Juvenile speckled paler. Song usually loud and delivered high in tree. Nest usually in bush or tree.

BLACKBIRD *Turdus merula*. One of the commonest birds of the region. Male distinctive, the only jet-black bird of the region that has a bright orange-yellow bill; smaller Starling (p. 303) is mottled and iridescent, with much shorter tail, bustling gait, and triangular outline in flight. Female darker and young more rufous than other common thrushes, with much less distinct spotting on breast. Mellow fluty song not repetitive like Song Thrush (p. 259) or loud and ringing like Mistle Thrush (p. 259). Calls include 'tchook, tchook', developing into a loud chattering scream when bird alarmed; a persistent 'pink, pink', used in going to roost and mobbing predators; and a high-pitched anxiety note, 'tsee'. Flight direct and impetuous, with a curious flicking motion of wings; usually flirts up tail on alighting; hops or runs; stands with head on one side listening for worms. Broad-leaved and coniferous forests, scrub, parks, gardens, orchards; a common town bird in the W. 10 in. (25 cm.).

●**RMW   Map 194**

RING OUZEL *Turdus torquatus*. Adult easily told from Blackbird by white gorget, coupled with pale patch in wing (especially marked in S European and Asiatic races *alpestris* and *amicorum*), but beware occasional partially albino Blackbirds, which can have similar gorget. Juvenile has more distinctly spotted breast than juvenile Blackbird. Song a simple fluty performance of two or three notes, often an elaboration of the clear piping call-note; also has a harsh grating 'tac, tac, tac', which may run into a loud chatter. Mountains and moorlands, especially lightly wooded slopes. 9½ in. (24 cm.).

●**Sm   Map 195**

FIELDFARE *Turdus pilaris*. Easily told from all other thrushes of the region by combination of blue-grey head and rump and chestnut back, but in flight at any distance closely resembles Mistle Thrush (p. 259), having the same white underwing flashes, and is then best told by distinctive call note, a chuckling 'chack, chack'. Song undistinguished, a medley of chuckles, squeaks and whistles, sometimes heard in chorus from migrant flocks in spring. Open coniferous and broad-leaved woods, and in Scandinavia also parks and gardens; in winter feeds on farmland and other open country. 10 in. (25·5 cm.).

●**MW(b)   Map 196**

BLACK-THROATED THRUSH *Turdus ruficollis atrogularis*. Male strikingly black and white, with upperparts slaty, throat and breast black and belly white. Female browner with throat white and breast streaked or spotted. Both show rufous beneath wings in flight. Cf. Red-throated Thrush (p. 260). Song simple, with some harsh notes; call a blackbird-like chuckle. Taiga and scattered subalpine scrub. 9¼ in. (23·5 cm.).

—**V**

albinistic

♀

BLACKBIRD

♂

♀

♂

RING OUZEL

FIELDFARE

♀

♂

BLACK-THROATED THRUSH

257

REDWING *Turdus iliacus.* The smallest of the commoner thrushes of the region, darker than most Song Thrushes, and easily told by creamy-white eyestripe and conspicuous reddish-chestnut flanks and underwing. Song briefer and flutier than Song Thrush, but rather stilted and repetitive, often accompanied by warbling subsong, which migrant parties collectively utter in late winter. Flight note a very high-pitched 'seeih', often heard from migrant flocks overhead at night, also a soft 'chup' and a harsher 'chittick' or 'chittuck'. Forests, especially birch, areas with scattered trees, and in Scandinavia in town gardens; in winter in farmland and other open country. 8¼ in. (21 cm.).

●rMW   Map 197

SONG THRUSH *Turdus philomelos.* Generally the commonest thrush of the region with dark spots on pale breast, distinguished from larger Mistle Thrush by warmer brown upperparts and no white in tail, from smaller Redwing by no eyestripe and buff underwing, from hen and young Blackbirds (p. 257) by much more distinct dark spotting on breast. Loud clear sometimes mimetic song, heard for greater part of year, easily told from other thrush songs by tendency to repeat each note. Chief call a short soft 'sipp', also a thin redwing-like 'seep' and a 'cheek' alarm note, like Blackbird's but higher-pitched. Flight more direct than Mistle Thrush; hops or runs; frequently stands with head on one side listening for worms. Woods and forests, scrub, town parks, orchards, frequent in suburbs in W and C Europe. Nest lined with mud. 9 in. (23 cm.).   ●RMW   Map 198

MISTLE THRUSH *Turdus viscivorus.* A large greyish thrush, with larger breast spots than Song Thrush, from which also distinguishable in flight by flash of white underwing (cf. Fieldfare, p. 257) and whitish tips to outer tail feathers. Loud ringing song, lacking both the fluty mellowness of the Blackbird (p. 257) and the repetitiveness of the Song Thrush; heard mainly in first half of year. Flight-note a harsh grating or churring chatter, like comb scraped against wood, quite distinct from other thrushes, except White's Thrush. Has a very characteristic flight, shared with Fieldfare, wings being closed at regular intervals but without producing a marked undulation. Coniferous and broad-leaved forests, areas with scattered trees, town parks, gardens; mainly in mountains in S of range, elsewhere a frequent suburban bird; after breeding frequents moors and open grasslands. 10½ in. (27 cm.).   ●Rs   Map 199

WHITE'S THRUSH *Zoothera dauma.* A vagrant from Siberia, larger than any breeding thrush of the region, distinguished from immature Mistle Thrush by golden-brown plumage, crescentic black marks all over both upper and underparts, and in markedly undulating flight also by black and white bands on underwing. Has a whistling song and a churring call like Mistle Thrush. Stays chiefly on ground; does not hop but runs. 10¾ in. (27 cm.).   —V

THRUSHES

REDWING

SONG THRUSH

MISTLE THRUSH

WHITE'S THRUSH

EYE-BROWED THRUSH *Turdus obscurus*. A small thrush, male like a small Redwing (p. 259), but some rufous extending to sides of unstreaked breast. Female browner. Calls a soft 'chuck' and a note like a Redwing but more liquid. Siberia. —V

AMERICAN ROBIN *Turdus migratorius*. One of the most frequent transatlantic passerine vagrants, though still of less than annual occurrence in Europe. In general character resembles a Blackbird. Calls 'kwik, kwik, kwik', like Blackbird, and a softer more song-thrush-like 'pit, pit'. —V

Dusky Thrush

NAUMANN'S THRUSH *Turdus naumanni naumanni*. Rufous tail distinctive. Both surfaces of wings chestnut. Female browner, with blackish breast and flank markings. Siberia. Dusky Thrush *T.n.euonomus* (—V) has tail and underparts blackish.

RED-THROATED THRUSH *Turdus ruficollis ruficollis*. The rufous counterpart of the Black-throated Thrush (p. 257 and below right), both sexes with a rufous tail. Siberia.

White's Thrush   Mistle Thrush   Song Thrush   Redwing

All the thrushes on this page are vagrants to the region, from either Siberia or North America, and like many of the region's vagrants (cf pp. 282–3, 312) they have occurred here mainly in autumn — either as juveniles blown off course by adverse winds on their first southward migration or as adults which may have undertaken an accidental "reversed migration". While none of the thrushes has been noted in Europe more than about 20 times, most of them have occurred in several different countries; recent records of the three American thrushes (American Robin, Olive-backed Thrush, Gray-cheeked Thrush) have however come mainly from the British Isles. Thrushes illustrated elsewhere in the book are shown below for comparison.

GRAY-CHEEKED THRUSH *Catharus minimus.* Like Olive-backed Thrush, but with grey cheeks; lacks eye ring and buff tinge on breast. Call a rather high-pitched 'quee-a'. North America. —V

OLIVE-BACKED THRUSH *Catharus ustulatus.* Like a diminutive Song Thrush (p. 259). Call 'whit' or in flight a short 'heep'. North America.   —V

SIBERIAN THRUSH *Turdus sibiricus.* Both sexes have white eye-stripe and show conspicuous white bar on underwing in flight. Male slaty black. Song a monotonous disyllabic fluty whistle. Siberia.   —V

Fieldfare   Black-throated Thrush   Ring Ouzel   Blackbird   261

BABBLERS: *Timaliidae.* The four species of the large genus *Turdoides* in the region all have uniform brown plumage, paler beneath, and superficially resemble thrushes, but with short rounded wings, not usually held close to the body, and a long, graduated, loosely hanging tail. Bill, legs and feet all strong, the bill slightly curved. Sexes alike. Almost always in parties. Poor fliers, they are constantly on the move in trees and bushes and on the ground, with jerky movements and brief flights, usually one after the other rather than together. Noisy, often with a loud, fairly musical song, often falling abruptly silent. Scrub dwellers.

FULVOUS BABBLER *Turdoides fulvus.* The only North African babbler, a large uniformly yellowish-brown bird with paler underparts, somewhat resembling a sandy-coloured Blackbird (p. 257) but with a longer tail and slightly decurved bill. Scrub in deserts and semi-deserts, especially acacia. 9¾ in. (25 cm.).

ARABIAN BABBLER *Turdoides squamiceps.* A plain earth-brown babbler, paler beneath, separated geographically from the next two species; feathers of crown tipped blackish, those of forehead stiff and scaly. Highly gregarious, in parties up to two dozen, which perform curious dances in the evening. The birds 'follow my leader' round a bush, each one hopping and then raising its tail and wagging it from side to side. After this they all fly off into a bush and noisily perform their preening toilet. Very inquisitive birds, they will fly down to inspect any strange object, and torment it if it proves to be alive and has the misfortune to be either smaller or less agile than themselves. Especially acacia scrub. 10½ in. (26·5 cm.).

COMMON BABBLER *Turdoides caudatus.* Plumage earth brown, tinged fulvous, faintly resembling a smallish long-tailed Mistle Thrush (p. 259) but with unspotted breast. Juvenile heavily streaked darker and spotted paler. Hops with a bouncing gait on the ground, trailing tail and nervously twitching wings. Parties in flight utter a low rippling note, 'which-which-which-ri-ri-ri-ri-ri', their long tails giving tham a miniature hen-pheasant appearance. Dry open country with scrub, cultivations, gardens. 9 in. (23 cm.).

IRAQ BABBLER *Turdoides altirostris.* Smaller than Common Babbler, differing also in its shorter weaker and more curved bill and especially in its unstreaked underparts. Juvenile quite distinct from juvenile Common Babbler, much paler above, with creamy buff cheeks, and underparts unstreaked creamy buff, with white chin and vent. More or less confined to reed-beds, palm groves and cultivations in Lower Iraq and south-western Iran, but can also be found among reeds as much as a mile from the shore. 8¾ in. (22 cm.).

BABBLERS

FULVOUS BABBLER

courtship
display

ARABIAN BABBLER

**COMMON
BABBLER**

IRAQ BABBLER

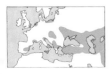

BEARDED TIT *Panurus biarmicus* (Timaliidae). Tit-like but related to the babblers (p. 263), not to the tits; the only small reed-bed bird with a long tail. Predominantly rufous; cock easily recognised by striking pattern of black 'moustaches' on grey head, also black under tail coverts; hen shares black and white wing-bars, otherwise lacks black; bill yellow, legs black. Juvenile brown with whitish throat and black back. Calls include characteristic metallic 'ching', 'dzu-dzu' and a kissing note. Flight weak and undulating. Confined to extensive reed-beds. 6½ in. (16·5 cm.).

⊙ **Rw   Map 200**

LONG-TAILED TIT *Aegithalos caudatus.* (Paridae; see p. 266). A small black, white and pink bird of more than half of whose length is occupied by its tail. Northern and eastern forms have pure white head; western forms have black stripe over eye, southern forms have grey back and grey eyestripe. Chief calls a soft 'tupp' and a spluttering 'tsirrup'; rarely heard song combines various call notes. Flight weak and undulating, often flying in a string from tree to tree. Broad-leaved and mixed woods and scrub, less frequent than other tits in parks and gardens. Unmistakable domed egg-shaped nest, woven of moss and cobwebs. 5½ in. (14 cm.).

● **R   Map 201**

PENDULINE TIT *Remiz pendulinus* (Paridae). A small long-tailed grey and brown bird, readily told by contrasting pale grey head and throat, black cheeks and chestnut mantle. Juvenile lacks black and chestnut. Caucasus race *caspius* is chestnut on crown, sometimes joining with chestnut on mantle. Calls, a low robin-like 'tsee' and a more tit-like 'tsi-tsi-tsi'. Flight somewhat resembles Blue Tit (p. 267). Marshes, fens, freshwater margins, with scrub or willow; nest flask-shaped. Spreading westwards. 4¼ in. (11 cm.).

—**V**

● **SUNBIRDS:** *Nectariniidae.* Old World equivalent of the hummingbirds, brilliantly variegated jewels that dart about from flower to flower, hovering to feed on nectar with usually long decurved bill.

ORANGE-TUFTED SUNBIRD or PALESTINE SUNBIRD *Nectarinia osea.* Breeding males have head, neck and upperparts metallic green, forehead violet, chin and throat metallic blue, and orange and yellow tufts at each side of breast. Non-breeding males and females olive-green with pale eyestripe and dark green tail. Dry open or rocky grassland. Nest bottle-shaped, usually in a thorn bush. 4–4½ in. (10–11·5 cm.).

PYGMY SUNBIRD or NILE VALLEY SUNBIRD *Anthreptes platurus.* Smaller than Orange-tufted Sunbird and easily distinguished by short bill; breeding male even more distinctive with very long tail (⅓ of total length) and green, violet and yellow plumage. Short-tailed olive-green non-breeding male and female resemble stout-billed leaf warblers (p. 237). Dry scrub, grassland; gardens in Nile Delta. 4–6 in. (10–15 cm.).

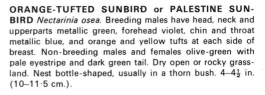

LONG-TAILED TIT
western race

southern race

northern and
eastern race

♂

♀

BEARDED TIT

adult

PENDULINE TIT

Caucasus

juv.

♂

♀

**ORANGE-TUFTED
SUNBIRD**

♂ breeding

♀

♂
winter

PYGMY SUNBIRD

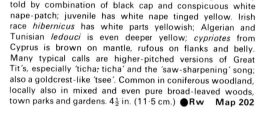

TITS : *Paridae*. pp. 265–9. Small active short-billed insectivorous birds, often flocking together, several species visiting gardens. Sexes alike; summer and winter plumage alike. Some species have an explosive hissing threat display on nest. Nests usually in holes, readily breeding in nest-boxes.

COAL TIT *Parus ater*. The smallest tit of the region, easily told by combination of black cap and conspicuous white nape-patch; juvenile has white nape tinged yellow. Irish race *hibernicus* has white parts yellowish; Algerian and Tunisian *ledouci* is even deeper yellow; *cypriotes* from Cyprus is brown on mantle, rufous on flanks and belly. Many typical calls are higher-pitched versions of Great Tit's, especially 'ticha; ticha' and the 'saw-sharpening' song; also a goldcrest-like 'tsee'. Common in coniferous woodland, locally also in mixed and even pure broad-leaved woods, town parks and gardens. $4\frac{1}{2}$ in. (11·5 cm.) ●Rw **Map 202**

GREAT TIT *Parus major*. A large tit, easily recognised by black and white head combined with broad black bib down centre of bright yellow underparts. Juveniles have black parts brownish and white parts yellowish. Extensive vocabulary includes a deceptively chaffinch-like 'pink' and a wide range of calls like those of other tits but louder. One form of song often rendered 'teacher, teacher', another likened to a saw being sharpened. Common in woodland, orchards, olive groves, town parks, gardens, heaths and other places with scattered trees. $5\frac{1}{2}$ in. (14 cm.).
●Rw **Map 203**

AZURE TIT *Parus cyanus*. The Asiatic counterpart of the Blue Tit, extending westwards across the plains of Russia, where it may hybridise with the Blue Tit. Larger, whiter and much less blue than Blue Tit, differing especially in its white head, white V on each wing, and longer tail. Juveniles are greyer, especially on the head. Typical call note like Long-tailed Tit's (p. 265) 'tsirrup'. Frequents broad-leaved scrub rather than forests, especially by fresh water, also birch-woods. $5\frac{1}{4}$ in. (13 cm.).

BLUE TIT *Parus caeruleus*. The only tit, indeed the only small bird of the region, appearing mainly blue and yellow; bright blue on head especially distinctive. Juvenile has white cheek and nape patches tinged yellow. In Canary Is. and N Africa head darker, mantle colour varies from grey through blue-grey to olive-green, and bill slightly longer and thinner. Race *palmensis* on La Palma has white belly; *ombriosus* on Hierro has olive-green back; *teneriffae* on the other islands has hardly any white on wings; and *ultramarinus* in N Africa is darker blue on mantle. Most typical of many calls is a rather scolding 'tsee-tsee-tsee-tsit'; cheerful song can be rendered 'tsee-tseee-tsu-tsuhuhuhu'. Common in broad-leaved woodland and areas with scattered trees, such as town parks and gardens, hedgerows, orchards and palm and olive groves; uncommon in coniferous woods. In winter frequent in reed-beds. In Canaries feeds on tree trunks like Treecreeper (p. 273). $4\frac{1}{2}$ in (11·5 cm.).
●Rw **Map 204**

TITS

adult
COAL TIT
juv

adult
Cyprus

adult
Algeria
Tunisia

juv.

Cyprus

GREAT TIT

AZURE TIT

BLUE TIT

Hierro   Palma   Gomera Tenerife   N Africa
                   Grand Canary

CRESTED TIT *Parus cristatus*. The only tit, and indeed the only really small bird of the region, with a crest. No wing-bar and white cheeks are useful pointers when crest cannot be seen. Vocabulary restricted to a rather soft trill, and the usual 'si-si-si. . . ' tit contact note. Mainly in coniferous woods, also in mixed woodland. 4½ in. (11·5 cm.). ○R **Map 205**

SIBERIAN TIT *Parus cinctus*. The northern counterpart of the Sombre Tit, like which it resembles a Marsh or Willow Tit as large as a Great Tit, but with much browner crown, nape and larger throat-patch. Voice willow-tit-like, but with a rather drawn-out 'eeez-eeez-eeez-eeez'-note. Coniferous and birch forests. 5¼ in. (13·5 cm.).

MARSH TIT *Parus palustris*. Marsh and Willow Tits are the only small tits with black crown, nape and chin, paler cheeks and underparts, distinguished from each other better by voice than by plumage. Adult Marsh Tit has glossy black crown and no pale patch on wing. Typical call note is 'pitchüü', often followed by a harsh 'tchay', less grating and nasal than corresponding note of Willow Tit, together with a distinctive scolding 'chicka-bee-bee-bee'. Song, a rather tuneless little rattle, 'schip-schip-schip' or 'schuppi-schuppi-schuppi' is quite different from either of Willow Tit's songs. Frequent in broad-leaved woodland and scrub, but with no special attachment to marshes. 4½ in. (11·5 cm.).
●R **Map 206**

WILLOW TIT *Parus montanus*. Very similar to Marsh Tit, but crown more sooty and has a sometimes obscure small pale patch on the secondaries. Northern race *borealis* is greyer, with white cheeks. Typical call note a grating, nasal 'tchay' or 'aig', sometimes preceded by 'chick' or 'chickit', but never by Marsh Tit's 'pitchüü'; also a characteristic thin 'eez-eez-eez' lacking from Marsh Tit's vocabulary. Never scolds like a Marsh Tit. Has two distinct songs, a liquid garden-warbler-like one quite unlike the song of any other tit and with a rather spasmodic delivery, and a more ringing, but slightly sad and wood-warbler-like 'piu-piu-piu'. Frequent in both broad-leaved and coniferous woodland and scrub, but showing no special preference for willows. Excavates own nest hole, unlike other tits. 4½ in. (11·5 cm.).
●R **Map 207**

SOMBRE TIT *Parus lugubris*. Like a rather drab great-tit-sized Marsh or Willow Tit, but with a larger black throat patch, browner-black crown (extending below eye) and nape and whiter cheeks. Cf. Siberian Tit. Asia Minor race *anatoliae* has crown and throat patch blacker. Much of its vocabulary is like Great Tit's (p. 267), but a distinctive note is rendered 'chrrrh' or 'churr-r-r'. Wooded and rocky country. 5½ in. (14 cm.).

TITS

CRESTED TIT

SIBERIAN TIT

MARSH TIT

WILLOW TIT

N Scandinavia

S Scandinavia
E Carpathians
Ukraine

SOMBRE TIT

Asia Minor
Transcaucasia

NUTHATCHES: *Sittidae*. Small tree-climbing birds, short-tailed and compact; sexes alike. The only birds which habitually descend trees head downwards, with jerky gait; feeding on small invertebrates, nuts and seeds, the tougher items being wedged into cracks in bark and hammered open. Hole nesters.

KRÜPER'S NUTHATCH *Sitta krüperi*. Similar to Corsican Nuthatch, but with a distinctive broad reddish-brown band on breast. Calls a soft single 'pwit' recalling Great Spotted Woodpecker's 'tick', a rippling 'pip, pip, pip, pip . . . .' and a harsh 'schwee'. Coniferous forests in Asia Minor eastwards to the Caucasus; very active and feeding tit-like on outer branches of pines. 5 in. (12·5 cm.).

CORSICAN NUTHATCH *Sitta whiteheadi*. Like a small Nuthatch with black crown (grey in hen) and conspicuous white stripe above black eyestripe; underparts pale. Vocabulary distinct and quieter, including a nasal jay-like note. Confined to pine forests in Corsica, where Nuthatch absent. 4¾ in. (12 cm.).

NUTHATCH *Sitta europaea*. Much the commonest and most widespread nuthatch in the region, blue-grey above, with underparts varying from white in the north to deep orange-buff with white belly in the south and west; black stripe through eye. Juvenile has no chestnut but some white in tail. The only bird with longish straight bill and this colour combination that is likely to be seen creeping about trees over most of Europe. Also known for habit of cracking hazel nuts. Wide vocabulary, includes loud ringing calls, e.g. typical 'chwit-chwit' or 'chwit-it-it', a sibilant long-tailed-tit-like 'tsirrup' and song, loud piping repetitions of 'twee', 'chu' or 'pee'. Always in trees, in forests, woods, copses, parkland and large gardens, where may visit bird tables; may accompany winter foraging parties of tits. Usually walls up nest holes with mud. 5½ in. (14 cm.). ●R **Map 208**

EASTERN ROCK NUTHATCH *Sitta tephronota*. Markedly larger than Rock Nuthatch, with longer, broader eyestripe and longer, stouter bill. Habitat similar to Rock Nuthatch, which it overlaps in Iraq, Iran and Armenia, but usually at greater elevations, above 3000 ft. 6 in. (15 cm.).

ROCK NUTHATCH *Sitta neumayer*. A south-eastern species very like Nuthatch, but coloration generally drabber, underparts paler and browner, no white on tail, and habitat quite distinct. In Iraq and Iran upperparts may be grey, and black stripe almost absent. Some calls resemble Nuthatch but others very varied from rich fluty cadences to jay-like screams; 'song' has rising and falling scale of shrill piping notes reminiscent of Tree Pipit (p. 209). Inland cliffs, gorges, hillsides and other rocky places, nesting in rock crevices walled up with mud. 5½ in. (14 cm.).

KABYLE NUTHATCH *Sitta ledanti*. Similar to Corsican Nuthatch, but with a less prominent white eyestripe and pinkish-beige underparts. Has a loud ringing fluty cry of 7-8 notes and a nasal jay-like call. Confined to coniferous forest on the Petite Kabyle, eastern Algeria, where first discovered in 1975.

NUTHATCHES

KRÜPER'S NUTHATCH

♂

CORSICAN NUTHATCH

♀

NUTHATCH

northern race

EASTERN ROCK NUTHATCH

**ROCK
NUTHATCH**

271

WALLCREEPER *Tichodroma muraria* (Sittidae). Despite its curved bill is more closely related to nuthatches than to treecreepers. Very distinctive with its constantly flicked bright red wing-patches; grey, white-spotted on wings and tail, with throat black, moulting to whitish in autumn. Song like Treecreeper but louder, on rising scale, habitually uttered while climbing. Flight butterflylike. Inland cliffs, rocky gorges, to snow-line in mountains, replacing the rock nuthatches (p. 271) high up; migrates lower down in winter, when often on stone buildings. 6½ in. (16·5 cm.)

—V

TREECREEPER *Certhia familiaris* (Certhiidae). The two treecreepers are the only small brown land birds of the region with curved beaks, and apart from the Wryneck (p. 197) the only ones that habitually creep mouse-like about tree-trunks, away from which they are hardly ever seen, except on a stone wall or in bat-like display flight. Presence more often detected by ear than by eye; song, 'tee-tee-tee-titidooee' and call-note, a rather prolonged 'tseee', both very high-pitched. Coniferous (especially spruce and fir) and mixed woodlands, only on mountains in the S; in British Isles also in broad-leaved woods, parks and gardens. Often with tit parties in winter. 5 in. (12·5 cm.).

●R   Map 209

SHORT-TOED TREECREEPER *Certhia brachydactyla*. Hard to separate from Treecreeper in the field, except by brownish flanks, voice and distribution. Song louder and less high-pitched, and call-note louder, more piping and sometimes trilling. Broad-leaved woods, parks, gardens and other areas with scattered trees, also, in Mediterranean area, coniferous forests. 5 in. (12·5 cm.).

WREN *Troglodytes troglodytes* (Troglodytidae). The smallest warm brown bird of the region, distinctive for its barred plumage, short, often cocked-up rufous tail and whirring flight. Vigorous clear warbling song is loud for so small a bird; call-note an irritable 'tic-tic-tic', often prolonged into a scolding trill. Wide range of habitats, from rocky mountain tops, sea cliffs and moors to forests, scrub, heaths, parks and gardens; common in town suburbs. May roost in domed nest after breeding season. 3¾ in. (9·5 cm.).

●Rm   Map 210

DIPPER *Cinclus cinclus* (Cinclidae). Unmistakable for conspicuous white front and habit of constantly bobbing on rock in midstream. Northern birds lack any rufous on underparts. Juvenile grey-brown above, whitish speckled darker below. Can swim both on and under surface, and dive from water or air; walks on stream-bed. Loud, rather wren-like song; call-notes 'zit, zit, zit' and a metallic 'clink, clink'. Only on fast streams in hills and mountains, but in winter may wander to lowland streams. 7 in. (18 cm.).

●Rw   Map 211

CREEPERS, WREN, DIPPER

winter

WALLCREEPER

summer

TREECREEPER

**SHORT-TOED
TREECREEPER**

WREN

adult

juv.

Britain
Central Europe

DIPPER

N Europe
S W Europe

273

BUNTINGS: *Emberizidae.* pp. 275–81. Mainly ground-living finch-like birds, of open country, with thick seed-eating bills; usually rather indifferent songsters. Male usually more brightly coloured than female. Flight fairly fast and bounding. Most species avoid human settlements.

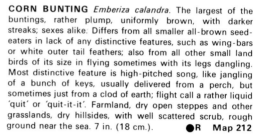

CORN BUNTING *Emberiza calandra.* The largest of the buntings, rather plump, uniformly brown, with darker streaks; sexes alike. Differs from all smaller all-brown seed-eaters in lack of any distinctive features, such as wing-bars or white outer tail feathers; also from all other small land birds of its size in flying sometimes with its legs dangling. Most distinctive feature is high-pitched song, like jangling of a bunch of keys, usually delivered from a perch, but sometimes just from a clod of earth; flight call a rather liquid 'quit' or 'quit-it-it'. Farmland, dry open steppes and other grasslands, dry hillsides, with well scattered scrub, rough ground near the sea. 7 in. (18 cm.). ●R **Map 212**

HOUSE BUNTING or STRIPED BUNTING *Emberiza striolata.* A small bunting, male being the only seed-eater with whole head, neck and upper breast uniform grey, and rest of plumage pale rufous or warm brown; female pale brown where male grey. Male has two less distinct whitish stripes instead of conspicuous black head stripes of Rock Bunting, with which it may consort. Song somewhat chaffinch-like; call a nasal 'tzswee'. In N Africa, a town and village bird, often as tame and semi-domesticated as House Sparrow; in S W Asia also in often remote rocky wadis, sometimes accompanying herds of sheep and goats. 5¼ in. (13·5 cm.).

ROCK BUNTING *Emberiza cia.* Male easily told by striking head pattern, grey with three black stripes, above, through and below eye; grey throat distinguishes from all other seed-eaters except House Bunting and much smaller Syrian Serin (p. 293). Unstreaked chestnut rump and pale rufous underparts also important identification features, especially in separating immature from young Ortolan and Cretzschmar's Buntings (p. 279). Female browner, duller and more streaked. Song a typical high-pitched bunting buzz, 'zi-zi-zi-zirr', often delivered from a rock with fluttering wings; call a sharp 'tzit', like Cirl Bunting (p. 277), and a bubbling twitter, 'tootootooc'. Rocky and stony hill sides, vineyards, gardens, wintering lower down. 6¼ in. (16 cm.).   —**V**

PINE BUNTING *Emberiza leucocephala.* A mainly brown and white bird, male with striking chestnut and white head pattern in breeding plumage, duller in winter; female like female Yellowhammer (p. 277) but white instead of yellow. Song resembles Chaffinch (p. 285). Open woodland, scrub, farmland, often near fresh water and along roads. Hybridises with Yellowhammer in W Siberia. 6½ in. (16·5 cm.).   —**V**

BUNTINGS

legs
dangling

CORN BUNTING

♂

HOUSE
BUNTING

♂
nai

♀

ROCK BUNTING

♂

♀

♂

winter

♂

PINE BUNTING

275

YELLOWHAMMER *Emberiza citrinella*. Male is the yellowest bird of the region (but cf. Yellow Wagtail, p. 214) and is the only mainly yellow one with chestnut back and rump. Female and juvenile browner and less yellow, but still with chestnut rump; white outer tail feathers conspicuous in flight at all ages. Cf. Cirl Bunting. High-pitched song has unmistakable pattern, popularly 'a little bit of bread and no cheese'; calls a sibilantly liquid 'twit-up' and a more grating 'twink' or 'twit'. Farmland, hedgerows, scrub, forest clearings and edges. 6½ in. (16·5 cm.).

●R Map 213

CIRL BUNTING *Emberiza cirlus*. From Yellowhammer male easily told by grey crown, black throat and greyish-green band across yellow breast; all ages have olive rump, which is only sure distinction of female and juvenile. Normal song quite different, a brief rattling trill, recalling Lesser Whitethroat (p. 231) but flatter, usually delivered from a tree where Yellowhammer prefers a bush; a rare variant sounds like Yellowhammer without the final 'cheese', sometimes heard from Yellowhammers too. Call 'zit', higher-pitched than Yellowhammer, also a wren-like churring alarm note. Farmland, hedgerows, areas with scattered trees and bushes. 6½ in. (16·5 cm.).

⊙R Map 214

YELLOW-BREASTED BUNTING *Emberiza aureola*. A small bunting, male very distinctive with dark head and yellow underparts, chestnut breast-band and white wing-patches, very conspicuous in flight. Female and juvenile differ from similar Yellowhammers chiefly in brown forehead, pale stripe down centre of crown, unstreaked centre of breast, indistinct pale wing-bars and less white in tail. Simple but loud and musical song, 'tü-li, tü-li, tü-li-ti, lü-li, li-lü-li', recalls Ortolan's (p. 279). Call a short 'zipp' and a soft 'trssit'. Open woodland and scrub. 5½ in. (14 cm.). —V

RED-HEADED BUNTING *Emberiza bruniceps*. Striking plumage of male, with uniformly chestnut head, throat and upper breast and bright yellow underparts makes it an attractive cage bird, so that males occurring in the West are presumably almost all escapes. Female like female House Sparrow (p. 299) but with pale yellow belly, under tail coverts, and rump. Song a loud pleasant whistle; call a musical 'tweet'. Scrub, in steppes, semi-deserts, and by fresh water. 6½ in. (16·5 cm.).

BLACK-HEADED BUNTING *Emberiza melanocephala*. Male differs from Cirl Bunting in its plain black head, from Yellow-breasted Bunting in its lack of chestnut breast-band, and from both in its lack of white in tail, which also, together with uniformly unstreaked underparts, differentiates female from females of these species and of Yellowhammer; pale chestnut rump separates from female Red-headed. Song more melodious than most buntings, beginning with a rather grating 'chit, chit, chit' phrase; calls 'chup', 'zitt' and 'zee'. Scrub, olive groves, hedgerows, gardens. 6½ in. (16·5 cm.).

—V

BUNTINGS

YELLOWHAMMER

♀ ♂

CIRL BUNTING

♀ ♂

YELLOW-BREASTED
BUNTING

♀ ♂

RED-HEADED BUNTING

♀ ♂

BLACK-HEADED BUNTING

277

gs dangling

ORTOLAN *Emberiza hortulana*. A not very brightly coloured bunting, mainly pinkish-brown with greyish-green head and breast and yellow throat, readily distinguished at close range by its white eye ring; female and juvenile successively duller and browner, with dark streaks on breast. In poor light throat pattern is a useful character, yellow underwing and reddish-brown bill and legs are also useful pointers. Cf. Cretzschmar's Bunting and Rock Bunting (p. 275). Rather mournful song consists of 6–8 'zeu' and 'zeee' notes, usually including a change of pitch; call a rather weak, cirl-bunting-like 'zit', also a flight-note, 'pwit' and a piping 'tseu'. Cultivations, and a wide range of country with scattered trees or shrubs, often in hills, sometimes in gardens. 6½ in. (16·5 cm.). ○**M**

Ortolan's 'territorial round flight'

CRETZSCHMAR'S BUNTING *Emberiza caesia*. In many ways very like Ortolan; adult has blue-grey instead of grey-green head and breast, and rufous instead of yellow throat, juvenile more buffish-chestnut, and like adult has whitish under-wing. Juvenile also differs from juvenile Rock Bunting (p. 275) only in its pink bill. Winter plumage duller. Song similar to Ortolan's, but briefer; call a loud, insistent 'styip'. Bare, rocky and sparsely vegetated hillsides and semi-deserts, usually on the ground, rarely perching in bushes; can be remarkably tame on migration. 6¼ in. (16 cm.). —**V**

GREY-NECKED BUNTING *Emberiza buchanani*. Very like both Ortolan and Cretzschmar's Bunting, but head all blue-grey, extending on to mantle, and breast and throat all linnet-red. Female duller. Song longer than Ortolan's, 'dze dze dze dzee-oo', with rising inflection but falling on the last note. Flight-notes include 'sip' and 'choup'. Dry open stony country with sparse vegetation, scattered bushes and rocky outcrops, above 7000 ft. 5¾ in. (14·5 cm.).

CINEREOUS BUNTING *Emberiza cineracea*. A yellow-headed bunting, with mainly greyish-brown plumage, but belly of Iran race *semenowi*, which migrates through or winters in Syria or Iraq, is yellow instead of grey; bill bluish. Female and juvenile duller, with streaks on throat. Brief bunting-like song typically has three long and two short notes; call 'kip'. An uncommon bird of high rocky slopes up to the tree limit, on migration in the deserts of the Middle East. Breeds on Mytilene in the Aegean. 6½ in. (16·5 cm.).

BUNTINGS

juv.

♂

ORTOLAN

♀

CRETZSCHMAR'S
BUNTING

♂

juv.

♀

GREY-NECKED
BUNTING

♂

♀

Syrian Desert, Iraq

♂

♀

CINEREOUS BUNTING

279

REED BUNTING *Emberiza schoeniclus*. Breeding male very distinctive with whole head black (browner in winter) relieved only by white moustachial streak, nape also white. Female and juvenile streaky brown; young males moulting into adult plumage have a triangular brown patch on breast. All ages and sexes show white feathers in tail when flying away. Cf. Little, Rustic and Lapland Buntings. Squeaky, staccato song, 'tweek, tweek, tweek, tititick'; chief call a yellow-wagtail-like 'tseep', also 'ching' and 'tsip'. Constantly flicks tail. Breeds in fens, reed-beds, rushy fields, freshwater margins, other marshy places, also in some areas, e.g. parts of England, in drier, yellowhammer-type habitats; in winter also on farmland. 6 in. (15 cm.).

●Rmw   Map 215

LITTLE BUNTING *Emberiza pusilla*. The smallest bunting of the N of the region, very like a small female Reed Bunting with rufous cheeks and crown. Song brief, twittering, almost robin-like; call a reed-bunting-like 'tsew', but alarm note, 'pwick' or 'tip, tip', quite distinct. Tundra scrub. 5¼ in. (13·5 cm.).

—A

RUSTIC BUNTING *Emberiza rustica*. Breeding male differs from Reed Bunting in its white throat and eyestripe and chestnut breast band; underparts also whiter than most other buntings; female and winter male have black parts browner. Female differs from female Reed Bunting especially in eyestripe not running in front of eye. May raise crest feathers. Song brief and warbling, recalling Robin (p. 253) or Hedgesparrow (p. 221); call a shrill 'tsip, tsip, tsip', like Little Bunting but louder. High northern forests, usually swampy. 5¾ in. (14·5 cm.).

—A

SNOW BUNTING *Plectrophenax nivalis*. Breeding male very black and white, with increasing admixtures of brown in winter male, female, immature and juvenile. Longish wings, gregarious habits (flocks are appropriately known as 'snowflakes'), and white wing-patches and underparts are distinctive at all times. Loud, sweet, rather repetitive song uttered from low song post or in aerial display flight; flight note a silvery rippling 'tirrirrirrip', mostly from flocks, numerous other notes (22 are described) include a soft 'twee' or 'tweet', a rather mournful whistling 'tew', and a disyllabic 'chis-ick'. Breeds on barren tundra, remote rocky sea shores and mountain tops; in winter mainly on coasts, also on hills inland. 6½ in. (16·5 cm.). ☉rmW   Map 216

LAPLAND BUNTING *Calcarius lapponicus*. Breeding male differs from male Reed Bunting in buff eyestripe, chestnut nape, whiter underparts and more black on sides of breast. Winter male lacks most of the black, as with female differs from female Reed Bunting especially in rufous nape and yellow bill. Song melodious, brief, somewhat recalling Skylark (p. 205); chief call a distinctive flat little trill, 'ticky-tick-tick', also 'teeu'. Runs on ground. Breeds on tundra, in winter on coasts and moors. 6 in. (15 cm.).

○Mw   Map 217

BUNTINGS

REED BUNTING

winter

♀

♂ summer

LITTLE BUNTING

♂

winter

♀ summer

RUSTIC
BUNTING

♂

♂

winter

♀ summer

SNOW BUNTING

APLAND BUNTING

ter

♀ summer

♂

281

PARULA WARBLER *Parula americana* (Parulidae). Yellow-green patch on back coupled with yellow throat and breast and conspicuous double wing-bar are distinctive, also male's dark breast-band. —V

RED-EYED VIREO *Vireo olivaceus* (Vireonidae). Vireos have heavier bills than warblers. Red-eyed has grey cap, black-bordered white eyestripe, no wing-bars. Immatures have brown eye. —V

adult

1st year

AMERICAN REDSTART *Setophaga ruticilla* (Parulidae). Very distinctive, male black with bright orange patches on wings and tail, female browner with yellow instead of orange, immature resembles female; a great fly-catcher. —V

adult ♂

imm.

MYRTLE WARBLER *Dendroica coronata* (Parulidae). Yellow rump is best field mark of all ages and in all seasons, coupled with white throat. Breeding male also has yellow crown and wing-patches. —V

♂

imm.

BALTIMORE ORIOLE *Icterus galbula* (Icteridae). Male in breeding plumage is only black and orange bird likely to be seen in region. Female and young more like female Golden Oriole (p. 303) but with white wing-bars. —V

RARE AMERICAN VISITORS: small passerines. An increasing number of North American passerines are being recorded as genuine vagrants in Western Europe. Only those which have occurred at least three times are shown here. Seven other species have occurred once or twice.

WHITE-THROATED SPARROW *Zonotrichia albicollis* (Emberizidae). White throat and yellow spot in front of eye, are best distinctions; no other American sparrow or bunting also has black and white striped crown. —**V**

FOX SPARROW *Passerella iliaca* (Emberizidae). Like a rather large House Sparrow (p. 299), with a conspicuous rufous rump and tail. —**V**

SLATE-COLORED JUNCO *Junco hyemalis* (Emberizidae). All dark grey except for white belly and conspicuous white outer tail feathers. —**V**

NORTHERN WATERTHRUSH *Seiurus noveboracensis* (Parulidae). Like a diminutive Song Thrush (p. 259) or a rather short-tailed Meadow Pipit (p. 209), but with streaks on underparts. Walks bobbingly, at edge of streams. —**V**

adult ♂

imm.

ROSE-BREASTED GROSBEAK *Pheucticus ludovicianus* (Emberizidae). Striped head and heavy bill of immature make it look much more like other seed-eaters than the red-breasted black and white adult, not yet seen in Europe. —**V**

283

Small thick-billed gregarious seed-eating birds, breeding mainly in habitats associated with trees, and with a characteristic bounding or dancing flight. Often better songsters than buntings. The principal groups are chaffinches, (below), carduelines (p. 287), trumpeter finches (p. 289), redpolls (p. 291), rose finches (p. 295) and crossbills (p. 297).

Finches, sparrows and buntings in winter on a feeding place for pheasants

BRAMBLING *Fringilla montifringilla.* Northern analogue of Chaffinch; best field mark is white rump, conspicuous when flying away, but orange-buff breast and shoulders also distinctive. Cock has head and mantle black in breeding season, otherwise brownish like hen and juvenile. Song resembles Greenfinch's 'dzhweee'; commonest call-note a rather harsh 'tsweék', flight note 'chucc-chucc'. Birchwoods and willow scrub of northern taiga; in winter in open country and under beeches or hornbeams, often flocking with Chaffinches. 5¾ in. (14·5 cm.). ●MW(b)　**Map 218**

CHAFFINCH *Fringilla coelebs.* Generally the commonest European finch, readily distinguished by combination of white shoulder-patch, white wing-bar and white in tail. Cock unmistakable with slate-blue head and nape, green rump and pinkish-brown underparts; mantle usually chestnut, but slate-blue in Canaries, greenish in Azores (*moreletti*) and Madeira *(maderensis)* and green in N Africa; main Canary form (*tintillon*) has bright green rump. Island and African forms also have black wings and black mark on forehead. Hen and juvenile yellowish-brown above, much darker in island forms, greyish below, and best told from other brown finches by conspicuous white shoulder-patch. Cheerful rattling song varies widely from region to region, and on Continent often ends in 'tick' recalling Great Spotted Woodpecker (p. 195). Commonest call-note, 'pink, pink' very like similar note of Great Tit (p. 267); also flight note, a soft 'tsup', casual 'tsit' and insistent warning 'wheet'; a confusing spring call is 'tsweee', reminiscent of both Greenfinch (p. 287) and Brambling. Call of Canary forms, 'choo, choo', 'chwee, chwee' or 'chwoopie'. Woods and forests, areas with scattered trees, heaths, farmland, orchards, town parks, gardens; frequent in town suburbs. In winter in more open country, often with other finches, and with bramblings under beeches 6 in. (15 cm.). ●RmW　**Map 219**

BLUE CHAFFINCH *Fringilla teydea.* Confined to Canary Is., this slate-blue chaffinch, the hen duller, is quite unmistakable, lacking the pinkish breast of the Canary forms of the common species. Song and call-notes like Chaffinch. Conifer forests high on Tenerife and Gran Canaria. 6½ in. (16·5 cm.).

FINCHES

♂ summer

♀

BRAMBLING

♂ winter

CHAFFINCH

♀

Madeira ♂

♂ N Africa

♂ Azores

♂

Canary Is. ♂

♂

♀

BLUE CHAFFINCH

GOLDFINCH *Carduelis carduelis.* A most distinctively plumaged finch, with red face, yellow wing-bars, whitish rump and black and white on head, wings and tail. Juvenile lacks red and is streaked, lack of yellow in tail separating it from young Greenfinch. Flight notably dancing. Song a series of tinkling variations on liquid 'tswitt-witt-witt' flight-note; call a rather harsh 'geez'. Habitat as Greenfinch; especially fond of orchards and in autumn of feeding on thistles and other tall plants. 4¾ in. (12 cm.).

●RS   Map 220

SISKIN *Carduelis spinus.* A small yellow-rumped dark-streaked yellowish-green finch, male distinguished from all other yellow-green finches by black chin and crown. Female and juvenile less yellow and more streaked, with no black on head. Distinguished from Serin (p. 293) at all ages by yellow patches at base of tail. Sweet twittering song often uttered in bat-like display flight; most frequent calls, 'tsuu' and 'tsyzing'. Coniferous or mixed woods, especially spruce; also sometimes in areas with scattered conifers. In winter often consorts with Redpolls (p. 291) on birches and alders. 4¾ in. (12 cm.).   ⊙ RMw   Map 221

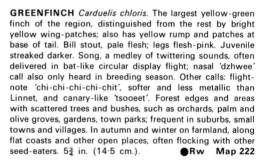

GREENFINCH *Carduelis chloris.* The largest yellow-green finch of the region, distinguished from the rest by bright yellow wing-patches; also has yellow rump and patches at base of tail. Bill stout, pale flesh; legs flesh-pink. Juvenile streaked darker. Song, a medley of twittering sounds, often delivered in bat-like circular display flight; nasal 'dzhwee' call also only heard in breeding season. Other calls: flight-note 'chi-chi-chi-chi-chit', softer and less metallic than Linnet, and canary-like 'tsooeet'. Forest edges and areas with scattered trees and bushes, such as orchards, palm and olive groves, gardens, town parks; frequent in suburbs, small towns and villages. In autumn and winter on farmland, along flat coasts and other open places, often flocking with other seed-eaters. 5¾ in. (14·5 cm.).   ●Rw   Map 222

BULLFINCH *Pyrrhula pyrrhula.* Male is unmistakable with black cap and red underparts, pinker female and juvenile almost equally so; white rump a conspicuous feature when flying away. Northern birds are larger and pale; Spanish birds *iberiae* are deeper red. Very rare Azores race *murina*, until recently believed to be extinct, has male like female. Generally rather shy, often revealing presence only by penetrating plangent low whistle 'deu', which also forms basis of feeble, creaky, often trisyllabic piping song. Woodland, scrub and orchards and large gardens near woodland cover; favours conifers, except in W Europe, where also in broad-leaved woods. 5¾–6¼ in. (14·5–16 cm.).

●Rw   Map 223

FINCHES

juv.

adult

GOLDFINCH

juv.

♂

♀

SISKIN

♂

BULLFINCH

♂

♀

juv.

♀

juv.

♂

Azores

GREENFINCH

287

Hawfinch winter

Brambling winter

Chaffinch winter

White-winged Grosbeak

HAWFINCH *Coccothraustes coccothraustes*. The largest European finch away from northern conifer belt, unmistakable with its outsize bill (grey-blue in summer, yellow in winter and juvenile), used to crack nuts and fruit stones. Mainly chestnut plumage, with black wing-tips and throat, white patch on wing and white border to tail; juvenile has throat yellow. Most frequent call a clipped robin-like 'tick', also a rather high-pitched sibilant 'tsip'; feeble bullfinch-like song is rarely heard. Most often detected by hearing 'tick' note and seeing dumpy form overhead in bounding flight, with white in wings and tail conspicuous. Broad-leaved and mixed woodland, large gardens, orchards and other areas with many scattered trees. 7 in. (18 cm.). ⊙ **Rm Map 224**

WHITE-WINGED GROSBEAK *Mycerobas carnipes*. Another huge-billed bird, black with white on wing and yellow rump and belly; female rather less yellow beneath. Mountains, 2800–3500 m. especially among junipers, N E Iran and Transcaspia.

DESERT FINCH *Rhodopechys obsoleta*. Very like Trumpeter Finch in general appearance and flight pattern; pale pinkish-brown, with black chin, pink patch on hindwing, and forewing marked black and white but appearing white in flight; markedly cleft tail black at tip; bill and feet black. Song fine, not unlike Song Thrush (p. 259). Distinctive call, a soft purring 'r-r-r-r-r-ee', falls in pitch and then rises. Open country with scattered trees and bushes near fresh water; often by roadsides and in gardens. Unlike Trumpeter Finch, readily perches in trees or bushes. 5¾ in. (14·5 cm.).

TRUMPETER FINCH *Rhodopechys githaginea*. Breeding male pale brown with pinkish sheen, grey crown and wings, dark brown tail, pale legs and bright red bill. Winter male and female duller, mainly grey with pinkish tinge and contrasting darker wing-tips, bill orange or yellowish-brown and pinkish legs; immatures and juveniles have no pink. Characteristic brief nasal 'trumpeting' call, 'resembling a child's trumpet incessantly repeated'. Stony deserts and rocky hills. 5 in. (12·5 cm.).

CRIMSON-WINGED FINCH *Rhodopechys sanguinea*. Larger than Trumpeter Finch, with pink only on wings, cheeks and tail, and readily distinguished by blackish brown crown; nape grey, legs dark. Female's pink is paler and crown only speckled black. Call-notes twittering and linnet-like. Rocky mountain tops and slopes with some scrub, not usually below 3500 ft. In winter feeds in cultivated fields lower down. 6 in. (15 cm.).

HAWFINCH, TRUMPETER FINCHES

♂ v.

♂

♀ HAWFINCH

♂

♀ DESERT FINCH

♂

winter

TRUMPETER FINCH

♂

♀

♂

CRIMSON-WINGED FINCH

♀

289

Redpolls and Linnets: *Acanthis.* Small brown finches, with short thick seed-eating bills, sometimes with red or pink patches in plumage. Gregarious, with a markedly undulating or dancing flight, and a canary-like anxiety note, 'tsooeet'.

REDPOLL *Acanthis flammea.* Redpolls are distinguished from Linnet and Twite by black chin; red forehead of adult and pink breast and rump of breeding male are also distinctive. Very variable in size and shade of brown plumage. Smallest form is dark British and Central European Lesser Redpoll *cabaret*; palest, with whiter wing-bars and rump (sometimes unstreaked) is northern Mealy Redpoll *flammea*; and largest is dark large-billed Greenland Redpoll *rostrata*, a winter visitor. Characteristic flight-note 'chuch-uch-uch', alternating with 'err', also forms basis of song, often delivered in circular song flight. Coniferous and birch woods, willow scrub, large gardens; in winter often on waterside alders with siskins and goldfinches. 5–6 in. (13–15 cm.).
●RSMW Map 225

ARCTIC REDPOLL *Acanthis hornemanni.* Paler than Redpoll, especially on head and back, with pure white unstreaked rump, wing-bars and underparts. Voice similar to Redpoll, but flight-notes less rapid. High Arctic tundra, wintering S to coasts of Scandinavia. 5 in. (13 cm.). **—V**

TWITE *Acanthis flavirostris.* The upland counterpart of the Linnet, sharing its whitish wing-bar but differing in its featureless brown plumage, apart from buff throat and male's pink rump. Can be told from Linnet and in summer also from Redpolls by bill colour, grey in summer, yellow in winter. Male is only small bird with pink on rump but not on breast or forehead. Turkish race *brevirostris* has brighter pink rump, much whiter in wing, and black spots on breast. Linnet-like flight-note and song, but nasal 'twa-it' call is distinctive. Open rocky and heathery ground, usually high on mountains, but in extreme NW down to sea-level; wintering also on open lower ground, especially near coast. 5¼ in. (13·5 cm.) **⊙Rsw Map 226**

LINNET *Acanthis cannabina.* Generally the commonest of the group in Europe, with prominent whitish wing-patch both at rest and in flight, and dark brown bill. Breeding male is only small brown bird with grey head as well as red breast and forehead, and always has much more chestnut on upperparts than twite or redpolls; red parts are pinkish in winter. Hen and juvenile lack red or pink and are much less chestnut. Turkish race *bella* paler with rump almost white. Flight note like Greenfinch (p. 287) but less melodious and higher-pitched; song a pleasant twittering medley, often in chorus. Frequent areas with plenty of low trees or bushes, such as heaths, maquis, woodland edges, hedgerows, large gardens, orchards and vineyards; often nests in loose colonies. In winter in more open habitats, such as farmland, saltmarshes and rough grassland near coast. 5¼ in. (13·5 cm.). **●RSw Map 227**

juv.

Iceland

REDPOLL

Mealy Redpoll

♀

♂

Lesser
Redpoll

♂

♀

ARCTIC REDPOLL

♂

TWITE

♂

winter

♂

Twite
Turkey

LINNET

♀

♂

Turkey

Serins: *Serinus.* Small to very small yellowish-green finches, most with very short stubby seed-eating bills. Flight notably dancing.

CANARY *Serinus canaria.* The Atlantic Islands analogue of the Serin, larger, greyer on the back and yellower on the underparts; female duller, juvenile more streaked. Song is that of .familiar cage bird, which is derived from it, often delivered in special display flight. Forests, orchards and gardens in Azores, Canaries and Madeira only. 5 in. (12·5 cm.).

SYRIAN SERIN *Serinus syriacus.* Slightly larger and generally paler and less streaked than Serin, and with bright golden-yellow forehead, pale yellow throat, and uniformly yellow unstreaked underparts; tail longer. Voice clear, varied. Cedars and other trees in the mountains of Syria and Lebanon, also in orchards. 5 in. (12·5 cm.).

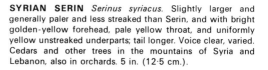

RED-FRONTED SERIN *Serinus pusillus.* One of the most distinctive finches, the black face of breeding plumage offsetting the fiery red forehead and still quite dark in winter; otherwise mostly rufous streaked darker, rump showing paler yellow; yellow patches in wings and at sides of tail. Also distinctive in flight, appearing dark fore and tawny aft, with red front only visible at short range. Song resembles Linnet (p. 291) or Goldfinch (p. 287) rather than Serin; call a trilling 'tsirrup' on a descending scale. Scrubby and grassy hillsides, especially with wild roses. 4¾ in. (12 cm.).

SERIN *Serinus serinus.* The smallest widespread European finch, yellowish-green with darker streaks and bright yellow rump; male also has bright yellow head and breast. Distinguished from slightly larger Siskin (p. 287) by very short bill, much more prominent yellow rump and no yellow at sides of tail; also lacks male Siskin's black on head and chin. Juvenile heavily streaked, rump not yellow. Jingling song like a whispering Corn Bunting (p. 275); flight-note 'tirrilillit' and anxiety note 'tsooeet', like cardueline finches. Edges of woodland, clumps and rows of trees, orchards, town parks, gardens; common in suburbs. 4½ in. (11·5 cm.).
—**A(b)**

CITRIL FINCH *Serinus citrinella.* Best distinguished from Serin and Siskin (p. 287) by grey nape and sides of neck and flanks, more greenish-yellow rump, and unstreaked underparts; no yellow at sides of tail. Bill nearer Siskin than Serin. Female duller; juvenile grey-brown, streaked below. Song siskin-like, often in circular display flight; twittering metallic flight-note. Mountain conifer forests and their edges; in Spain also in birch-holly woods. In autumn and winter also on open rocky ground on lower slopes. 4¾ in. (12 cm.). —**V**

SERINS

Domestic Canary

CANARY

♀

♂

juv.

SYRIAN SERIN

juv

RED-FRONTED
SERIN

juv.

♂

♀

SERIN

♂

♀

Corsica

juv.

CITRIL FINCH

293

Rosefinches: *Carpodacus*. A mainly Asiatic genus of rather large stout-billed bullfinch-like seed-eaters, the males with much red or pink in their plumage, the females all brownish and streaked; tail cleft. Flight undulating, like other finches.

COMMON ROSEFINCH or SCARLET GROSBEAK
Carpodacus erythrinus. Much the most widespread rosefinch and the commonest in Europe, where it is spreading westwards. Male has head, breast and rump bright red, tail and wings dark brown, with pale double wing-bar. Amount of red varies considerably, some with more and others with less red than the one illustrated. Female and immature (the latter much the most often seen in British Isles) are like slim Corn Bunting (p. 275) with pale double wing-bar. Song a clear piping 'tiu-tiu-fi-tiu'; call 'twee-eek' reminiscent of Chaffinch (p. 285) and Twite (p. 291). Woodland and forest edges, thickets by rivers in taiga, scrub, gardens, orchards and cultivated areas. 5¾ in. (14·5 cm.) —A

Corn Bunting, p. 275   House Sparrow ♀ p. 297   Common Rosefinch imm., p. 295

PALLAS'S ROSEFINCH *Carpodacus roseus*. Intermediate between Great and Common Rosefinches, male having smaller white spots on crown and chin than Great Rosefinch and being browner on back, wings and tail than Common Rosefinch. Female pinkish on rump. In flight male appears a bright pink bird with a long tail. Rather silent, but has short subdued whistle. High forest and scrub in Siberia and Central Asia, rarely wandering to Russia and C Europe. 6 in. (15 cm.).

SINAI ROSEFINCH *Carpodacus synoicus*. Larger than Trumpeter Finch (p. 289) and male redder, especially on head, breast and rump, but has no pink on wings, and bill never red. Female brown with pinkish tinge. Song melodious, varied; alarm note a high-pitched 'tweet'. Very local in sandy and rocky deserts. 5¾ in. (14·5 cm.).

GREAT ROSEFINCH *Carpodacus rubicilla*. The largest and reddest rosefinch of the region, the male distinguished by white spots on dark red crown and breast; female grey-brown, markedly streaked on breast. Flying birds look dark at a distance. Flight slow, dipping, hops on ground. High rocky slopes and scrub in the Caucasus, above the rhododendron zone, in winter in scrub in higher valleys. 8 in. (20 cm.).

ROSEFINCHES

COMMON
ROSEFINCH

♂

♀

PALLAS'S
ROSEFINCH

♂

♀

SINAI ROSEFINCH

♂

♀

GREAT
ROSEFINCH

♀

♂

295

Crossbills: *Loxia.* Large finches, unique among all the birds of the region for the crossed mandibles with which, using a distinctive criss-cross motion of the head, they dexterously extract seeds from fir, pine, spruce and larch cones, their almost exclusive diet. Plumage of adult males generally red, of immature males orange-red, of females olive-brown with yellower rump and underparts, and of juveniles brown with darker streaks; all with wings and deeply cleft tail dark brown. Associated almost exclusively with coniferous trees, and periodically erupting westwards as far as Ireland.

CROSSBILL *Loxia curvirostra.* Much the commonest and most widespread crossbill, erupting at irregular intervals far to the W and S of main breeding range. Plumage as above, with no wing-bars. N African race *poliogyna* has males almost always orange, females grey with hardly any olive. When at too great a distance for crossed mandibles to be seen, large size, distinctive feeding motion and very characteristic metallic 'jip-jip' flight and contact note are good field marks. Song a rather staccato series of bell-like metallic notes, based on 'jip'. Coniferous forest, especially spruce and fir; during irruptions also at isolated conifer clumps or trees, sometimes in towns and villages. 6½ in. (16·5 cm.).   ⊙ **RW   Map 228**

PARROT CROSSBILL *Loxia pytyopsittacus.* Slightly larger than Crossbill, and distinguishable with some difficulty and only at close range by larger head, much stouter bill, almost like a Hawfinch (p. 289) with crossed mandibles. Much more often seen in pine forests than other crossbills, and so rarely mixes with them; very rare away from the northern conifer belt. 6¾ in. (17 cm.).   **—V**

WHITE-WINGED CROSSBILL *Loxia leucoptera.* Smaller than the two other crossbills, and easily told by conspicuous chaffinch-like double white wing-bars, paler in juvenile. Male brighter red and female paler than Crossbill, and bill rather less heavy. Song a series of loud, almost canary-like, undulating trills of varying pitches; flight call less metallic than Crossbill, 'chif, chif', also a more musical 'peet'. Still more restricted in range than Parrot Crossbill, showing a marked preference for larches. 5¾ in. (14·5 cm.).   **—V**

PINE GROSBEAK *Pinicola enucleator.* The largest finch of the region, as big as a Starling (p. 303), resembling an outsize White-winged Crossbill with a stout but uncrossed bill. Adult male mainly red, female and immature male mainly greenish-yellow; white wing-bars more conspicuous than in Common Rosefinch (p. 295), which also has less stout bill. Song a loud whistling, twanging medley; call-note a loud clear trisyllabic whistle, with a more musical alarm-note. High northern conifer and birch forests, especially larch and spruce, very rarely erupting westwards. 8 in. (20 cm.).   **—V**

CROSSBILLS

♂

♀

♂

Algeria

♂

juv.

CROSSBILL

♂

PARROT-
CROSSBILL
♂

♀

♂

WHITE-WINGED
CROSSBILL

♀

♂

♂

imm.

PINE GROSBEAK

SPARROWS : *Ploceidae.* pp. 299–301. Generally rather dull-plumaged thick-billed finch-like birds, differing from the finches (p. 285) especially in having a rudimentary first primary and their tails not cleft. Flight direct or bounding.

SPANISH SPARROW *Passer hispaniolensis.* Male differs from male House Sparrow in chestnut crown, whiter cheeks, black breast, black streaks on flanks and more conspicuous dark streaking on back. Female and juvenile also have streaks on flanks, white cheeks and darker back. Voice deeper than House Sparrow, especially a contralto 'chup'. Scrub, especially by dry or wet river beds, olive groves, date palms, areas with scattered trees; flocks in cultivated land likely to be hybrids, cf. House Sparrow. In Canary Is. replaces House Sparrow. 5¾ in. (14·5 cm.).   —V

TREE SPARROW *Passer montanus.* Both sexes distinguished from slightly larger male House Sparrow by chestnut crown, yellowish-brown rump, smaller black throat bib, and black patch on cheek. Voice similar, but harder and higher-pitched; a quick 'chip, chip' and the 'teck, teck' flight note are especially characteristic. Open woodland and areas with scattered trees, nesting in holes, and nestboxes. More closely associated with man than Spanish Sparrow but much less than House Sparrow. 5½ in. (14 cm.).
●Rw   Map 229

HOUSE SPARROW *Passer domesticus.* The archetypal small brown bird, male readily told by chestnut mantle, grey crown and rump, and black chin and throat. Female and young undistinguished except for single pale wing-bar. Male Italian Sparrow *italiae,* an intergrade with Spanish Sparrow, has chestnut crown, more black on breast, and whiter cheeks and underparts; similar hybrid populations scattered through Mediterranean basin. Vocabulary of chirps and cheeps, with a double 'chissick', sometimes strung together as a rudimentary song, often in chorus. Highly gregarious, inhabiting human settlements of all kinds, including city centres, often feeding in associated cultivated areas. Usually nests on a building but also in hedges. 5¾ in. (14·5 cm.).   ●R   Map 230

DEAD SEA SPARROW or SCRUB SPARROW *Passer moabiticus.* Smaller than House Sparrow, male differing especially in conspicuous yellow patches on black throat; female paler. Male has rhythmical house-sparrow-like call. Often flocks with Spanish Sparrow. Tamarisk, poplar and other bushes and scrub near water, but very local. 4¾ in. (12 cm.).

DESERT SPARROW *Passer simplex.* A quite distinct sparrow, generally pale buff, though male has some black on throat, lores, wings and tail, and in breeding season a black bill. Black on wings shows as bar in flight. Has a house-sparrow-like chatter. Wadis and sandy and grassy areas in deserts, where it is the only buff-coloured seed-eater. Replaces House Sparrow in some villages. 5¼ in. (13·5 cm.).

SPARROWS

SPANISH SPARROW

TREE SPARROW

Italian Sparrow

♀

♂

HOUSE SPARROW

♀

♂

DEAD SEA SPARROW

♀

♂

DESERT SPARROW

SNOW FINCH *Montifringilla nivalis.* A long, grey-headed, black-throated, finch-like alpine sparrow, dull chestnut above, creamy white below. Its strikingly black and white wings and tail, especially noticeable in flight, recall pied appearance of Snow Bunting (p. 281), which however has white head and rarely if ever overlaps its range. Female has browner head and less white in wings and tail; juvenile duller still. Bill black, turning yellow in winter. Has habit of perching erect and flicking tail. Song a rather monotonous 'sitticher, sitticher'; chief calls a grating 'tsweek' and a softer 'pitsch'. Rocky and stony mountain tops and slopes, descending lower down in winter, when often near huts and houses. 7 in. (18 cm.).

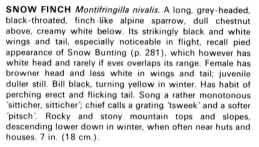

ROCK SPARROW *Petronia petronia.* Like a pale female House Sparrow, but with long pale eye-stripes and another long pale stripe down centre of crown. Pale yellow upper breast patch and white spots in tail often hard to see in field. Juvenile lacks yellow on breast. Various more or less house-sparrow-like notes, including highly characteristic 'tut', a wheezy 'chwee' and goldfinch-like 'pey-i'. Rocky mountain slopes, stony ground, desert edges, all with or without vegetation; farmland, often near hollow trees; villages, especially with ruins. 5½ in. (14 cm.).

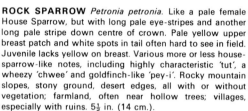

YELLOW-THROATED SPARROW *Petronia xanthocollis.* Differs from Rock Sparrow in having chestnut shoulder patch and two whitish wing-bars but no pale stripes on head. Female has paler chestnut shoulders and no yellow on throat. Song a monotonous 'chip-chip-chock'. Areas with scattered trees, such as cultivations, gardens and light deciduous forest; often in villages but always nests in tree-holes and will use nestboxes. 5 in. (12.5 cm.).

PALE ROCK SPARROW *Petronia brachydactyla.* A plain dull brown greenfinch-sized seed-eater, lacking crown stripe and yellow breast patch of Rock Sparrow, but with strikingly darker-patterned wing coverts, tail more conspicuously white-tipped and with dark bar near tip and chestnut near base. White undertail coverts fairly conspicuous. Musical whistling song, 'tee-zee' ending in cicada-like trill, resembles cardueline finches; 'twee-ou' call distinctive and similarly cardueline. Desert or semi-desert, with bushes; sometimes in large flocks among crops. 5½ in. (14 cm.).

WAXBILL *Estrilda astrild* (Estrildidae). A tiny finch-like bird, with white cheeks and black under tail coverts contrasting with red belly; tail long, graduated. Bill of adult coral-red, of immature black. Flight note 'tzep' or 'tjüküp'. In reeds near vegetable fields, where they feed in flocks. Introduced in Portugal, near Obidos. 3¾ in. (9·95 cm.).

SPARROWS, WAXBILL

juv.

adult summer

adult winter

SNOW FINCH

Snow Bunting p. 281

juv.

adult

ROCK SPARROW

adult

YELLOW-THROATED SPARROW

adult

adult

WAXBILL

PALE ROCK SPARROW

STARLINGS: *Sturnidae.* Medium-sized, highly gregarious, stocky land birds, with short tail, strong legs and bill, running not hopping on the ground. Sexes alike. Flight fast and direct, often carrying out spectacular mass movements.

STARLING *Sturnus vulgaris.* Adult blackish, iridescent with green and purple, especially in summer, and spangled with pale spots, especially in winter; bill yellow in summer. Juvenile dull brown with paler throat and unspotted breast. Differs from Blackbird (p. 257) at all times by shorter tail, bustling gait and triangular shape of wings in flight. Cf. Spotless and Rose-coloured Starlings. Chattering, whistling, mimetic song, sounding like several birds in whispered conversation, often delivered in chorus. Has many other clipped and often mimicked notes; hunger-cry of young an insistent 'cheerr'. Open woods, areas with scattered trees, cultivations, parks, gardens, villages, towns; after breeding often on hills and moors, roosting communally in plantations and reed-beds and on trees and buildings in city centres. 8½ in. (21·5 cm.). **●RmW Map 231**

ROSE-COLOURED STARLING *Sturnus roseus.* Crested adult is only medium-sized black and pink land bird, but juvenile can only be told from young Starling by paler plumage, pale rump, pink legs and yellow base of bill. Habits similar to Starling, but with rather more musical notes mixed with the grating ones in song. Breeds in dry grass steppes, with low rocky hills, following the locust swarms; erupts westwards at irregular intervals. 8½ in. (21·5 cm.). **—A**

SPOTLESS STARLING *Sturnus unicolor.* Adult differs from Starling in being completely unspotted in breeding plumage, though this hard to detect except at close range, and only slightly spotted in winter; juvenile darker than juvenile Starling. Habits and habitat similar, but voice louder. 8¼ in. (21 cm.).

TRISTRAM'S GRACKLE *Onycognathus tristramii.* Very local, blackbird-sized, all glossy blue-violet, except for large chestnut patch on each wing, conspicuous in flight. Female greyish on head and neck. Song sweet, wild and weirdly melancholy. Fond of collective aerial manoeuvres. Wild rocky ravines, e.g. at Petra, Jordan. 10 in. (25 cm.).

GOLDEN ORIOLE *Oriolus oriolus* (Oriolidae). Male is only medium-sized black and yellow land bird, but is very retiring and hard to glimpse among the foliage. Female and young are sometimes confused with Green Woodpecker (p. 193), whose juvenile lacks red on head), but bill much shorter and less stout, and orioles never crouch on boles or branches like woodpeckers. Male has distinctive loud mellow fluty song, 'weela-weeo'; both sexes make a cat-like squalling cry. Flight woodpecker-like, undulating on a long wave-length. Broad-leaved woods, and forests, areas with scattered trees, parks, large gardens. 9½ in. (24 cm.). **○M(b) Map 232**

imm.

juv.

winter

summer

imm.

STARLING

juv.

adult summer

**ROSE-COLOURED
STARLING**

summer

winter

SPOTLESS STARLING

♀

♂

TRISTRAM'S GRACKLE

♀

♂

GOLDEN ORIOLE

CROWS: Corvidae. pp. 305–9. The largest and most advanced perching birds, with robust bill and legs, a high degree of intelligence and unmelodious song. Sexes alike. Usually gregarious. Nest in tree or rock ledge.

JAY *Garrulus glandarius*. Plumage very variable, but no other medium-sized or large land bird combines a white rump, very conspicuous when flying away, and blue and white wing patches; tail black, often jerked. Black and white feathers on crown can be erected to form a crest. Harsh scolding screech, 'skaaak, skaaak' is a most distinctive field character; also makes loud crow-like screeches, a ringing kiew' and some curious creaking notes. Has no proper song, but may utter, sometimes collectively, a crooning, warbling, mimetic subsong, interspersed with less pleasing notes. Usually rather silent in breeding season. Flight markedly undulating, rather weak; hops on ground. Usually singly or in small parties, but larger numbers collect in spring. Forests, areas with numerous scattered trees, parks, orchards, large gardens, occasionally in towns. Fond of acorns in autumn, which it also collects and buries. 13½ in. (34 cm.).

●Rw   **Map 233**

Cyprus

N Russia
Central Urals

Asia Minor
S Russia

SIBERIAN JAY *Perisoreus infaustus*. Rather dull brown, with rufous in wing, rump and tail especially conspicuous in flight. General outline jay-like, but tail relatively longer and bill less stout. Calls a harsh 'chair', a brisker 'kook, kook' and a disyllabic 'whisk-ee', but rather retiring in breeding season. Coniferous forests of the taiga, mainly of spruce, also among birches, and in winter on outskirts of human settlements. Climbs out to tips of pine branches to feed on cones. 12 in. (30·5 cm.).

NUTCRACKER *Nucifraga caryocatactes*. The only brown bird of its size that is covered with white spots, with white on tail and under tail coverts very noticeable in flight. Like Jay has only a warbling subsong; normal call a rather high-pitched and far-carrying caw, also a nightjar-like trilling alarm note and various harsh croaking calls. Flight markedly undulating and jay-like; frequently perches on topmost point of a tree; hops on ground. Forests, especially coniferous; in the Alps especially associated with the Arolla pine *Pinus cembra*, on whose seeds it feeds; in Scandinavia feeds on hazel nuts and stores them as Jays do acorns. Thin-billed Siberian race *macrorhynchos* erupts westwards at irregular intervals. 12½ in. (32 cm.).   **—V**

Britain

W Europe

JAY

Middle East

Atlas range

N W Africa

SIBERIAN JAY

NUTCRACKER

MAGPIE *Pica pica.* One of the most distinctive birds of the region, the only large black and white land bird with a long graduated tail; purple-blue gloss on body feathers and green gloss on tail can only be seen at close quarters or in bright sunlight. Juvenile has much shorter tail. Has no true song, and babbling subsong is rarely heard, but a musical 'chook, chook' is associated with spring ceremonial gatherings. Characteristic call is a loud harsh chattering or chuckling note, but beware imitations of this by Jay (p. 305); rasping chatter of Grey Squirrel can also be confused with it. Flight weaker than typical crows, appearing slightly unbalanced by long tail; on ground walks, or hops sideways. Flocks small, except at roosts and in spring gatherings. Areas with scattered trees and scrub, from tundra and semi-desert to farmland and town suburbs; in Norway and elsewhere a common town bird. Nest large and domed. 18 in. (46 cm.).

●R   Map 234

AZURE-WINGED MAGPIE *Cyanopica cyanus.* Very distinctive, with jet black head and nape, wings and long graduated tail blue and white throat. Gregarious and noisy, constantly uttering a rather peevish 'zhreee' on a rising scale. Flight and other behaviour similar to Magpie. Open woodland and areas with scattered trees, such as olive groves, orchards and large gardens. 13½ in. (34 cm.).

CHOUGH *Pyrrhocorax pyrrhocorax.* The only all black bird of the region with red bill and legs, which distinguish it at once from both Alpine Chough and the black *Corvus* crows (pp. 309 and 311). Lack of grey on nape separates it easily from smaller Jackdaw (p. 311). Juvenile's bill tinged orange. Starling-like chattering subsong is rare; one common call-note is like a young Jackdaw's 'kyow', another is more gull-like than corvine, and a third 'k'chuf' has given the bird its English name. Flight much more buoyant than other black corvids, and performs aerobatics like Raven (p. 309); both walks and hops. Flocks usually small. Steep, ragged cliffs, both in mountains and on the coast. Nest in a rock crevice or sea cave. 15½ in. (39.5 cm.).   ☉R   Map 235

Alpine Chough adult   Chough juv.   Chough adult

ALPINE CHOUGH *Pyrrhocorax graculus.* The only all black bird of the region with yellow bill and red legs, the shorter yellow bill readily distinguishing it from the usually much less frequent Chough; also has less glossy plumage and shorter tail. Juvenile differs from juvenile Chough in its blackish legs and yellow bill. Flight and other behaviour very similar to Chough, but most frequent call quite distinct, a musically metallic whistling 'chirrish', often uttered communally by flocks, e.g. while mobbing large predators; also a shorter sharper 'tchiupp' comparable to Chough's 't'chuf'. High rocky mountains with steep cliffs and crags, up to the snow line. 15 in. (38 cm.).

N African race

MAGPIE

AZURE-WINGED MAGPIE

juv.

CHOUGH

adult

ALPINE CHOUGH   307

CROWS: *Corvus.* pp. 309–311. The typical crows are all black in plumage, sometimes with an admixture of grey, and are usually regarded as the most advanced in evolution, the most intelligent and the most adaptable of all birds. All are distinguished from both Red-billed and Alpine Choughs (p. 307) by their black bill and legs.

RAVEN *Corvus corax.* The largest all-black bird of the region; adult can be told from all other crows by huge size, as large as a Buzzard (p. 77), stouter bill and distinctive voice. Even juvenile shows the greater length of bill, head and neck projecting in front which can give adult an almost Maltese-cross appearance on wing. Cf. Brown-necked and Fan-tailed Ravens. Has longer neck and stouter bill than smaller Carrion Crow (p. 311) and Rook (p. 311). Chief call a deep croaking 'pruk, pruk'; beware similar less deep note occasionally heard from Rook. Flies rather heavily, but often soars and in spring performs remarkable aerobatics, 'tumbling', flying upside down and nose diving; walks, rather majestically. When common will flock, especially to roost, but in breeding season usually in ones, twos or family parties. Widespread on open and hilly country from tundra to sea coast and desert; frequent on sea cliffs and in woods and crags on hill and mountain sides. Usually nests on a rock ledge, but sometimes in a tree; one of the earliest birds to start nesting. 25 in. (64 cm.). ●R **Map 236**

Raven in flight   Raven   Crow

BROWN-NECKED RAVEN *Corvus ruficollis.* A desert crow in many ways more like a Rook or Carrion Crow (p. 311) than a Raven, the brownish tinge of the nape and neck being hard to see in the field except at close range in good light. Juvenile lacks brown tinge till first autumn moult; in adult brown becomes more noticeable as plumage wears after moult. Bill appreciably less stout than Raven and wings more pointed. Cf. Fan-tailed Raven. Voice more cawing, like a Rook, or Carrion Crow (p. 311), and includes a bell-like note. In N Africa largely confined to *Artemisia* (wormwood) steppe, with scattered jujube trees, in which and not on crags, it always nests. 19½ in. (50 cm.).

FAN-TAILED RAVEN *Corvus rhipidurus.* A noticeably short-tailed all black crow, with a most distinctive bat-like outline in flight; bill stout, shorter than Raven, with upturned bristles at base, visible only at short range. Can show a bronzy brown tinge, but tail and bill always distinguish from Brown-necked Raven. Voice still higher-pitched than Brown-necked Raven, almost approaching Chough (p. 307); has a varied repertoire of notes. Frequently indulges in collective aerobatics, taking full advantage of thermals; has singular habit of walking with bill open as if panting. Cliffs, crags and rocks, often at nearby human settlements, as at Aqaba, Jordan. Nests in cliffs and rocks only. 18½ in. (47 cm.).

RAVENS

RAVEN

BROWN-NECKED RAVEN

often *not* brown on neck

FAN-TAILED RAVEN

ROOK *Corvus frugilegus*. Adult is the only large black bird with a bare face patch. All ages can be told from Carrion Crow by purplish gloss and baggy appearance of thigh-feathers; from Jackdaw by larger size and no grey on nape; cf. also Raven (p. 309). No song; harsh 'caw' and 'caah' notes are more deliberate and prolonged than Carrion Crow, and not usually repeated thrice; also has extensive range of other calls, including a misleadingly raven-like croak and a 'ki-ook' recalling Herring Gull (p. 151). Flight rather heavy; walks sedately. Intensely gregarious throughout year, frequently consorting with Jackdaws; nests communally in trees, though odd pairs occasionally nest away from main rookery. Farmland and grasslands with plenty of scattered trees or small woods, feeding in more open country and on sea shore in winter. 18 in. (46 cm.). ●Rw **Map 237**

CARRION CROW *Corvus corone corone*. Differs from the same-sized Rook in its greenish gloss and tight-fitting thigh feathers, from adult Rook also in feathered base of bill; from smaller Jackdaw by no grey on nape; cf. also Raven (p. 309). Chief calls, often repeated three times, are an abrupt, jerky rasping 'keerght' and 'kaaah' and a higher-pitched 'keerk' not unlike an old-fashioned motor-horn. Flight rather heavy; walks, and sidles with ungainly hops. Normally goes singly, or in pairs or family parties, but where common will flock, especially to roost. All types of country except tundra, desert and bare mountain tops; frequent in farmland, moorland, sea cliffs, town parks and suburbs. Nest usually in tree, sometimes on rock ledges. 18½ in. (47 cm.). ●Rw **Map 238**

Carrion Crow × Hooded Crow hybrids

HOODED CROW *Corvus corone cornix* differs from all other black crows in its grey body, but intermediates with Carrion Crow occur. Voice, flight, habits and habitat, as Carrion Crow. 18½ in. (47 cm.). ● Rw **Map 239**

JACKDAW *Corvus monedula*. The smallest black crow and the only black bird with a grey nape. Typical notes are higher-pitched than the larger black crows; a clipped metallic 'kow' or 'kyow', and a softer 'chack', both of which may be repeated several times with an antiphonal effect. Both flight and gait much quicker and jerkier than those of the larger black crows. Open and cultivated country with rocks, crags and old trees, frequent on sea coast and in towns and villages, especially around cathedrals, castles and ruins. Nests in holes in trees, rocks and buildings. 13 in. (33 cm.). ●Rw **Map 240**

CROWS

adult   ROOK

juv.

CARRION CROW

HOODED CROW

JACKDAW

eastern race

311

List of accidentals

Black-and-white Warbler

Birds which have either been recorded as accidental vagrants in the area, or which breed on its extreme south-eastern edge and are not otherwise mentioned in the text.

Species	Scientific Name	Origin	Recorded
Ostrich	*Struthio camelus*	Arabia	Jordan
Wandering Albatross	*Diomedea exulans*	S. Oceans	Sicily, Portugal
Southern Giant Petrel	*Macronectes giganteus*	S. Oceans	English Channel
Capped Petrel	*Pterodroma hasitata*	Caribbean	Britain
Jouanin's Petrel	*Bulweria fallax*	Indian Ocean	Israel
Swinhoe's Petrel	*Oceanodroma monorhis*	W. Pacific	Israel
Pink-backed Pelican	*Pelecanus rufescens*	Africa	Egypt, Israel
Least Bittern	*Ixobrychus exilis*	N. America	Iceland, Azores
Schrenk's Little Bittern	*I. eurhythmus*	E. Asia	Germany, Italy
Dwarf Bittern	*Ardeirallus sturmii*	Africa	Canaries
Green-backed Heron	*Butorides striatus*	Africa	Sinai
Green Heron	*B. virescens*	N. America	Britain
Marabou Stork	*Leptoptilos crumeniferus*	Africa	Israel
Lesser Flamingo	*Phoenicopterus minor*	Africa	Mauritania, Spain
Spur-winged Goose	*Plectropterus gambensis*	Africa	Egypt
Fulvous Tree Duck	*Dendrocygna bicolor*	Africa	Morocco, Spain
Black Duck	*Anas rubripes*	N. America	Britain, Ireland
Cape Teal	*A. capensis*	Africa	Cyrenaica
Hooded Vulture	*Necrosyrtes monachus*	Africa	W. Sahara
Bateleur	*Terathopius ecaudatus*	Arabia	Iraq
American Kestrel	*Falco sparverius*	N. America	Britain, Denmark
Sandhill Crane	*Grus canadensis*	N. America	Britain
Semipalmated Plover	*Charadrius semipalmatus*	N. America	Britain
Eskimo Curlew	*Numenius borealis*	N. America	Britain, Ireland
Long-toed Stint	*Calidris subminuta*	Siberia	Sweden
Ring-billed Gull	*Larus delawarensis*	N. America	Britain, Germany
Laughing Gull	*L. atricilla*	N. America	Britain
Franklin's Gull	*L. pipixcan*	N. America	Britain
Forster's Tern	*Sterna forsteri*	N. America	Iceland
Brown Noddy	*Anous stolidus*	Tropical Seas	Germany
Parakeet Auklet	*Cyclorrhynchus psittacula*	N. Pacific	Sweden
Eastern Stockdove	*Columba eversmanni*	Asia	Russia
Yellow-bellied Sapsucker	*Sphyrapicus varius*	N. America	Britain
Blyth's Pipit	*Anthus godlewskii*	E. Asia	Finland
Brown Thrasher	*Toxostoma rufum*	N. America	Britain
Catbird	*Dumetella carolinensis*	N. America	Germany
Gray's Grasshopper Warbler	*Locustella fasciolata*	Asia	Denmark, France
Thick-billed Warbler	*Acrocephalus aedon*	Asia	Britain
Plain Willow Warbler	*Phylloscopus neglectus*	S. Asia	*Breeds* Iran
Siberian Blue Robin	*Luscinia cyane*	E. Asia	Sark, C.I.
Eastern Pied Wheatear	*Oenanthe picata*	S. Asia	*Breeds* Iran, Jordan
Veery	*Catharus fuscescens*	N. America	Britain
Hermit Thrush	*C. guttatus*	N. America	Britain, Iceland, Germany
Tickell's Thrush	*Turdus unicolor*	Asia	Germany
Siberian Meadow Bunting	*Emberiza cioides*	Asia	Italy
Yellow-browed Bunting	*E. chrysophrys*	Asia	Belgium, France

Chestnut Bunting	*E. rutila*	Asia	Netherlands, France
Black-faced Bunting	*E. spodocephala*	Asia	Germany
Pallas's Reed Bunting	*E. pallasi*	Asia	Russia, Denmark, Britain
Song Sparrow	*Zonotrichia melodia*	N. America	Britain
White-crowned Sparrow	*Z. leucophrys*	N. America	Britain
Rufous-sided Towhee	*Pipilo crythrophthalmus*	N. America	Britain
Indigo Bunting	*Passerina cyanea*	N. America	Iceland
Scarlet Tanager	*Piranga olivacea*	N. America	Britain
Summer Tanager	*P. rubra*	N. America	Britain
Black and White Warbler	*Mniotilta varia*	N. America	Britain
Tennessee Warbler	*Vermivora peregrina*	N. America	Britain
Yellow Warbler	*Dendroica petechia*	N. America	Britain
Cape May Warbler	*D. tigrina*	N. America	Britain
Black-throated Green Warbler	*D. virens*	N. America	Germany
Blackpoll Warbler	*D. striata*	N. America	Britain
Ovenbird	*Seiurus aurocapillus*	N. America	Britain
Yellowthroat	*Geothlypis trichas*	N. America	Britain
Hooded Warbler	*Wilsonia citrina*	N. America	Britain
Bobolink	*Dolichonyx oryzivorus*	N. America	Britain
Oriental Greenfinch	*Carduelis sinica*	Asia	Denmark, Germany
Mongolian Trumpeter Finch	*Rhodopechys mongolica*	Asia	*Breeds* Iran
Evening Grosbeak	*Coccothraustes vespertinus*	N. America	Britain
Daurian Jackdaw	*Corvus dauricus*	Asia	Finland

Index of English Names

314

Index of Scientific Names

318

Maps of bird distribution in the British Isles

Of the 468 different species of birds which have been recorded in Britain and Ireland, about 200 breed here regularly. A further 27 have bred here at one time or another, in some cases (e.g. Black-winged Stilt, Bee-eater) on only one or two occasions, in others (e.g. Hoopoe and Golden Oriole) at fairly frequent intervals, and in yet others (e.g. White-tailed Eagle, Great Bustard) regularly in the past until they were wiped out by persecution or environmental changes. Some species have only recently been recorded nesting for the first time in the British Isles, and some of these (e.g. Little Ringed Plover, Collared Dove, Redwing and Firecrest) have all become established within the last 10-30 years. A number of breeders have also become re-established in this period (e.g. Osprey, Avocet, Black-tailed Godwit, Ruff, Savi's Warbler), and several others may be on the point of becoming established (e.g. Serin, Fieldfare, Snowy Owl). So it is a curious fact that more species of birds are now known to be breeding in the British Isles than at any other point in history.

The 240 maps on the following pages show the distribution in the British Isles of all the 200 regularly **breeding species,** with the exception of a few very localised birds, which include some introduced species such as the Golden Pheasant and Ruddy Duck. Also mapped are those species which visit us regularly but which do not nest here. These fall into two main categories: **winter visitors** from northern Eurasia (e.g. various species of wildfowl and, among the passerines, Waxwing, Shore Lark and Great Grey Shrike), and **passage migrants,** especially waders, most of which breed in Arctic and sub-Arctic regions and pass through the British Isles on migration to and from their winter quarters in lower latitudes.

Four types of shading are used on the maps according to the example below.

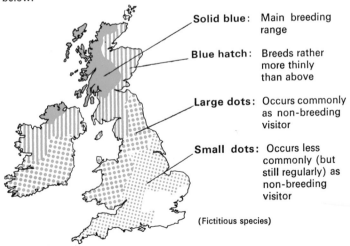

Solid blue: Main breeding range

Blue hatch: Breeds rather more thinly than above

Large dots: Occurs commonly as non-breeding visitor

Small dots: Occurs less commonly (but still regularly) as non-breeding visitor

(Fictitious species)

For explanation of the abundance and status symbols, see page 7. Page numbers refer to main text descriptions.

1 Great Northern Diver
⊙ W(b), p. 20

2 Black-throated Diver
⊙ RW, p. 20

3 Red-throated Diver
⊙ RmW, p. 20

4 Great Crested Grebe
● Rw, p. 22

5 Red-necked Grebe
⊙ W, p. 22

6 Slavonian Grebe
⊙ rW, p. 22

7 Black-necked Grebe
⊙ sMW, p. 22

8 Little Grebe
● Rw, p. 22

9 Fulmar
● Sr, p. 24

10 Manx Shearwater
⊙ Sm, p. 26

11 Great Shearwater
○ M, p. 26

12 Sooty Shearwater
○ M, p. 26

13 Storm Petrel
⊙ Sm, p. 28

14 Leach's Petrel
○ Sm, p. 28

15 Gannet
● Smr, p. 30

16 Shag
● R, p. 32

17 Cormorant
● Rmw, p. 32

18 Grey Heron
● Rw, p. 34

19 Bittern
⊙ Rw, p. 38

20 Spoonbill
○ M, p. 40

21 Mute Swan
● R, p. 44

22 Whooper Swan
⊙ W(b), p. 44

23 Bewick's Swan
⊙ W, p. 44

24 Greylag Goose
⊙ rW, p. 46

25 Bean Goose
○ W, p. 46

26 Pink-footed Goose
⊙ W, p. 46

27 White-fronted Goose
⊙ W, p. 46

28 Brent Goose
⊙ W, p. 48

29 Barnacle Goose
⊙ W, p. 48

30 Canada Goose
● R, p. 48

31 Shelduck
● Rw, p. 50

32 Mallard
● Rw, p. 52

33 Gadwall
⊙ RsW, p. 52

34 Wigeon
● rmW, p. 52

35 Teal
● RmW, p. 54

36 Garganey
⊙ Sm, p. 54

37 Pintail
● rmW, p. 56

38 Shoveler
● rsmW, p. 56

39 Tufted Duck
● RW, p. 58

40 Scaup
⊙ mW(b), p. 58

41 Pochard
● rmW, p. 58

42 Eider
● Rw, p. 60

43 Common Scoter
● rMW, p. 62

44 Velvet Scoter
⊙ mW, p. 62

45 Goldeneye
● mW(b), p. 64

46 Long-tailed Duck
⊙ W(b), p. 64

47 Goosander
● rW, p. 66

48 Red-breasted Merganser
● RW, p. 66

49 Smew
⊙ W, p. 66

50 Osprey
○ sM, p. 70

51 Red Kite
⊙ R, p. 72

52 Sparrowhawk
● Rmw, p. 74

53 Buzzard
● Rmw, p. 76

54 Honey Buzzard
○ Sm, p. 76

55 Golden Eagle
⊙ R, p. 78

56 Marsh Harrier
⊙ SRm, p. 86

57 Hen-Harrier
⊙ RmW, p. 86

58 Montagu's Harrier
⊙ Sm, p. 86

59 Peregrine
⊙ Rmw, p. 92

60 Hobby
⊙ Sm, p. 94

61 Merlin
⊙ Rsmw, p. 94

62 Kestrel
● Rsmw, p. 94

63 Red Grouse
● R, p. 96

64 Ptarmigan
⊙ R, p. 96

65 Black Grouse
● R, p. 98

66 Capercaillie
◉ R, p. 98

67 Red-legged Partridge
● R, p. 102

68 Partridge
● R, p. 102

69 Quail
○ S, p. 104

70 Pheasant
● R, p. 106

71 Water Rail
◉ RmW, p. 114

72 Spotted Crake
○ SMw, p. 114

73 Corncrake
◉ Sm, p. 114

74 Moorhen
● RW, p. 116

75 Coot
● RW, p. 116

76 Oystercatcher
● RsmW, p. 118

77 Avocet
◉ Srm, p. 118

78 Ringed Plover
● RMW, p. 120

79 Little Ringed Plover
◉ S, p. 120

80 Kentish Plover
○ M(b), p. 120

81 Golden Plover
● RMW, p. 122

82 Grey Plover
⊙ MW, p. 122

83 Dotterel
○ SM, p. 122

84 Turnstone
● MW, p. 122

85 Lapwing
● RSMW, p. 124

86 Curlew Sandpiper
⊙ M, p. 126

87 Dunlin
● rsMW. p. 126

88 Temminck's Stint
○ M(b), p. 126

89 Little Stint
⊙ Mw, p. 126

90 Knot
● MW, p. 128

91 Sanderling
● MW, p. 128

92 Purple Sandpiper
⊙ MW, p. 128

93 Grey Phalarope
⊙ Mw, p. 128

94 Red-necked Phalarope
○ sm, p. 128

95 Redshank
● RMW, p. 130

96 Spotted Redshank
● Mw, p. 130

97 Greenshank
● sMw, p. 130

98 Common Sandpiper
● SmW, p. 132

99 Wood Sandpiper
⊙ sM, p. 132

100 Green Sandpiper
● Mw(b), p. 132

101 Ruff
⊙ sMw, p. 132

102 Curlew
● RsmW, p. 138

103 Whimbrel
● sMw, p. 138

104 Black-tailed Godwit
⊙ sMW, p. 138

105 Bar-tailed Godwit
● MW, p. 138

106 Woodcock
● RmW, p. 140

107 Jack Snipe
● MW, p. 140

108 Snipe
● RmW, p. 140

109 Stone Curlew
⊙ S, p. 142

110 Great Skua
⊙ Sm, p. 144

111 Arctic Skua
● Sm, p. 144

112 Black-headed Gull
● RsmW, p. 148

113 Little Gull
⊙ Mw, p. 148

114 Herring Gull
● RW, p. 150

115 Lesser Black-back
● Srm, p. 150

116 Great Black-back
● RW, p. 150

117 Glaucous Gull
⊙ W, p. 150

118 Iceland Gull
○ W, p. 150

119 Common Gull
● Rmw, p. 152

120 Kittiwake
● RSmw, p. 152

121 Sandwich Tern
● Sm, p. 158

122 Common Tern
● Sm, p. 160

123 Arctic Tern
● Sm, p. 160

124 Roseate Tern
⊙ Sm, p. 160

125 Little Tern
● Sm, p. 160

126 Black Tern
⊙ sM(b), p. 162

127 Razorbill
● Rsw, p. 164

128 Guillemot
● Rsw, p. 164

129 Puffin
⊙ rSw, p. 164

130 Black Guillemot
⊙ R, p. 164

131 Little Auk
⊙ W, p. 164

132 Rock Dove
⊙ R, p. 170

133 Stock Dove
● Rw, p. 170

134 Woodpigeon
● Rw, p. 170

135 Collared Dove
● R, p. 172

136 Turtle Dove
● Sm, p. 172

137 Cuckoo
● Sm, p. 174

138 Barn Owl
● R, p. 176

139 Long-eared Owl
⊙ Rmw, p. 178

140 Short-eared Owl
● RsmW, p. 178

141 Little Owl
● R, p. 180

142 Tawny Owl
● R, p. 182

143 Nightjar
⊙ Sm, p. 184

144 Swift
● Sm, p. 186

145 Kingfisher
● R, p. 190

146 Hoopoe
○ M(b), p. 190

147 Green Woodpecker
● R, p. 192

148 Great Spotted Woodpecker
● Rmw, p. 194

149 Lesser Spotted Woodpecker
⊙ R, p. 196

150 Wryneck
○ sM, p. 196

151 Shore Lark
○ W, p. 198

152 Woodlark
⊙ R, p. 204

153 Skylark
● RmW, p. 204

154 Swallow
● Sm, p. 206

155 Sand Martin
● Sm, p. 206

156 House Martin
● Sm, p. 206

157 Tree Pipit
● Sm, p. 208

158 Meadow Pipit
● SrMW, p. 208

159 Rock Pipit
● Rw, p. 210

160 Pied Wagtail
● RSM, p. 212

161 Grey Wagtail
● Rs, p. 212

162 Yellow Wagtail
● Sm, p. 212

163 Waxwing
○ mW, p. 216

164 Great Grey Shrike
⊙ mW, p. 218

165 Red-backed Shrike
⊙ SM, p. 218

166 Hedgesparrow
● Rm, p. 220

167 Grasshopper Warbler
● S, p. 222

168 Savi's Warbler
○ S, p. 222

169 Reed Warbler
● Sm, p. 224

170 Marsh Warbler
○ Sm, p. 224

171 Sedge Warbler
● Sm, p. 226

172 Whitethroat
● Sm, p. 230

173 Lesser Whitethroat
● Sm, p. 230

174 Garden Warbler
● Sm, p. 230

175 Barred Warbler
— A, p. 230

176 Blackcap
● Smw, p. 232

77 Dartford Warbler
⊙ R, p. 234

178 Willow Warbler
● Sm, p. 236

179 Chiffchaff
● Smw, p. 236

180 Wood Warbler
● Sm, p. 236

81 Goldcrest
● RMW, p. 238

182 Firecrest
⊙ sMw, p. 238

183 Spotted Flycatcher
● Sm, p. 240

184 Pied Flycatcher
● SM, p. 240

85 Red-breasted Flycatcher
— A, p. 240

186 Stonechat
● Rs, p. 242

187 Whinchat
● Sm, p. 242

188 Wheatear
● SM, p. 244

89 Black Redstart
⊙ SMw, p. 250

190 Redstart
● Sm, p. 250

191 Robin
● Rsmw, p. 252

192 Bluethroat
○ M(b), p. 252

193 Nightingale
● S, p. 254

194 Blackbird
● RMW, p. 256

195 Ring Ouzel
● Sm, p. 256

196 Fieldfare
● MW(b), p. 256

197 Redwing
● rMW, p. 258

198 Song Thrush
● RMW, p. 258

199 Mistle Thrush
● Rs, p. 258

200 Bearded Tit
⊙ Rw, p. 264

201 Long-tailed Tit
● R, p. 264

202 Coal Tit
● Rw, p. 266

203 Great Tit
● Rw, p. 266

204 Blue Tit
● Rw, p. 266

205 Crested Tit
○ R, p. 268

206 Marsh Tit
● R, p. 268

207 Willow Tit
● R, p. 268

208 Nuthatch
● R, p. 270

09 Treecreeper
● R, p. 272

210 Wren
● Rm, p. 272

211 Dipper
● Rw, p. 272

212 Corn Bunting
● R, p. 274

13 Yellowhammer
● R, p. 276

214 Cirl Bunting
⊙ R, p. 276

215 Reed Bunting
● Rmw, p. 280

216 Snow Bunting
⊙ rmW, p. 280

17 Lapland Bunting
○ Mw, p. 280

218 Brambling
● MW(b), p. 284

219 Chaffinch
● RmW, p. 284

220 Goldfinch
● RS, p. 286

21 Siskin
⊙ RMw, p. 286

222 Greenfinch
● Rw, p. 286

223 Bullfinch
● Rw, p. 286

224 Hawfinch
⊙ Rm, p. 288

225 Redpoll
● RSMW, p. 290

226 Twite
⊙ Rsw, p. 290

227 Linnet
● RSw, p. 290

228 Crossbill
⊙ RW, p. 296

229 Tree Sparrow
● Rw, p. 298

230 House Sparrow
● R, p. 298

231 Starling
● RmW, p. 302

232 Golden Oriole
○ M(b), p. 302

233 Jay
● Rw, p. 304

234 Magpie
● R, p. 306

235 Chough
⊙ R, p. 306

236 Raven
● R, p. 308

237 Rook
● Rw, p. 310

238 Carrion Crow
● Rw, p. 310

239 Hooded Crow
● Rw, p. 310

240 Jackdaw
● Rw, p. 310